EXACTING CLAM No. 15 — Winter 2024
CONTENTS

Front cover: "The Road to Serfdom" by Tyler C. Gore
Interior illustrations by Guillermo Stitch

ISBN: 978-1-963846-32-4 (paperback)
          978-1-963846-33-1 (ebook)

exactingclam.com

Exacting Clam is a quarterly publication from Sagging Meniscus.

Contributing Editors: Jake Goldsmith, Tomoé Hill, Kurt Luchs, Melissa McCarthy, M.J. Nicholls, Mike Silverton, Thomas Walton
Contributing Metaclamician: Christopher Boucher
Senior Editors: Jeff Chon, Elizabeth Cooperman, Tyler C. Gore, Doug Nufer
Fiction Editor: Charles Holdefer • *Poetry Editor:* Aaron Anstett • *Reviews Editor:* Jesi Bender
Assistant Editors: Rayne Haas, Nina Mazariegos, Nora Schobel, Kim Kerner
Executive Editor: Guillermo Stitch
Publisher: Jacob Smullyan

Jake Goldsmith

On Conservation

What does it mean to *conserve*? Across the entire ideological spectrum there is talk of conserving and preserving land, nature, culture, and history. There's little considered thought about what that means, and all the bitter ironies. Walking through old buildings I feel conflicting impulses. One is what I'd glibly call *Goethe's Feeling*, trying to find a real and compelling connection to ancient history among silent architecture—though I'm not in Rome:

Tell me you stones, O speak, you towering palaces!
Streets, say a word! Spirit of this place, are you dumb?
All things are alive in your sacred walls
eternal Ipswich, only for me all's still.

Chaucer lived in Ipswich. But going to Ipswich today you may experience a local form of Paris Syndrome, as is the case in over-expectant Asian tourists: despair at the dirt and grime of modern Britain, with just a thin haunted shadow of history hiding around dark corners near Betfred and a dozen phone-repair-cum-vape emporiums. Another impulse is *conservative*, in the older, perhaps better meaning of the word—pastoral, nurturing, rural, wanting to preserve deteriorating architecture and dying nature rather than lower taxes and build a mega pork-and-chicken factory near King's Lynn, polluting nearby rivers or squashing badgers in my brand-new BMW. It becomes increasingly difficult to feel something; something the heathen me can never call spiritual, in ancient spaces and in pretty landscapes. I want to preserve churches but I don't want, or need, some comforting myth to make my sentimentality worth more. It's rude to suggest that only the God-bothering can *really* have a true and deeper connection with the past, with the stones, with life, as if the intensity of their conceit, so fantastical, maybe approaching delusion, can be an intense gratification and justification for wanting nice things, rather than anything perverse. I don't need to believe in any elevated metaphysics or theological dogma to recognise a good building and a good story.

Occasionally I do feel something, but it's more about the prospect of losing things. It would be a deep shame to demolish a thousand-year-old building (disregarding any listed status), in disuse or not, or replace some other landscape, to build an identikit housing estate. This appears very obvious, although I am no so-called *nimby*. I would very much like the propagation of more housing, and better housing, though there's a question of not, in Ruskin's words, producing such "comfortless and unhonoured dwellings", and it's insulting to think that we somehow cannot do this; when we are otherwise so abundant and wealthy.

It's difficult for me to walk far. Illness restricts my ability to wander through forests and picturesque countryside, so any experience of the rolling hills of Suffolk is rarer, more precious, less common or boring. Countryside is worth a lot and is easy to lose. It takes more effort to repair it and sustain it.

Much of the modern world is so quickened, so hastily built up and torn down again in destructive renewal. We often mock Americans for having little history or no old buildings. Americans mock themselves for this; Americans visiting Britain marvel at quaint brick cottages and structures older than nations . . . But America does have history, and has known beauty in the sort of dated pre-modern architecture many of us love: particularly civic architecture. The United States produced some of the grandest and most beautiful train stations to ever exist. They destroyed them. There's always an irony to what we call *conservatism*: the historian J. G. A. Pocock asked American conservatives what was it of their culture they wanted to conserve? They do no good job at conserving much at all, and are far better at societal arson and insurrections. America is a land of radical destruction before much else. The most vocal self-proclaimed modern conservatives have no motivation to preserve democracy and the rule of law and instead prefer a radical free-market and devastating, authoritarian, counter-revolutionary violence—all while corruptibly preaching *freedom*. It brings to mind Samuel Johnson's bitter indictment: "How is it that the loudest yelps for *liberty* come from the drivers of Negroes?"

I've never been a conservative, in a fairer sense or with any mixture of right-wing demagoguery. It's well-noted, indeed obvious, that deregulatory capitalism, Friedmanism or Hayekian economies on crack, are antithetical to conservation, conservatism, and the preservation of culture, of local tradition, or nature. A less corporatist variety of conservatism, even anti-capitalist conservatism, may be less destructive but cannot protect life and does more to neuter and impoverish it. Parochial, inflexible defenders of culture do more, in bleak irony, to dull, stagnate, and kill custom and tradition. We can, however, navigate ideas and borrow their elements without subscribing to projects or even to fundamental principles; much like a thief appropriating wealth for better use.

I don't expect much, but sometimes we need a basic reminding. We have many sentiments, often conflicting, with labels that are always inadequate, and we all dip into the pool of ideas robbing each other. In this way, we can regard certain virtues, practices, values, without the baggage and the burdens of impoverished dogmas. Most people don't know what they want and give themselves silly names. Ideologies claim virtues they never maintain, and the gulf between ideas and regimes remains unbridgeable.

It might seem peculiar that I'm having this struggle, yet there is a popular sentiment, a decent and compassionate sentiment, to preserve culture and architecture, art, objects, local spaces, living beings, that is definitely not reactionary and cruel or exclusionary. But mean and unsavoury sorts, and righteous ideologies, are so vocal, in a fetishistic way, about the preservation of things that one can mistakenly believe the wish to protect and conserve, and not so callously replace old things, is a nasty or even exclusively right-wing disposition. This mistake is understandable when so many rose-tinted and perverse nostalgists, ahistorical and false recoverers of history, proliferate in modern spaces—and modernity does little to be a good caretaker. Or when opponents of the right care less about antiques . . . Modernity may often hurt us; we make this situation worse if we let others claim dominion over the past. We do ourselves a disservice if we let our opponents monopolise symbols, images, and ideas, let alone practical activities. If a misbehaving conservative says it's bad to neglect a Norman castle, that doesn't mean it's now good to do so. Heritage and history, very obviously, are not exclusively the domain of cultural conservatives—yet we can somehow forget this: we allow them to steal it. More progressive and fairer-minded people are mistaken, in wanting to improve our lot, if they do away with any old thing just because it's dated, pressing ever-onward with the newfangled and fashionable.

At the risk of snobbery, one can say that poverty and deprivation may impose a particular condition, a ruinous and deprived state where one may not believe in much: judging how they are seen, noting the neglect of their welfare, the distressed state of their immediate environment, and the opacity of political institutions—one may ask: *Why should I care?* Why would one care for community and culture, let alone a few classical buildings, birds, and musty heritage sites when little care is afforded to you and immediate vices are easier? We can condemn this as callous, and poverty cannot be a blasé excuse for bad behaviour, but is it not understandable, and readily attested to, that a poor state of affairs may lead this way? And who is the author of this state of affairs? We ask a lot of people. Those who demand so much, in the realm of ideas, still maintain a world where waste and cheap clothes matter more than anything so sentimental and quaint as virtue or the conservation of trees.

I want to wear older clothes. Not out of a sense of nostalgic sentimentality, which still might creep in, but because it's better to maintain an old outfit than wear through new garments like meals. Clothing should not be so wasteful; so effluent. Society should not be, either. If we want to conserve the past, or physical representations of the past, then we need a more equal and judicious present.

The liking of history should not mean cultivating crude and cruel ideas. Such an attachment makes more sense as a reprieve, an escape, a guard against a world where so much may soon be lost in any number of ecological catastrophes or democratic upheavals, often with little hope. Nostalgia for what's lost forever need not be so obscene. In rare moments we can really feel the past, the stones do speak, and it need not always be so terrible.

MELISSA McCARTHY

SCARS, SCHERIE, SILENCE

BOOK

De-wax your ears, untie yourselves from the mast; in this piece I'll be harking back to *The Odyssey*, first written down circa 750 BC. The book, the physical text I'm working from, is my Penguin Classics paperback, revised edition from 1991 (which is when I embarked on A-Level Greek), as translated by E.V. Rieu then updated by his son D.C.H. Rieu in consultation with P. Jones. They're super-scholarly, which makes it surprising that the page headers throughout Book 19 (and only Book 19, out of the 24 books, of around 600 lines each) misspell the title of the work as *The Oddyssey*. I think it's a typesetting error, this strange reduplication of the "d." Or a stuttering, an echo.

On opening the cover, the first, verso page gives the authors' biogs, and explains, "The Greeks believed that *The Odyssey* was composed by Homer. In our ignorance of the man, his life and his work, we are free to believe it or not"—not a bad approach, to take towards this and indeed every other book.

I was revisiting *The Odyssey* because I had some scars from playing football, and I wanted to compare and contrast with exactly how Odysseus got the damage on his leg—he has a wound, which, as I'll outline below, is an important plot-point. The headline story of *The Odyssey* most people know—post-war adventures and return—but the level of detail and odd-ness is less familiar; I'll go into some of it here. The whole work, which began in an oral tradition, has a complex structure, full of loop-backs, prophecies, and stories-within-stories. But by the second half this has calmed down somewhat, and there's a straightforward third-person narrative, explaining what happens now that Odysseus has arrived home in Ithaca after ten years fighting at Troy, and ten years adventuring back. With such a long absence, and suitors infesting his palace, he feels it would be more prudent not to reveal himself straight away. So what does he do?

ODYSSEUS'S CLAIMS

He's come home, twenty years on and in disguise as a beggar; various people ask him who he is, and he gives a range of answers. To his son Telemachus he admits his true identity. Telemachus demurs, "You are not my father, you are not Odysseus; some divine power is playing me a trick to make my grief all the more bitter." But they work it out.

In the conversations before and after this, Odysseus takes a different tack, declining to say accurately who he is. First he meets Eumaeus, a faithful swineherd, and to him, Odysseus claims to be a Cretan, Castor's son, who's been shipwrecked at Thesprotia in north-west Greece. "It was there," explains in-disguise Odysseus, "that I heard of Odysseus. The King told me that he had entertained and befriended him on his homeward way and showed me what a fortune in copper, gold and wrought iron Odysseus had amassed. [. . .] He added that Odysseus had gone to Dodona to learn the will of Zeus from the great oak-tree that is sacred to the god, and to discover how he ought to approach his own rich island of Ithaca after so long an absence, openly or in disguise." There's a ship on stand-by, just ready to bring Odysseus home, in-disguise Odysseus tells Eumaeus. So this is a story that Odysseus confects—that he has heard that Odysseus is soon to be coming home, from Dodona.

The third person Odysseus talks to is his own wife, Penelope, and when pressed, he offers her a similar story, saying that he is Aethon, from Cnossos in Crete. In this role, he goes one up on his previous claim to have heard of Odysseus; he says that he's even met him, long ago, when Odysseus first set off for Troy, but was storm-blown to Crete and had to stay there twelve days.

This pretend-Aethon consoles the distraught Penelope, saying, as in the previous tale he spun for Eumaeus, that the Thesprotians are about to send Odysseus back, laden with riches. "This very month," reports Aethon, "Odysseus will be here, between the waning of the old moon and the waxing of the new." He's just popped out; he's gone, says Odysseus for a second time, "to Dodona to find out the will of Zeus from the great oak-tree that is sacred to the god."

The sceptical Penelope fears that "Odysseus will not come home nor will you secure your passage from here; for we have no leaders of men like Odysseus (if ever there was such a man)." And this aside is heart-breaking, with the element of doubt, an encroaching sense that perhaps the man she has remembered and longed for, for so long, never really was. The persistence of memory is going very shimmery, here.

Truth-adjacent

These stories, while sleightful, are close to the truth—Odysseus *has* been deposited home by a friendly king on whose shores he was shipwrecked, at Scherie. He *is* just close to a full return, and unsure about concealment or disguise. It's just that Odysseus steps back a person, he detaches himself and pretends to be, not the man he really is, but someone who only encountered him. He's claiming a role here as an evangelist, precursor, harbinger. He duplicates or stutters, setting up a little distance between himself—in disguise, in the flesh, on Ithaca, actually talking now—and the in-story character of Odysseus, the described Odysseus whom his listeners receive, whose arrival is imminent.

He's done something similar before in Book 9, tricking Polyphemus the Cyclops by claiming that his name is not Odysseus but Οὖτις, that is, "outis," or, "no-one." So when his neighbours ask why he's shouting in agony, Polyphemus tells them that "No-one has blinded me." And they, not great readers of context and tone, think, well that's all right then.

It's Borgesian, or J.L. Borges is Homerian, in setting up this overlap, displacement, eventual collision, between a person telling a story, a person in a story, whoever tries to escape and ends up clashing straight into the character they fled or were all along. Think, for example, of "Ibn-Hakam al-Bokhari, Murdered in His Labyrinth" of 1949, "a wanderer, who, before becoming no one in death, would recall once having been a king, or having pretended to be a king." This is the opposite of Odysseus, pretending not to be his kingly self, so that he can return again better, re-return. In a way he is projecting another body through narrative: there's him here speaking, but he claims there is somebody else, too. He uses linguistic displacement to doppleganger himself.

Place and prophecy

All this instability and complexity of identity is interesting, but I was also caught by one of the geographical details in the story. What's this place that twice Odysseus in disguise claims that the actual Odysseus (who's fictional; it's just a cover story he's telling his swineherd and his wife) has gone to? It's Dodona.

Internet research tells me that Dodona is the site of much archaeological inquiry into its history as a religious site from the second millennium BC. There's a current focus on a huge collection of lamellae, or little lead oracular tablets, dug up in the 1930s, onto which were written, in many languages, questions for Apollo to answer. Such as, "Aristomachos asks whether he should sail out and work with Straton." I'd be more worried for Straton, whose lamella asks, whether he will get back the money he has lent Aristion. Someone else, unnamed, just asks, "If I will win the dispute." Fragments of story and poetry, in the prayers and questions.

Less materially, my Everyman *A Smaller Classical Dictionary* (1937 version with a wine-dark cloth cover) explains that Dodona is: "the most ancient oracle in Greece, situated in Epirus; founded by the Pelasgians, and dedicated to Zeus. The responses of the oracle were given from lofty oaks or beech trees. The will of the god was declared by the wind rustling through the trees, and in order to render the sounds more distinct, brazen vessels were suspended on the branches of the trees. These sounds were interpreted in early times by men, but afterwards by aged women." The wind rustles through the oak and beech trees (and there are wind chimes, but these are deeply annoying, so I, being "free to believe it or not," will ignore the suggestion of their presence), and the priests interpret this message from the god into human words. This is a beautiful idea.

It's a slightly different technique to how they did things at Delphi, the later, rather more famous oracular centre in Greece. Here, the Pythian priestess would sit on a tripod over a thin chasm, and breath in intoxicating vapours. The *Smaller* explains, "the words which she uttered after exhaling the vapour were believed to contain the revelations of Apollo. They were carefully written down by the priests, and afterwards communicated by hexameter verse to the persons who had come to consult the oracle. The oracle is said to have been discovered by its having thrown into convulsions some goats which had strayed to the mouth of the cave."

I propose that life would be greatly enhanced if we revived many of these traditions—tripping goats, communicating in hexameter verse, listening to older women's interpretation of noise—and all the other ancient world modes of prophecy and seeing: looking at the flight patterns and the in-sky behaviour of birds, the running-around paths of birds when they come out to eat grain, the livers of birds when you chop them up.

At the exchange

Is there an equivalent now, in our modern, media age? An echo, a duplication that struck me was an instance from television's *Twin Peaks*, created by D. Lynch and M. Frost between 1990 and 2017. This epic work contains 48 episodes (the same as the number of books in the *Iliad* and *Odyssey* combined), 48 episodes of around 55 minutes each. It's a modern-day Odyssey about identity, war, and double lives, about whether a person can recover their proper body and come home safely, after two decades. And it contains a brilliant snippet of dialogue from Episode 1, broadcast in 1990, in which Lucy, a switchboard operator at the sheriff's office, wants to put through a call to the visiting FBI agent. She says, "Agent Cooper, I've got a call for you from a Mr Albert Rosenfeld, it sounds like long distance. It has that . . . open air sound, you know, where it sounds like wind blowing, like wind blowing through trees."

Coop takes the call, though it's not Apollonian prophecy wanting to talk to him, but Albert, a cynical but endearing pathologist. What's Lucy hearing—is it a quality of the voice, being distorted as it comes, or is it the noise of the information conduit itself, the sound of the inside of the phone lines, the long, internal echo of the wires? All messages have content then distance; signal and noise. We want the communication to come through, and sometimes it does, by speaking. Messages and verbal reports keep on arriving, made more interesting by various degrees of interpretation, interference, or downright lies.

The information that has come through to me, in the course of thinking about these artworks, is that Dodona appears to be the birthplace of listening hard for the message. This would be good in itself. But the story complicates, because while it's the place Odysseus on Ithaca twice tells people that Odysseus has gone to for prophecy and will shortly be returning from, to be precise, it isn't. He says that he, another he, has gone to get advice from the wind whistling through the trees, but he's not actually doing that; he hasn't gone to Dodona. There isn't a message being translated for him, converted from the wind through the trees into guidance on how to proceed. He isn't there listening; he's already home. The oracle's instruction was only a story, in a story.

Scars and self

But if the spoken and received word is unreliable, unstable, there's one more mode of revelation for Odysseus. After his conversation with Penelope, Odysseus-as-Aethon is offered a bed for the night, and his old nurse, Eurycleia, undertakes to wash his feet. While she's doing this, she recognises a scar on his leg, above the knee, and the story tracks back to explain how, as a boy, Odysseus went to visit his grandfather, who took him hunting for a mighty boar on the slopes of Parnassus. He did spear and kill the boar, but it gored a long flesh-wound into his leg, which healed to give the scar that Eurycleia now touches and recognises. From it, she instantly knows that this is Odysseus who has returned.

This detail, this twist in the revelation, has nothing to do with voices, listening, storytelling. But it's lovely. Does it tell me what I wanted to know, give me insight into my own scars and travels? Not really. It has set me thinking about how much of our understanding—of the self, of others—comes from words, articulation, and how much comes flooding back through a physical encounter with a marking from the past. Sometimes no oracle, interpretation, or conveyance was needed. Not a lot of reading; just a touch.

KURT LUCHS

THE INCREDIBLY SEXY WORLD OF COLLECTOR'S PLATES

In 1979 I was looking to make a career change. Since graduating from Wheaton North High School in the top five percent of my class and dropping out of college after a fruitless year, I had been employed as a janitor at a bakery and a Volkswagen dealership, a shipping clerk at the Theosophical Publishing House, a groundskeeper at the Theosophical Society, a stockroom clerk at a small electronics plant, a purchasing agent at the same plant, a purchasing agent at a small factory where the owner threw hammers at you when he was angry (yes, we called him Thor), a life insurance agent, and a call center rep selling subscriptions to the *Chicago Tribune* (aka "The World's Greatest Newspaper").

In the evenings and on weekends I was writing and performing sketch comedy with three of my siblings as the Luchs Brothers (formerly Chinaman's Chance, until we became good enough to use our real names). My passion project in the world of regional comedy had led to several creative opportunities that had changed my life. A Midwestern underground newspaper called the *Prairie Sun* invited the Luchs Brothers to write a weekly humor column. The editor, Bill Knight, gave us complete freedom and ten dollars a column, the former being far more important than the latter. Even then I had some idea just how unusual and valuable that editorial empowerment was.

With four of us to share the writing, each of only had to come up with one column per month. We could have been topical, like most humor writers then and now. Instead, we chose the much more challenging path of writing literary humor meant to be perennial in the vein of the *New Yorker* and the early *National Lampoon*. The column eventually led to a book and many other things, but that's another story. What's relevant to this tale is that it taught me to write. The

Prairie Sun then let me write concert and film reviews as well, which led to the opportunity to write book reviews for another regional paper whose name will go to the grave with me for reasons that are nobody else's business. Most of my reviews were of books published by Little, Brown & Company, because they were the only major publishing house that would send me books to review. Anything else I reviewed I had to buy myself.

One book published by Little, Brown & Co. that I reviewed was *The Track to Bralgu*, a collection of short stories by B. Wongar, an Australian aborigine writing under a pseudonym for political reasons. It was a very fine book and I gave it a strong recommendation. As far as I can tell the book sank like a stone in this country, unnoticed by anyone except me, though it launched B. Wongar's career in Australia. The reason this little review in a little regional paper matters to this account is that it landed me my first full-time job as a writer and editor.

The magazine that hired me was a new one called *Plate World*, a trade publication designed to boost the sales and appreciation for collector's plates. What are collector's plates? you might well ask, seeing as they have almost disappeared from public consciousness. For a brief, precious time, they were a way for people with limited means and no knowledge of art to have something nice to hang on the wall. The people who bought collector's plates could not afford a real painting, not even a bad one, nor did they have the taste to buy and frame prints by Van Gogh or Monet. In other words, the buyers of collector's plates were simply honest, hard-working Americans trying to beautify their homes. *Plate World* was their magazine. Most of them had no idea that both the magazine and the industry it celebrated had been created out of whole cloth by one of the most ingenious hucksters ever to grace our shores, J. Roderick MacArthur of the prominent MacArthur family.

All watchers of PBS are familiar with the John D. and Catherine T. MacArthur Foundation, "a catalyst for change." Well, J. Roderick, aka Rod, was John D.'s son, not by Catherine T. but by John D.'s first wife, the former Louise Ingalls. Is your head spinning like a collector's plate yet? Despite being born into wealth, Rod was a self-made man in every way that mattered, and one of life's truly colorful characters. He worked for the Associated Press in Mexico and served with the French army in the ambulance corps during World War II, helping liberate the country so the French could finally take their hands down.

He met his wife there too, Christiane L'Entendart, whom he married in 1947 when he was 27 years old. I never heard him call her anything but "Chri-Chri," his affectionate nickname for her. Their marriage was very French, very continental in the sense that, while he truly adored her, he also considered it his duty to dally with anything in a dress. Over the years a number of employees had reportedly found him in flagrante in the company elevator with one female or another. I'm happy to say I never had the pleasure myself.

Rod started out in his father's insurance business but, I suspect, grew restive at the limited opportunities for boondoggling offered in that staid industry. An independent entrepreneur at heart, he noticed the rapidly growing popularity of collector's plates, and intuited that someone with a vision could unify that market and reap rich rewards in the process. He founded the Bradford Exchange to do just that in 1973.

It was a brainchild worthy of P. T. Barnum. When you control ninety percent of a market, as Bradford eventually did, it is not hard to rig and manipulate the entity purporting to objectively measure the worth of various products in that market. In other words, the Bradford Exchange had a lot in common with the New York Stock Exchange, of which it was a brilliant parody. John T. had provided some backing for the venture. In 1975, seemingly jealous of his son's successful idea, he seized control of the company and locked up all of the inventory in its Northbrook warehouse just outside of Chicago. Rod did not take that lying down. He organized an expedition to raid the warehouse in the dead of night. He reestablished the business on his own and in so doing earned his father's enmity and estrangement, along with his grudging respect.

By 1979 Rod realized that a thriving market should have a publication of record. He created *Plate World* magazine and hired Don DeMicheal

as editor and publisher. DeMicheal had edited the top jazz magazine *DownBeat* during some of its best years. He was also a jazz drummer and vibraphonist of some note, working with Chuck Hedges and Art Hodes, among many others. With Rod's approval, and after they had both read my review of *The Track to Bralgu*, Don hired me as associate editor of *Plate World*.

It was my first job as a writer and editor, and I was thrilled to get it because I had no formal qualifications. I didn't care that the subject was collector's plates. I would've been happy to write about bubonic plague or wire-haired schnauzers, two things I despise. My real education began the minute Don brought me aboard and sent back my first story with dozens of red marks on every page. He taught me more about writing and editing than any course I ever took or anyone else I ever knew.

Our staff was small. In addition to Don and myself, there was the office manager Vivienne, a gargoyle of uncertain age with a voice like a bullfrog and a face like wet cement; the business manager Marvin, a very smart and funny guy who became a friend; the art director Michael, a veteran of bombing missions in Vietnam who clearly suffered from PTSD; and Jackie, the vivacious administrative assistant who managed to conduct simultaneous affairs with myself, Marvin, and a college professor of hers who was more than twice her age. She kept these other relationships compartmentalized and I didn't learn of them until sometime later. In addition to being our business manager, Marvin was Bradford's spy in the house of love, reporting on the inner workings of *Plate World* to our corporate manager named Tony, who reported directly to Rod.

When I describe the world of collector's plates as "incredibly sexy," I am referring both to the company culture established at the Bradford Exchange by J. Roderick MacArthur, and to the collector's plate industry itself, which of course included all kinds of people, but also, it seemed to me, a preponderance of individuals who might fit equally well at Playboy magazine. Everybody was sleeping with everybody else. Everyone who was married was cheating and getting divorced, and everyone who was divorced was running wild.

As for me, Jackie was my office romance, but there were others. The job entailed national and international travel, which led to some odd situations indeed. A trip to Atlantic City to cover a plate convention is, in the words of Steely Dan, "etched upon my mind." For starters, I won $500 at blackjack and was ejected bodily from a casino for card counting, one of the greatest honors of my life. A ravishing brunette who had been playing at the same table followed me outside, we had some drinks, and she spent the night in my room. I was not card counting at the time, but a gentleman never tells.

On another occasion I was in Fort Lauderdale interviewing Herschell Gordon Lewis, best known as the director of *2,000 Maniacs* and other cult films much admired by Sam Raimi and Quentin Tarantino. Lewis would return to film-making later. At the time, however, he ran a marketing consulting company and was an expert on collector's plates. Throughout the evening, he and his wife Margo, a stunning brunette, plied me with martinis. (You may have gleaned that I have a weakness for brunettes, but in my defense I will say I am equally partial to redheads and in an emergency have even occasionally deigned to notice a blonde.) At some point Herschell suggested I join them in their hot tub. I knew exactly what he meant but pretended not to and protested weakly that I had no bathing suit. Margo batted her smoldering eyelashes and said, "You won't need one." This had about the same impact on me as the special effects in the Irwin Allen disaster picture *Earthquake*. My god she was gorgeous!

I barely escaped with my nonexistent virtue intact because, to paraphrase Woody Allen, I could never get naked with a man of my gender. More's the pity. And to add to my shame, I felt I had let the Bradford team down. J. Roderick MacArthur would've jumped into that hot tub in a second.

I got to meet a number of celebrities who had become associated with collector's plates. Some impressed me as human beings, others did not.

One who did was Red Skelton who, when I interviewed him in 1981, was just about the last survivor of the golden age of comedy, the generation that had traversed the whole modern world of entertainment, from vaudeville to radio to films to television. Being in my twenties and still involved in comedy myself, I felt I had been summoned to Mount Olympus to meet one of the gods. After telling one of my comedy friends about it (okay, let's not be coy, it was Emo Phillips), we began a tradition of ending every one of our phone calls to each other with the line that Skelton used to end his television programs, "May gawd bless!" I was not terribly taken with his corny clown paintings, of which he turned out at least 1,000 in his lifetime. But I left his Palm Springs home convinced of his utter sincerity in trying to honor the world of comedy with these very personal works. I also learned that he earned up to $2.5 million dollars per year from his artwork, more than he had ever made in Hollywood. And I was frankly amazed to discover he also wrote thousands of songs and other musical compositions, many of them licensed by Muzak, the famous "elevator music" company.

Skelton lived not very far from German-born actress Elke Sommer, another star who dabbled in art, some of which landed on collector's plates. While she made many, many films, for me her greatest on-screen achievement was playing the female lead opposite Peter Sellers in the Pink Panther sequel *A Shot in the Dark*, still one of the funniest movies ever made. She was proud of her paintings and rightly so; I thought they were quite good, actually. However, my main motive in securing an interview was to get a peek at the artist at work, because she famously liked to paint in the nude.

Supposedly she would paint beside her backyard swimming pool—the fence was unusually high—and then at the end of the day she would dive into the pool and wash off any splashes of paint left on her person. Naturally, as a student of the artistic process, I was eager to observe this ritual firsthand. Regrettably, it was not to be. I asked the question as politely as I could about five different ways, until Elke finally said, "Kurt, you're a nice boy with a nice German name, but this is simply not going to happen." I left her home a sadder and wiser man regarding the ways of women and the ways of art.

One of my last assignments for *Plate World* was to cover a reception being given for Shirley Temple Black to publicize a series of collector's plates bearing her image from her time as America's best-known child star. This was at a meeting room in a Los Angeles hotel, I can't recall which one, sometime in the summer of 1981. I had no idea what to expect. I was quite familiar with her films, including those she made as she transitioned to more adult roles, such as *The Bachelor and the Bobby Soxer* (1947), with Cary Grant and Myrna Loy. But I knew next to nothing about what she had been up to since retiring from film acting around 1950.

The room was filled with people, all of them wanting to say hello, introduce themselves to her or have their pictures taken with her. I got her attention by offering to buy her a drink. As we stepped over to the bar she said, reading my mind, "Please, not a Shirley Temple. Way too sweet. Make it a martini." We spent the next two hours sipping our drinks and deeply engrossed in a conversation that wandered to all four corners of the earth. I shamelessly monopolized her, as she did me, both of us happily ignoring the reason we were supposed to be there. Those were two of the most fascinating, unforgettable hours of my life, and it is no exaggeration to say that they changed me, as I now suspect she meant them to do. She was someone who wanted to make a difference, if possible, to every person she met.

She talked a little about her work in television after leaving films, and about raising her first daughter after leaving her first husband, the abusive alcoholic actor John Agar. She was still completely in love with her second husband, Charles Alden Black, the father of her son and her other daughter. What she wanted to discuss more than anything, though, was books, ideas and the state of the world. The first thing she wanted to know was, what was the last book I had read? I believe my answer is what caused her to give me two hours of her time. I told her I was reading everything by Graham Greene, and mentioned two novels set in Africa, *The Heart of the Matter* (1948) and *A Burnt-Out Case* (1960). That's when I learned she had recently spent four years as the U.S. Ambassador to Ghana. I later found out that she got the post because Henry Kissinger had overheard her discussing South West Africa at a cocktail party, and was stunned by her level of knowledge.

"Graham Greene is a brilliant writer," she said, "but he's awfully anti-American."

"Can you blame him?" I said. My political philosophy at the time was amorphous, albeit generally leftward.

"Yes!" she said. "Who is he to equate our national sins with those of the Soviet Union? We don't have gulags. Haven't you read Solzhenitsyn?"

"I've read *One Day in Life of Ivan Denisovich*," I said. My parents had owned it.

"That's good," she said. "But you've got to read *The Gulag Archipelago*. That'll set you straight."

All I could do was nod. This was embarrassing. I was supposed to be the writer, the reader, but Shirley Temple was revealing large gaps in my knowledge. Who was interviewing who? By that time I didn't care. I was too fascinated by this incredibly intelligent, well-read woman. Who, by the way, was still very beautiful at age 53. She showed absolutely no trace of ever having been a child star. She was no emotional train wreck like Judy Garland and so many others. She was so completely self-possessed and yet so focused on things outside herself, things she felt mattered.

"What do you know about economics?" she said.

At that point I simply had to laugh, and she did too.

"It's becoming clear to me that I am somewhat uninformed," I said, "but I have actually read *The Communist Manifesto* by Mr. Marx and *The Wealth of Nations* by Mr. Smith."

"And?" she said.

"Well," I said, "the part where Smith goes on about the Corn Laws for seventy pages nearly put me to sleep, but he does make a pretty good case for capitalism. What surprised me about Marx is that he admits capitalism works. I wonder how many of his followers know he said that? He just predicts that it will be overtaken by socialism, which he says is even more wonderful, and then the state will wither away, and we'll all be in heaven. Except the state never seems to wither away, does it?"

"It does not," she said. "I was in Czechoslovakia in the summer of 1968 when the Soviets sent ten thousand tanks in. I've seen with my own eyes how the state does not wither away."

Neither of us knew it at the time of our conversation, but she would later serve as U.S. Ambassador to Czechoslovakia from 1989 to 1992 after the fall of the Iron Curtain. She told me of seeing a woman protester shot down in the street in 1968 by Russian soldiers, a sight she would never forget. Then she returned to the present.

"Everything you know about economics is hundreds of years old," she said. "You need to read the Austrian economists. Start with Hayek and Mises. *The Road to Serfdom* by Hayek is a book everyone should read."

I promised I would. I would've promised anything to keep that conversation going. Our time together was up, however. I realized we hadn't even finished our drinks. The thing is, I kept my promise. I read that book and many more exploring all sides of the capitalism versus socialism debate.

One result was that a year later I took a job with the human rights arm of a religious relief organization working in the Soviet bloc. I spent the next six years publicizing the plight of prisoners of conscience suffering in Soviet gulags, working to free them, support their families and help them all emigrate. I traveled and met with them in Russia, Ukraine, Estonia, Siberia (technically part of Russia but practically a separate country), East Germany, Kazakhstan, Kirghizstan and Uzbekistan, harassed and spied on by the KGB every step of the way. (Later I twice visited communist China, but that was to adopt my two daughters.) I continued to study the failures of socialism, and also the foundations of our own freedoms, now more precious to me than ever.

Eventually Gorbachev came to power in the Soviet Union, and things loosened up. He released many—though not all—political prisoners. The Iron Curtain collapsed in 1989, and I moved on to other pursuits. I now regret that I never dropped a note to Shirley Temple letting her know the impact our lone conversation had made on me. I'm sure she would have appreciated knowing that there was one person, at least, who didn't feel that her rendition of her signature child star song, "On the Good Ship Lollipop," was her greatest accomplishment in life.

KURT LUCHS

THE LETTER BOX

The evening after my father's memorial service, most of his seven children and their spouses gathered at the home of our youngest sister. It had been a rough day, to put it mildly. Only three of us attended and spoke at the service. It had taken me a week of soul-searching sleeplessness to come up with half a dozen positive things I could say about him, this monster, this horror of a human being who had haunted and tormented our childhoods and continued to cast twisted shadows over our broken psyches until he drew his last breath. Good riddance to bad rubbish, as Johnny Rotten said when Elvis died.

I did speak at the service because there were a few good things I could say about him, and because myself and my siblings were the only ones there who had any inkling of his dark side, his true nature. The others had known only his superficial charm and sense of humor, which cast a powerful spell in the way of all narcissists everywhere. The service was for them, not for us. We had no desire to spoil their illusions.

Once we were alone with each other we were free to speak the truth. Only we found there was no longer any need to do so. Years of Jungian therapy had freed me as much as anything ever could from his baleful influence. Toward the end I was even able to establish an arms-length relationship with him, the only kind possible. Like many people after a wake or a funeral, we found ourselves thinking mainly of the funny moments, most of them still horrific, but also unintentionally hilarious.

Some of us were old enough to remember the night of our middle sister's birth. Our mother had delivered her first child, our older sister, in a hospital. She never did that again. The rest of us all had home births, some more complicated than others. This one wasn't complicated until our mother went into the final throes of labor in the bathtub, screaming for our father to come help her, and he wouldn't leave their bedroom because he was watching the end of *Caesar's Hour*,

comedian Sid Caesar's successor to *Your Show of Shows*. It was probably a rerun, something he had already seen. But he was going to see it again, baby and blood-filled bathtub be damned. Our mother screamed one last time and pushed our sister out. After a slap on the bottom our sister started screaming too, a howl out of all proportion to her size. That finally brought our father running into the bathroom.

"What are you doing to our child?" he yelled, scooping the baby into his arms, where she did indeed stop crying for a bit. He looked on her with pride, this creature he had done so much to help beget and so little to help get born. We laughed ourselves silly just thinking about it.

After a few more such memories there was a knock on our sister's door. It was our father's second wife. Technically she was our stepmother, though none of us thought of her that way. They had lived in a million-dollar Chicago condo across the street from the John Hancock Tower and Water Tower Place, seldom venturing out to the suburbs to see any of us. Usually we came to them. What was she doing here now, in the evening rain? She hadn't been invited to this gathering. We had remembered our father her way at the memorial service. This gathering was for us. She asked me if I would carry a box in from her car. I did. She said she had been going through his things and realized that this box contained letters and other mementoes from before he knew her. She felt it was more appropriate for us to have them. And then she was gone. None of us ever saw her again.

Two or three of us dug into the box and began opening and reading aloud from a lifetime's correspondence. In most cases our father had not kept copies of his letters. The letter box contained only the replies that his own missives had generated. Nearly all of them were from women, and what's more, women who were known to us because we had met them, they had been guests at our parents' legendary house parties, and sometimes when he had taken a couple of us into the city to visit museums or whatever, we would stop with him at one of their apartments.

The letters quickly revealed that he had slept with, or tried to sleep with, every woman he had ever worked with, along with others he met through them or their friends. Many mysteries suddenly became crystal clear: his frequent need to work nights and weekends, for one thing. And despite his seemingly herculean efforts, he was always getting fired, which plunged our household into extended periods of economic hardship. Even when he was working we were always behind on our bills. Now it all made sense. It turns out you can only sleep with the boss's wife or the account manager's girlfriend so many times before they bounce you out on your ear. The revolving door of employment and unemployment worked for him romantically, however. He would move on to a new office full of fresh potential conquests. At the same time, many of his old affairs continued for years.

Where did he find the time and energy for all this sex? Partly by his de facto abandonment of his wife and children. He spent as little time with us as possible, and that was fine with us. Too often when he did come home he seemed to be bubbling over with rage and frustration, and would hit the first child he saw. Oddly, he never hit our mother, though they would conduct screaming arguments late into the night. That sound would be what we fell asleep to, those of us who could sleep. Even more oddly, our parents often had angry sex, which I now understand was probably on those nights when his current girlfriend had failed to come across.

Another puzzle was also solved for me by those letters. At one point our father took a sudden interest in continuing education. Neither of our parents had attended college, though their house contained more books, of a higher level and on a greater variety of subjects, than any other house I encountered in my youth. Perhaps both of our parents nursed an itch to prove their intellectual worthiness academically. Anyway, our father signed up for night classes in paleontology and astronomy at Northwestern University. Even more surprising, he invited me to accompany him as an underage observer. Naturally I said yes. Up until then he had done little or nothing to encourage the growth of my mind, other than allowing me free reign in their home library. That was more than enough for me. Usually the only time he referred to my intelligence was to say I was too smart to make such-and-

such a mistake, right before he hit me. I loved the night classes, and they gave me a reason to love my father, a rare occurrence indeed.

And then I pulled a certain envelope from the letter box. It was from a young woman at one of my father's jobs, who had been trying to finish her degree, and whom we had apparently bumped into at the night classes. It was a break-up letter. She accused him, rightfully I now saw, of being a terrible boyfriend and a terrible father who only brought his son to night classes as a beard, a cover for his affair. No wonder that after class he would dismiss me to take the train back to Wheaton, Illinois alone, while he stayed downtown to "finish his homework." I was gratified when I read her comment that I studied harder and knew the material better than he did, even though I would receive no credit. And I recalled that the night classes stopped when the woman started to enjoy conversing with me more than with my father. In this and many other ways he was much more like a resentful, disgruntled older brother than like a father.

Our excavation of the letter box had begun with laughter as we read aloud the juicier and sillier passages from letter after letter. I wish I could quote some of them now verbatim. Unfortunately, after that night my youngest sister decided unilaterally to burn the contents of the box, save for a few Korean War-era items that she donated to the war museum at Cantigny Park. Our father had been a sharpshooter in the Marines, volunteering as soon as he realized he had knocked up our mother with our older sister, thus escaping briefly what he regarded as the pure hell of parental responsibility.

Not all of the Korean War items got donated to the war museum. Among them were some startlingly detailed drawings of the goings-on at a Korean brothel. Aside from their skill, which was considerable, these sickened us. Our laughter dwindled into embarrassed silence. We barely noticed the other drawings, mostly of Disney characters (he was a lifelong frustrated cartoonist, one of his more endearing traits, actually).

The final straw came with a packet of letters from one of the few male correspondents represented in the box. They were from his oldest friend, who had attended high school with him in

Glen Ellyn, Illinois. Some of the letters dated from that period—the late 1940s—and they were . . . disturbing is the word. They adopted the identities of high-ranking Nazis, whose military exploits they admired (hopefully not their ideology), and spoke jokingly of subduing the American masses and having their way with American females.

Our mother was one of the females they mentioned. Both letter writers referred to her as "the delicious Jeannine," although neither had dated or bedded her yet. I say both letter writers because this was one of the few instances where the bundle included our father's half of the correspondence. The reason was soon revealed. The later letters between these old buddies dated from the early 1970s. His friend explained in the final letter why he was breaking off the friendship for good, and returning my father's correspondence to him.

When our father got our mother pregnant and promptly enlisted in the Marines, his friend also enlisted, but chose the Navy. Our father returned after the Korean War ended. He went into advertising as a copywriter at the Leo Burnett agency in Chicago, becoming one of the original Mad Men. His friend stayed in the Navy, rising to the rank of admiral. He married and had several children. We saw him occasionally when he was on leave, traveling to or from his base command in San Diego. He would bring exotic gifts for us children: immense and very dangerous firecrackers from Spain, almost the size of sticks of dynamite, and origami kites from Japan which were so aerodynamically sound that on a windy day you could tie the cord to a railing or a tree branch and the kite would just keep going. They were like living things you didn't have to mind.

These gifts, which never had to pass through customs, made us the envy of all other children in our neighborhood. I think the admiral brought them because he saw our plight. He was one of the only visitors to our home who spent enough time there to recognize the deep neglect and abuse. And he knew our parents, not the facades of their public personalities but their true natures, their twisted roots. He took pity on us. And perhaps even then he was thinking that Jeannine was still delicious.

A few years later our parents' marriage was finally coming apart due to our father's womanizing and also our mother's affairs (mostly brief ineffectual attempts at revenge). The admiral came back into our life. Our parents were separated. Our father took an apartment in the city while we stayed in the family home with our mother. She had spent decades popping out unwanted and almost completely ignored children and sinking into postpartum depression, a little-understood malady in those days. She was completely tied down, which suited our father's lifestyle perfectly. She had never held a job or learned how to drive. Now she was forced to do both. The admiral visited. She cried on his shoulder. Later that night, when they no doubt assumed we were asleep, we could hear them having very sloppy and noisy sex.

The admiral's amorous visits continued off and on. Our mother enjoyed throwing this fact in our father's face, and we enjoyed it a little too. Still, we did not share her delusion that he would abandon his wife and children to rescue her from her soon-to-be ex and seven unwanted offspring. Our father wrote a letter to the admiral bewailing his betrayal (as if he wouldn't have seduced his friend's wife if given the chance). The admiral's reply was devastating. He laid out our father's innumerable failings in precise detail. I wish I had that letter in front of me right now. The one phrase I can recall is this: "You are the author of your own distress."

By the time we had dug far enough into the letter box to read those words, there were no more laughs in us, and no more tears either. We were done with the whole sordid business. We closed the box and went our separate ways. It was then that a thought occurred to each of us: why had his second wife felt it appropriate to drop this bundle of joy on our sister's doorstep? She must have known exactly what was in the letter box. She had most likely opened every envelope, or enough of them to get the picture. What could have been her motive for bringing it to us, and on this night of all nights? You have the facts, ladies and gentlemen of the jury. I don't believe any summation or closing argument is required.

In a few years she remarried, and if Facebook posts are any indication, they seem quite happy. I wish them well. We never let on that we knew she had met her new husband at the hospital where their respective spouses were dying. She took care of our father for the last decade of his life, after a botched operation had left him with a damaged heart and damaged lungs. He never moved again without a wheelchair or a walker, and he never breathed without an oxygen tank. She nursed him very devotedly, and he appeared to return her affection, though we knew him for the hollow man he was, incapable of love, or at least, of human love. I still remember one gray Saturday when they were delighting in their utterly terrible dog. He said that the dog was the only creature he had ever really cared for in his life.

Lawrence Winkler

A Rose in Every Cheek

The name *Pakistan* literally means *'Land of the Pure'* in Urdu and Persian. Figuratively, it is also an acronym of its five regions—*P*unjab, *A*fghan province, *K*ashmir, *S*ind, and Baluchi*stan*. There is no *'i'* in team, or the acronym, but they threw it in anyway, as in 'kiss my ease of pronunciation.' I thought it more accurately represented *P*overty, *A*narchy, *K*orruption, *I*lliteracy, and the suffix *–stan*, Persian for 'place of.'

The poverty part came along slow and hard. Because *'P'* also stood for pea vetch, used to make *kesari dal*, poor man's lentils. It caused poor man's paralysis of the lower limbs, convulsions, and death, a condition known as lathyrism, or *Kalayakhanja* in ancient India. The culprit was a motor neuron mitochondrial poison called ODAP, an analogue of the amino acid neurotransmitter, glutamate. And glutamate was waiting for us in spades, in a side junction limbo, in a jar, on the far side of Radhan.

Julie had taken it out of her daypack. It was a big and black, with a red and yellow label, and white letters where the skull and crossbones should have been. Robyn brought out chapattis and a knife. When Julie opened the jar, the compartment filled with the smell of salt, seaweed, and bloody stools.

"Vegemite?" She asked, grouting the cracks in the bread.

"No thanks." I demurred.

"It's good for you." Said Robyn.

"No, it's not." I replied. "It contains a ton of glutamate, which, in extracellular excess, causes excitotoxicity as part of the ischemic cascade associated with strokes and epilepsy and lathyrism and autism and ALS and Alzheimer's. It's also almost ten per cent salt. So, it's not good for you."

"Course it is." Julie said. And they broke into song:

'We're happy little Vegemites As bright as bright can be.
We all enjoy our Vegemite For breakfast, lunch, and tea.
Our mummies say we're growing stronger Every single week,
Because we love our Vegemite, We all adore our Vegemite
It puts a rose in every cheek.'

". . . and mental retardation." I finished.

Outside the barred window, roving packs of feral canine skin and gristle, cadaveric to the points of their bones coming through their hides, were hunting their next heartbeat. They would have eaten their shadows if they'd had the energy to catch them. I took a chapatti, already prepasted with black adhesive, and tossed it out into the night. *He just smiled and gave me a vegemite sandwich . . . You better run, you better take cover.*

A miniature mushroom dust cloud rose off the desert soil. Wild dogs converged on the commotion from every degree of the compass, biting and snapping at each other to get there first. But 'there' was surrounded by an invisible force field that stopped them in their tracks, no less than five feet from the source. They all turned in unison, dejected and defeated, and skulked away slow, tails between their legs. An occasional yelp reverberated out into the darkness. The Vegemite twins were as silent.

"A rose in every cheek." I said.

Marvin Cohen

John Milton's Just-Discovered Novel

(Who brought it to light? Jim Ruoff, who's been teaching a John Milton course so long in college that something snapped, something had to give—and it did: this brainchild, a work by that innovator of the English novel, John Milton.)

John Milton never wrote a novel, it was really too early in literary history for him to milk his fiery muse into that particular pail or genre.

So many years later that the world was beyond recognition, it was Jim Ruoff's turn to be living, and so suitably he was born on the American west coast. English John Milton had by then long been dead.

Jim Ruoff "discovered" Milton. He read different kinds of Milton"ian" poems, from tiny to epic. Also the sterling, lordly Milton"ic" prose, impassionately grandiloquent, magnificently rhetorical. What a style! Jim Ruoff admired enviously, "I can't *do* it," he thought; "but at least I can *champion* it. That way, I partake, in its glory. Whatever Milton did, is thereby mine, as I advocate it, endorse it, push it, extol it. The magic of his genius, then, lives in me. It's like maybe an adorer of a celebrity stealing a lock of his hair. Then part of him is here, forever."

So Milton became, in a way, Jim Ruoff's "property." Permission to read him had to come through Jim Ruoff. Milton was his "franchise." He had "rights" to the "concession" of Milton. It's like a Pope in the old days being entitled to grant "indulgences"—for a small fee or consideration: much to Martin Luther''s indignation, thus indirectly leading to that famous "reform" known as Protestantism, which today is all branched and twigged out into so many splinter factions that they're all united by at least the one tree.

Anyone in the world who dared even to *wish* to read part or whole of any Miltonic work had to apply for Jim Ruoff's permission. To do him credit, Jim Ruoff was generously liberal in bestowing upon democratic literacy that enormous privilege. The publicity was good—both for Mil-

ton and Jim Ruoff. Milton''s name was enhanced by that of Jim Ruoff, just as Jim Ruoff's growing fame owed in strict fact so essentially much to the firm literary tradition of that old English Master.

That's called symbiosis; they fed off each other, the dead man writhing in his live writing, and the live American man who *owned* the great reputation of the former. Owned by association and possession; by entrepreneurship; by expert backing and adroit management.

"John Milton and Jim Ruoff"—the world coupled them, like "ham and eggs," like "Gilbert and Sullivan," like "Shakespeare and Hamlet," like "love and sex," like "Freud and neurosis," like "Gargantua and Pantagruel," like "death and eternity."

It was a thriving partnership. "I owe my flourishing enterprise," exulted Jim Ruoff, "to the grafting on—to live me—of the still sappy branch of the great dead Miltonic tree. Now the sap flows and rises again. I'm doing Milton justice. Mutually, I'm *profiting* by him, as well. It's an ideal arrangement, a mutually beneficial deal; and it was clever of me to latch on to him. I'm on to a good thing. It's an endless milking of an ever fertile cow.

"However, he never wrote a novel. The 'novel' form hadn't been developed then, that's why. Well, it's not too late. Since I've 'taken him over,' *I'll* write one, *for* him—*in his name. He'll* get the credit, not me. It's a small debt to pay, but I'll pay it."

That was Jim Ruoff's decision of honor. And he stuck to his word.

He did good by John Milton. John Milton was his "charge": like an orphan being the "charge" of a foster father or the ward of some surrogate parent. So Jim Ruoff was "charged" with his mission: to engender, belatedly (hopefully not *too* belatedly), a yet undiscovered (but still. unwritten) "novel" authored by old John Milton. A novel far "ahead of its time."

"I'll prove," resolved Jim Ruoff, in a firm clench of determination, "that John Milton was 'avant-garde.' Then today's young bohemian literary terrors will respect and venerate John Milton and plant him new seeds of homage. Such awe will redound, of course, to *my* authorship—secretly. But John Milton will be the author. His old Muse has come out of her pensioned-off retirement chamber to personally 'authorize' me to do this. By divine right, by official sanction, by solemn ordinance, I'll discharge this office entrusted by an almost holy writ to my writing hand. Have I the skill for it? Is it within my craftsmanship, thus to fabricate so long delayed and so historically shocking a sudden artifice? It shall be! I'm sworn to it! By the Holy Milton, I make this sacred vow, May he guide my hand, from his oblivion-brooding shadows where his soul keeps purgatory. Inspire me, Miltonic Muse! Ignite bright invention's fuse. And be our grafted souls ever fused."

So Jim Ruoff was hard at work writing Milton's novel. It was a perspired labor of love. He kept at it, with a superhuman frenzy of determination, like a demon driven by an even fiercer demon.

He'll get it done, at this rate. It's tremendous.

Then he stops short. He takes stock, from the qualm or scruple of compunction that almost ruins the might of his zealous resolve.

He's devastated by this thought: "I'm Milton's parasite! Alas, 'tis so!"

He'll kill himself, and entitle the deed "Parasite Lost." But then unkill himself, to entitle "Parasite Regained."

His com*pun*ction was thus purged by the *pun*; so he resumed his heroic novel. The style was sheer Milton—grander than ever.

"This style is an anachronism from the point of view of the Twentieth Century it's being written in. Nevertheless, I'll follow through, and persist in it."

Now the unveiling of the new-found masterpiece. The world waits.

It's been printed in millions of copies; today is publishing day. All the critics are wearing their Sunday best.

It's a long-lost masterpiece! Come to light! John Milton wrote the first great novel in English, to go with the only great English epic and all those marvelous sonnets and other poems and that mighty cannon of imperishable prose.

Now it's found he was the innovator of the novel! Jim Ruoff takes a bow. He says to the press (and to the television cameras, to be up to date), "I found it among his old papers. Scholarship just had neglected to unearth it, that's all. Everybody took it for granted that all of Milton had already come to light. So no one bothered, till me, to look again. Not only did I look, but I found. Read the novel and enjoy it. No advance copies have been distributed to the critics yet. Copies are being issued to critics *today*, the general *public* publication day. That's fair and uneffete of me, impartial to all. Read it. You'll find it worthy of the Master. It's in his unmistakable style. Let no one doubt me. This is no hoax. I want no cynical skeptic playing detective in suspecting me of some fraudulent act on behalf of some of Milton's glory rubbing off on me. *Milton* wrote it, I didn't. I've been instrumental in *bringing it out*: that's the extent of my service. My modesty doesn't exceed it. In humility, I withdraw. I've brought forward this book. It speaks from, of, and by Milton. All glory to him."

The applause drowned out further words. Then all the world took the book home to read. Verdict?: *Sublime*. Milton has done it again! Cutting through all these years, even into the era of the automobile and the airplane, the radio, the television, and the birth control pill.

It was translated into every tongue. It's our newest Old Classic. The university English Departments quickly revamp their schedules to include it.

What's it about? What!? You haven't read it? You're the only one that hasn't. Read it. Catch up with the rage. Read it. The sublime crime of Milton's self-proclaimed alter-ego, that genius of prank, that serious perpetrator of a believed farce, that credulity-enforcer: Jim Ruoff; Milton incarnate.

[This is the first English publication of a piece that originally appeared in Norwegian in 'Vinduet vol28/#3, 1974'. Marvin Cohen often names his characters after his acquaintances; there is no necessary resemblance between the real and the un-real. Marvin writes of the real James E. Ruoff: "I loved him. As City College's Literature Head, he got me once a week adjunct jobs as creative writing teacher despite my lack of any college degree, and as always I really needed the salary. He himself was a specialist in John Milton. We became good friends."]

Thomas Walton

Unsavory Thoughts

Connivance

When my daughter was in seventh grade, she told me they watched a video about Hiroshima in her history class.

"It was so terrible, Papa. Their skin was peeling off, and the radiation turned people into zombies. The whole city was gone. All the people in it, and children who had nothing to do with the war. Papa, people melted or burned, and their eyes fell out. Even their bones were gone. Some people became ants. They called them ants. Their skin sort of just rotted on their bodies and they walked in straight lines, slowly. Papa, their brains were eaten by the radiation, and babies exploded or melted or just disappeared. Did you know about this, Papa? Did you know that happened?"

"Yes."

We were quiet then. I felt accused. And guilty. Was it me who dropped the bomb? Should I have told her about it? And the Holocaust? Have they studied that? Pol Pot? Dresden? The Salem Witch Trials? Does she know about R. Kelly? Should I tell her about Hugh Heffner and the Playboy Mansion? The Branch Davidians? Jefferey Epstein? Jeffrey Dahmer? Jeffrey Goldblum in *The Fly*? Am I the bearer of human atrocities? Is this what I've passed down? What mad and incomprehensible inheritance have I given her?

I was walking her home from school. I was carrying her clarinet. The day was cold and cloudy but then there was a little break, the sun fell through the sky and it was as if the air had flowered. Every aerosol filled with light, and the leaves and cars and street signs all seemed so brilliant, so fine and so lovely.

And then the clouds closed over again, and the air dulled again, dampened and grew cold again.

"Papa, it was so terrible."

You're Not a Woman Again

We were in the museum looking at various ancient Roman artifacts. We weren't in Rome. We were in the Rome Room at the museum. The artifacts were encased in plexiglass cubes. We like to go to the Rome Room after we see whatever exhibits are happening in the main galleries. It's somehow grounding. I can't explain it, I just notice that that's what we do. Every time we go to the museum.

We were having some sort of fight, this particular time. In fact, we were having a fight we'd had several times. A hundred times. About the baby. A baby. The baby I didn't want but she did. Not that I didn't want the baby, I just didn't want to go out of our way to have it. The baby. If it happened, great. If not, well . . . I didn't like having this fight because every time we had it we arrived at an impasse. The same impasse. Nothing was resolved. It was baffling to me that we kept having it. The fight. The less we had the baby, the more we had the fight. The fight seemed to have a mind of its own. The fight was having us.

"You don't understand," she always said, "you're not a woman."

This was her coup de grâce, and I learned that it was best not to respond to this. I learned that early on, many fights ago. The hard way. So this time I didn't respond. Again.

We were standing in front of an amphora. I think it was Greek, or maybe Etruscan, despite the fact that we were in the Rome Room. The amphoras were used to store oil or wine. I was thinking it would take a lot of wine to fill up one of the amphoras. Did the wine they drank back then taste like the wine we drink now? I started to crave a glass of wine. The painting running around the amphora was odd. I didn't recognize the scene.

"What is this? Dionysus?" I asked.

"You think everything's Dionysus," she said, annoyed.

"Well it usually is when it's on a jug of wine," I said. "Who do you think it is?"

"It looks like Diana to me."

"Okay . . ." I looked more closely. She was usually right about these things. "Okay, Diana then . . . what's she doing?"

We both leaned in and slowly walked around the plexiglass, trying to decipher the scene scratched into the clay, or painted on it. It was hard to say.

"It's a bit weird, don't you think?" I said, hoping to move beyond the fight.

"I think it's a child," she said.

"Maybe the moon . . ." I said.

"Probably. She's goddess of the hunt, and of the moon, and of childbirth."

"Jeezus," I said.

"What? I didn't paint it . . ." she said.

"Can we just look at the art?" I said.

"We are looking at the art," she said, "and this is a painting of Diana, goddess of childbirth."

"Okay, fine."

She smiled sarcastically, "I'm going back to the Frankenthaler exhibit."

She left and I let her go without saying anything else. I didn't follow her. It's nicer to be alone in a museum anyway. I looked at the vase again. There was what looked like a couple (the expectant parents?) lounging in a field. Lying in the grass. The moon up above. Maybe our fight is as old as Time. Maybe if we were the couple on the vase, we could just offer Diana a lamb and be done with it. It's not like I didn't want a baby. I just didn't necessarily think it was a good idea. I thought it might even be a bad idea. We weren't trying not to. It just wasn't happening. And she was bothered by it, and I didn't care. Not that I didn't care, I just thought, oh well, there you go, it's not happening.

I walked around the vase again, the jar, the amphora. Maybe it's not a deer, I thought. I mean, it had antlers and hoofs, but the face was like a man's face. Sad. Resigned. Useless. It could be Dionysus after all. Just because she says it's Diana doesn't mean it is . . . I thought about the wine again. It would be nice to drink wine out of something like that.

A Note On Revision

Writers have strong opinions about revision. Some love it, some hate it. Some think a work only gets worse by revising, some that it only gets better. The "raw vs. the cooked" has been cooked to death.

For me, I find my work generally gets more intelligent as I revise. Not that the writing necessarily gets better. It's just that the things that I'm saying grow more thoughtful the more I consider them, the more I go over them. Sometimes this self-reflection allows me to think better of including this or that nasty remark. So I edit it out. Sometimes not. Sometimes I miss a few things.

I do reach a certain point, though, where the revision process has to end. This is because, as the work gains in thoughtfulness and consideration, so too does the notion that I probably shouldn't publish it. That, for those few unfortunate souls who will read it, it will only cause offense, suffering and regret. So, as my manuscript becomes more intelligent with every revision, I eventually reach a point where I think to myself, "you know, you probably shouldn't publish this. You'll only make enemies. Maybe just go for a walk instead."

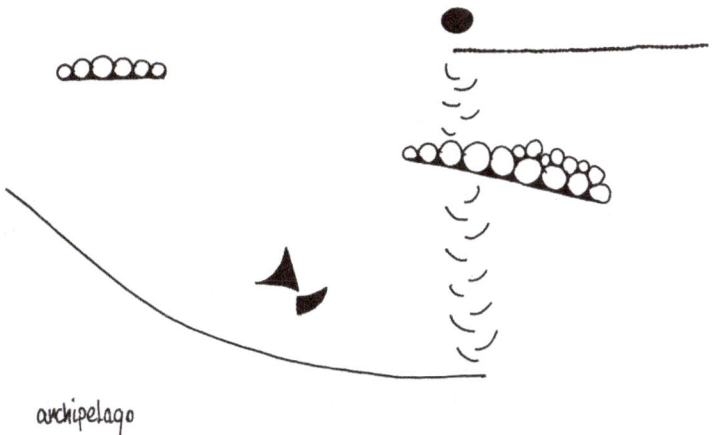

archipelago

KURT LUCHS

STILL FRESH AND FUNNY AFTER ALL THESE YEARS

THE ENDURING SUBVERSIVE CHARM OF KENNETH KOCH'S BIGGEST AND MOST SERIOUS JOKE

I'm tired of thinking about poetry.

Let's stop here by this cool mountain stream and consider instead how some of the great screeds of history could be improved by the judicious application of humor. For example, take Martin Luther's *95 Theses*, surely the most popular screed to be nailed to the door of All Saints' Church in Witttenberg, Germany, in 1517. But, let's face it, if you weren't in the burning-heretics-at-the-stake business, this document was pretty dull and dreary stuff. What if he had named it *96 Theses* and if number 96 was: "Be it hereby revealed in Holy Writ and divine revelation that Mrs. Luther's blueberry pies are more scrumptious than anything available in the Vatican Bake Shoppe." His point would've been made, the Reformation still would've happened, yet possibly without bloodshed and with much better desserts.

Or take this gem in *Quotations from Chairman Mao Tse-Tung* (aka *The Little Red Book*): "Learn to 'play the piano.' In playing the piano, all ten fingers are in motion; it will not do to move some fingers and not the others." What if he had changed it to: "Learn to 'play the piano' like Chico Marx." Quite possibly the Cultural Revolution might have taken a different turn, and China could have spared itself the deaths of tens of millions due to political purges and the implementation of Mao's insane ideas on socialist agriculture.

I could go on. Anyway, you get the point. Contrary to what Mary Poppins says, it's not a spoonful of sugar that makes the medicine go down, but rather a dollop of humor. Which brings us to the most famous screed in the history of poetry,

"Fresh Air" by Kenneth Koch. This full-frontal assault on the failed verse of the time was written in 1956 and published in the poet's 1962 volume *Thank You and Other Poems* (Evergreen). Koch performed it at many readings and it was certainly infamous long before it was put into a book (I can't find that it was ever published in a magazine first, but if you know better, drop me a line).

The most amazing thing about the poem is how it combines a truly savage attack on bad contemporary poetry with large helpings of humor and genuine lyricism. It manages to authoritatively condemn inferior work while offering an example of superior work and loads of laughs. It is not simply an angry polemic (though make no mistake, there is plenty of anger in it). As all great literature should be, it is first and foremost tremendously engaging and entertaining. Let's look at how Koch achieved that.

The poem is in five parts, numbered, not named. It begins with an imaginary scene:

> At the Poem Society a black-haired man stands
> up to say
> "You make me sick with all your talk about
> restraint and mature talent!
> Haven't you ever looked out the window at a
> painting by Matisse,
> Or did you always stay in hotels where there
> were too many spiders crawling on your
> visages?
> Did you ever glance inside a bottle of sparking
> pop,
> Or see a citizen split in two by the lightning?
> I am afraid you have never smiled at the
> hibernation
> Of bear cubs except that you see in it some deep
> relation
> To human suffering and wishes, oh what a
> bunch of crackpots!"

Now that is another "Shot Heard 'Round the World"! Not as deadly as the bullets fired at Lexington and Concord, perhaps, but every bit as revolutionary, and ultimately just as fatal to the literary fatuities of the moment. He writes in a long free-verse line clearly inspired by Whitman, as Allen Ginsberg was doing at exactly the same time. The exclamation points are also Whitmanesque, as they are in Ginsberg's work. I know comparisons are odious, but if I may make one—I often feel that Ginsberg throws in exclamation points to try to whip up an excitement that is not actually present in the poet or the poem, whereas the same exclamation points erupt from a Koch poem because of an authentic excitement that cannot be contained. Long before Warren Zevon popularized the term, Koch was the original Excitable Boy.

Another thing to notice about the opening volley of these first nine lines: the ghastly "Poem Society" would appear to be a stand-in for a non-fictional organization. My first guess was the Modern Poetry Association (MPA), the former publisher of Poetry magazine. It was founded in 1941 and was only 15 years old when Koch wrote this. However, he mentions the MPA by name near the end of the poem. So here he must be making fun of the Academy of American Poets, founded in 1934.

As he does throughout the poem, Koch mixes drop-dead funny jokes ("Or did you always stay in hotels where there were too many spiders crawling on your visages?") with moments of surprising lyricism. When he asks, "Haven't you ever looked out the window at a painting by Matisse," is he saying that it takes the eye of an artist to perceive potential art in every mundane moment? Or does he mean that reality is constantly supplying us with visions of boundless beauty and wonder all around us all the time, comparable to the work of our best artists? It's a striking phrase any way you look at it. Of course it is also a reminder that the New York School poets saw themselves as leading a literary revolution that followed in the wake of great painters.

Two other seemingly straightforward lines—"Did you ever glance inside a bottle of sparkling pop, / Or see a citizen split in two by the lightning?"—also contain layers of meaning. Koch is an inveterate celebrator of the simple pleasures of everyday American life, such as baseball and pop. But notice how he refers to the pop. He invites us to glance inside it, not merely at it, which would show the bubbles of carbonation forming and releasing, and at the same bring our ears close enough to hear the fizz. Thus the image contains a hidden sound. And then he leaps right into the image of "a citizen split in two by the lightning."

The first section of the poem takes place at a meeting of the Poem Society. An argument is already underway as we come on the scene, an argument about what modern poetry is versus what it should be. Koch didn't have to recap what was going on in poetry in 1956, because his fellow poets were well aware of it. Still, it may be helpful to remind a contemporary audience of what the issues were. Poets born in the last decades of the 19th century—Yeats, Pound, Eliot, Williams, H. D. and all the rest—had wrought a revolution in poetry in the first decades of the 20th century. It had been a total war, organized by Pound more than anyone else, and victory had been total as well. As always happens, though, victory brings its own problems. The former revolutionaries become the new establishment. Instead of following the excellent advice from Pound to "make it new," many poets opted to make it like Pound, and Eliot, and the other leaders of the revolution. After all, imitation is the sincerest form of plagiarism.

At the same time as most poets were failing in their creative duties (which, to be honest, is what most poets are doing most of the time in any age), the literary world was tilting toward critics as if literature was really something to do with them, as opposed to writers and readers. William Empson's book *Seven Types of Ambiguity* became the cornerstone of the New Criticism, along with *The Well Wrought Urn* by Cleanth Brooks. So pernicious was the influence of these noxious tomes that writers started using them as blueprints for their work. The most pathetic example was Robert Lowell, for many years regarded as one of the best poets in the country. If you are in any degree a fan of Lowell, you'd better step away from this essay now, because in my view if you threw his entire life's work into the mouth of an active volcano, our literature would be vastly improved.

Even Eliot took part in this madness, claiming that it was the poet's job to provide an "objective correlative" to impart his or her vision to the reader. What rubbish! Eliot never once in his life sat down at his desk trying to think of an objective correlative. The only American author who might've had the intellect to approach the job that way would've been Henry James. And in the end he was just like the rest of us: staring at the blank page while shudders of horror and desperation wracked his frame, sweating blood until he managed to come up with something he hoped was new. In his case, it usually was. Would that all of us were so fortunate.

Back to the poem! We haven't even made it through the first part. Here's a bit more of that:

> A blond man stands up and says,
> "He is right! Why should we be organized to defend the kingdom
> Of dullness? There are so many slimy people connected with poetry,
> Too, and people who know nothing about it!
> I am not recommending that poets like each other and organize to fight them,
> But simply that lightning should strike them.

There follows a kind poetry slam between the chairman of the Poem Society—an ugly little man whose voice "had the sound of water leaving a vaseline bathtub"—and the black-haired man, the blond man and half a dozen of their friends. It's no contest. At the end of it, the chairman "Wilted away like a cigarette paper on which the bumblebees have urinated," The meeting adjourns and the other poets can't help but go on singing:

> And together they sang the new poem of the twentieth century,
> Which, though influenced by Mallarme, Shelley, Byron, and Whitman,
> Plus a million other poets, is still entirely original
> And is so exciting that it cannot be here repeated.

This would be a good place to mention the lack of critical appreciation and approval for Koch, both during and after the formative years of the New York School and for some time after. In a way this withholding of recognition applied to the whole movement. Yet it applied even more to Koch for one simple, silly reason. As Koch's student Ron Padgett explained in his introduction to Koch's *Selected Poems* (Library of America 2006), "In the dominant atmosphere of the somewhat depressed and solemn academic poetry of the 1950s and 60s Koch had been, after all, a disarming rarity: a highly sophisticated

and serious comic poet." This comment is still more perceptive and profound than it might appear. How many readers are even aware that a comic poet can be serious, despite the examples of much of the work of Shakespeare, Byron, Wilde, Pound and Cummings? Precious few is the not at all amusing answer.

One example of the critical dismissal of Koch can be found in the otherwise excellent volume *Alone with America: Essays on the Art of Poetry in the United States Since 1950* by poet and critic Richard Howard. The book was a rare work of poetic criticism that was really about the poems, not the critic. It greatly enhanced our understanding of an entire generation of poets that, up until then, had been underappreciated. In it, Howard examines the work of the three best-known (at that time) New York School poets, Ashbery, O'Hara and Koch. He undervalues all of them, but for Koch he cannot seem to utter a single kind word. Not that he denigrates him directly either. Here is the phrase that really sticks in my craw: "This outcry is from Koch's rhetorical manifesto 'Fresh Air,' a screed which explains, or at least explodes, the fallacies of all other poets except Kenneth Koch." As we have seen from the passages of the poem already quoted, this is a damnable lie. Koch is very quick, even eager, to credit the many inspirations and antecedents for the poetry that he and his friends were writing.

This is even more apparent in the second part of the poem, which begins with this ginger outcry:

> "Oh to be seventeen years old
> Once again," sang the red-haired man, "and not know that poetry
> Is ruled with the scepter of the dumb, the deaf, and the creepy!'

There follows another litany of poets, this time asking hard questions and starting to make important distinctions between poets whose work is useful to those of us writing in the present, and poets whose work is not useful to us:

> Who are the great poets of our time, and what are their names?

> Yeats of the baleful influence, Auden of the
>   baleful influence, Eliot of the baleful
>   influence
> (Is Eliot a great poet? no one knows), Hardy,
>   Stevens, Williams (is Hardy of our time?),
> Hopkins (is Hopkins of our time?), Rilke (is Rilke
>   of our time?), Lorca (is Lorca of our time?),
>   who is still of our time?
> Mallarmé, Valéry, Apollinaire, Éluard, Reverdy,
>   French poets are still of our time,
> Pasternak and Mayakovsky, is Jouve still of our
>   time?

Let me admit here, I never heard the name of French poet Pierre Jean Jouve before reading this poem, though he was nominated five times for a Nobel Prize. In any case, this passage puts forth the idea that a poet can be great yet not of our time, and thus, not so useful to us. For the record, the question of whether Eliot is a great poet is one that Eliot himself could not answer. In an interview with the *Paris Review* in 1959, when asked whether he was assured of his reputation, he said something like no, and how could anyone be so assured (I don't have it front of me)?

Interestingly, Koch does not question whether Stevens or Williams are still of our time, nor does he accuse them of having a baleful influence. At the time he wrote this Stevens had just died. Williams died in 1963, one year after this poem was collected into a book.

Also in 1963, Robert Bly published his own screed, an essay called "A Wrong Turning in American Poetry," in the Chicago-based magazine *Choice*. It too is a powerful critique of the effete, denatured, academic verse so common in the fifties. Bly goes Koch one better (or worse) by naming contemporaries. The American poetry scene was much smaller then, with far fewer periodicals, and only a handful that really mattered. The essay caused a scandal and a sensation in a way that would be impossible today. Every poet in the country read it, terrified of finding themselves mentioned in it. Bly made himself some lifelong enemies with it, which of course is bound to happen when you take a stand, any stand. One difference between Bly's essay and Koch's poem is that there are many cruel smiles in the essay but no laughs. Also, Bly seeks inspiration more in the Hispanic and German-speaking poets than in the

French. As far as he's concerned, Lorca and Rilke are certainly of our time. He further name-checks Pablo Neruda and Juan Ramon Jimenez, among others. The essay deserves to be revisited on the occasion of its sixtieth anniversary. And I mean to do that at another place and time. The only other thing to say about it here is that it almost completely and unfairly ignores the work of the New York School poets.

As part two of the poem barrels to a close, Koch asks plaintively, "Where are young poets in America, they are trembling in publishing houses and universities." A little further on, he exclaims, "Oh what worms they are! they wish to perfect their form." The final stanza of part two yearns for some genuine poetry while simultaneously offering us some:

> Is there no voice to cry out from the wind and
>   say what it is like to be the wind,
> To be roughed up by the trees and bring music
>   from the scattered houses
> Of the stones, and to be in such intimate
>   relationship with the sea
> That you cannot understand it? Is there no one
>   who feels like a pair of pants?

Those last two lines are particularly good. First he reminds us that if we knew anything about the sea we would know how little we know. Then he brings us back down to earth with the thought that poetry also lives in the wonderful mundanity of a pair of pants. Love that!

In part three of "Fresh Air" Koch fantasizes most delightfully about the prospect of taking violent personal action against bad poetry. It begins: "Summer in the trees. 'It is time to strangle several bad poets.'" And then the Strangler—a stand-in for Koch, no doubt—comes down the chimney like Santa Claus and throttles a versifier who clearly has it coming. There are white and pink roses in the room that are "slightly agitated by the struggle." On the bright side, "They are safe now, no one will compare them to the sea."

The penultimate section of the poem, part four, is the shortest. Koch uses it to lampoon some of the leading poetry outlets of his time. I find it fascinating that nearly seven decades later most of them are still with us. Whether they remain deserving of a similar critique today is a question each of us must answer for ourselves. Certainly they had earned the licking that Koch gave them. He takes accurate aim at "the poetry / Written by the men with their eyes on the myth / And the Missus and the midterms in the *Hudson Review*" and laments, "what is one to do / With the rest of one's day that lies blasted to ruins / All bluely about one, what is one to do?" He has no recourse, it seems. The end lines of this part contain an especially clever twist:

> And supposing one goes to the Hudson Review
> With a pack of matches and sets fire to the
>   building?
> One ends up in prison with trial subscriptions
> To the Partisan, Sewanee and Kenyon Review!

The last section of the poem, part five, is the longest and makes for a rousing conclusion. Koch invokes the title phrase, fresh air, and personifies it as a female art student toward whom he feels both admiring and amorous. He is so worked up at this point that he can't decide whether he and little Miss Fresh Air should "paint the poets" (as so many New York poets painted him and his friends), "Give them a little inspiration," or "be sea air! be noxious! kill them, if you must, but stop their poetry!" As it happens, fresh air leaves, and things take a turn for the worse. Despite the author's best intentions to banish all superfluous references to classical mythology from modern poetry, the myths intrude anyway. Suddenly he's babbling about a gull that becomes a swan that becomes Zeus, Achilles and Helen. He lets out a cry: "One more mistake and I get thrown out of the Modern Poetry Association, help! Why are there no adjectives around?"

The poet appears to be subjected to some kind of forced reeducation, ending with a suggestion that he imitate a horse which is emptying its bowels, as horses sometimes do. He renders all of this in a delicate and roundabout way of course. Koch asks pitifully, "Is there no other way to fertilize minds?"

Just when neither the narrator nor the reader can stand any more, a serving girl enters. She is in fact the art student, fresh air, in a different guise (which, ironically, is exactly what happens in such ancient mythic classics as *The Odyssey*, where the gods are always assuming different forms in their efforts to punish or aid humanity). The poet and his girl are literally walking off into the sunset—or sunrise, it isn't clear—and waving goodbye to the odd ghastly presences that have haunted the poem: "Good luck to you, Strangler!" "Goodbye, manure!" And finally:

> Until tomorrow, then, scum floating on the
>   surface of poetry! goodbye for a moment,
>   refuse that happens to land in poetry's
>   boundaries! adieu, stale eggs teaching
>   imbeciles poetry to bolster your own egos!
>   [...]

> Ah, but the scum is deep! Come, let me help you!
>   and soon we pass into the clear blue water
>   [...]

> Hello, sea! good morning, sea! hello, clarity and
>   excitement, you great expanse of
> green—

> O green, beneath which all of them shall drown!

I have read and reread this mighty poem countless times. It never fails to make me laugh, and to rouse me back to my mission. It continues to remind me that it is always the right time for renewal, for a return to first principles, to a primal way of seeing, listening and singing. Great art is not made by committee or groupthink, whether aesthetic or political or even spiritual. No one ever has or ever will workshop or MFA a great poem into being. Only a voice crying in the wilderness can bring true wildness and imagination back into our literature, which is too often oh-so-tame and trying oh-so-hard to pretend to be something else.

NOTE: While I used many resources for this essay and have quoted from some of them, the most helpful book was one I did not have occasion to quote from directly, *The Last Avant-Garde* by David Lehman (Doubleday 1998). For me, this is the most penetrating and insightful book about the New York School poets, and I say that knowing it has lots of worthy competition. If you are at all interested in that movement or Kenneth Koch or "Fresh Air," you owe it to yourself to read this book.

Kurt Luchs

A Villanelle for Kenneth

There is nobody quite like Kenneth Koch,
No one in this world or any other
Having such serious fun with a joke.

If poetry's the egg, he is the yolk.
The nine muses call Kenneth their mother.
There is nobody quite like Kenneth Koch.

His brilliant flame always brings forth some smoke
From critics Kenneth would gladly smother,
Having such serious fun with a joke.

Said he, "Our poets are bankrupt! They're broke!
I'd kill them all if I had my druthers!"
There is nobody quite like Kenneth Koch.

Ashbery, Schuyler, O'Hara and Koch,
The New York School is our Band of Brothers
Having such serious fun with a joke.

Let every frog that dares rhyme feebly croak,
"Kenneth is gone! There won't be another.
There is nobody quite like Kenneth Koch
Having such serious fun with a joke."

To the Night Belongs a Tree

The Stories of Guadalupe Dueñas (1910–2002)

The dry sickle of the bell rocks in its casement in the street. The cemetery's black wings and mottled marbled silhouettes receive Miss Silvia's coffin through their lowering gate. That lady will never come out again. Dresses, slips, tie pins, buckles, hats, ribbons, silks, and shrouds from a bygone century pass like ghosts across the pages of *Tiene la noche un árbol,* the 1954 collection of Mexican gothic stories by Guadalupe Dueñas of Jalisco, Mexico, a girl gone spinster in the eyes of her society, whose austere tales of terror and death seem at first to stand in contrast to the pragmatic, jolly persona she would exude in interviews and speeches in the 1960s. Yet why should humor and death be strange bedfellows? Guadalupe Dueñas might reply that they always go hand in hand.

It seems appropriate to begin with Dueñas' diction, ornate and precise, fully a product of the educated caste of early 20th century Mexico, of her private Catholic schooling and classes at Mexico's finest Universidad Nacional Autónoma de Mexico (UNAM). You will catch Dueñas describing the orange tree, the cypress, the trellis and wellhead in the courtyard, and inside the gated house the moderate opulence pertaining to a mid-century upper class Mexican household: the rooms, passageways, stairs, canopied beds, crucifixes and mirrors of a small princess's secret castle. Everything, but especially the flora and fauna, the stories devoted to spiders and fleas, seems to be the product of lonely hours and years shut into gardens, into empty spaces in large houses.

The stories themselves could easily be described as cousins to those of Shirley Jackson, the North American horror writer. They are tales of loneliness, madness and death. And as in Jackson's work, there is a strong transgressive undercurrent that runs against abuse of power from the patriarchy, the gender inequality and social prejudice that always hemmed Dueñas in. Even in protest, in the story 'I.Q. Test', after her first-person character has dolled herself up to apply for a serious position in a bank, the experience of the woman applicant is reduced to that of a patient in a madhouse, as she is subjected to a barrage of humiliating psychological tests, and finally, when her application is successful, placed behind a barred window where a lineup of men attempt one by one to flirt with her.

And yet Dueñas was a staunch Catholic, a true believer by her own account, and as eldest of fourteen children a traditional mother figure in many ways.

She did not do hallucinogenic mushrooms, she said, but loved a good sherry.

Dueñas' diction and delivery provide a perfect backdrop for her relentlessly satiric tone: the little bald man is surprised by a woman's alacrity ('I.Q. Test'), her pet chimp has decided to leave her ('My Chimpanzee'), the line of people waiting for stamps is a procession to the confessional, the postmaster a deaf octogenarian judge ('The Post Office'), and again and again we are reminded drily of each human being's final doom, while exterior characters are worrying about day-to-day minutiae. 'But one day, *the day that always comes,*' she writes in 'The Dying Man' (Dueñas 33, emphasis mine), and we know which day she means.

Dueñas' tone is sardonic, skeptical in the extreme, humorous but never light. '[The man] asked me who I thought was the most famous Mexican who had ever lived. Naturally I told him Our Lord Jesus Christ! Maybe he was Jewish, he got disgusted and changed the subject' (from 'I.Q. Test', Dueñas 17). The story 'Me Talking Like a Cow', which is also a commentary on her reception by society, begins with the line, 'If I had been born a cow I would have been content' (Dueñas 70).

She fills her stories with ferns and vines, willow trees, wood floors, skylights, mosses, and the curse of the lonely child that plays in the patio: splinters and nails. Dead bodies are hurled into patio wells. There is the abusive Aunt Carlota, the man in the ruby shirt and dancing shoes who may have murdered Miss Silvia, or loved her to death, and the shoeshine man with hands like iguana bellies who reeks of horse piss, whose hands no one would want them to touch, 'and yet this thing talks' ('The Rats', Dueñas 78). With just the hint of the supernatural, which Dueñas never deigns to explain, her words open up worlds.

Pita Dueñas, as she was known to her contemporaries, came from a bit of a batty family. Her words, not mine: 'una familia chiflada' (Espejo 5). Her father would hunt cats, trapping or shooting them with a musket that had belonged to the Emperor Maximiliano, boil them in large cauldrons in their kitchen, and eat them. Pita was born second, after the unfortunate death of her three-day-old sister Mariquita. The story goes that Pita's father, after sitting for most of a day next to the dead baby's crib, head bowed in silence, brined the body in a large glass chile jar and placed the dead baby on the sideboard. Mariquita spent most of Pita's childhood in different nooks and crannies in the family's different residences, 'usually on top of the wardrobe,' but also everywhere else apparently except in the parlor, because what would guests think? Pita referred to her sister in a 1967 speech as 'Mariquita la del bote—Mariquita, the one in the jar' (Mortiz 60), presumably to belly laughs from the audience, and the mummified sibling received several pages in *Tiene la noche un árbol* called 'Mariquita's Story'.

¡Una familia chiflada! is a large chunk of the iceberg, one must suppose. Guadalupe Dueñas' father Miguel Dueñas Padilla was a fallen priest from an aristocratic background who had given up his vows upon meeting Guadalupe's fifteen-year-old mother, Guadalupe de la Madrid Garcia, first cousin to former Mexican President Miguel de la Madrid. He placed the minor into a school until she came of age, and then they married. The father was relentless with his Catholicism, while the mother was essentially secular. The newlyweds moved to Guadalajara, away from both extended families, however, and Dueñas later said that she 'didn't know anybody' as a child, so that when she finally got out into society, though apparently not as a quinceñera or willing candidate for advances from eligible men, she felt she had no part either in the Church or the world.

Again, her father Miguel did not fall far from his priestly ways, and the opulent Catholicism of old Mexico breathes and rustles and fumes in Dueñas' writings. Miguel would wake the children up for mass at six am with the words 'Jesus lives!', and young Pita would mutter, 'I hope he dies!'

'[My father] woke me up, I was cold, and we had to go to church for mass . . . All this upset me' (Carrizales 1–3).

But she spent her youth interned in Teresita Catholic schools surrounded by nuns and rosaries, votive candles and wafting incense, and would fantasize about one day becoming a saint. *Tiene la noche un árbol* is full of visions of the chapels, votive nooks, cemeteries and of course the religious fervor and hypocrisy of the day.

There is also a duality of perspective in many of Dueñas' stories that is at first confusing, and reflects the author's own belonging 'neither to this sphere nor to the other' (cf. Carrizales), as the reader is thrust from one highly subjective viewpoint to another. In 'At the Shadow's Touch' the story begins with the protagonist Raquel snapping awake in a sumptuous bed, but almost immediately we are with her on a train, and then at the doorstoop of the Spinsters Moncada, then listening to the man on the train again, and then inside the house (Dueñas 36 ff.), as though being shuttered between scenes of a film, which perhaps foreshadows Dueñas' later success as a screenwriter. The story 'Judit' (Dueñas 83 ff.) shifts dizzyingly between the inner monologues of the star-crossed lovers Ricardo and Judit.

Dueñas also uses frequent parentheticals within direct speech to represent interjections of dialogue or thought. In the following, between the student Rosita, who shows up at writing school with mirrors, seashells, and a little bag of sand which she arranges on her desk, and wants to be a mermaid, and her frustrated instructor Mr. Nebrija, Rosita delivers her farewell monologue while Mr. Nebrija's exclamations remain in parentheses:

'. . . but there are other things of which even your imagination is unaware. (I do not want speeches, shut up!) Mr. Nebrija, to be a mermaid, a real mermaid, not just in the flesh, is a privilege of women who, like me, are mermaids by choice (what stupidity). You do not understand, but you too, hungry for knowledge, have dedicated to this, excuse me for saying, the most succulent juices of your spirit. (Good, that's enough!)*

—'Backwards' (Dueñas 50)

Some critics have taken the bestiary approach to dissecting Duenas' diminutive corpus, by enumerating her creatures: the tortured toad, leafcutter ants like a stream of blood, hummingbirds or 'rose boozers', the pigeons, turtledoves, rats, fleas, the spider, the cow, the Saint Bernard. Were these the author's only friends, living as she did apart, growing up with rich, absentee parents, eschewing love after just one failed attempt, suspicious of the Church, in which she used to sit and read except during the Sacrament, yet having religion, feeling it inside her? The theme of fauna, especially malevolent, as in 'The Spider', or otherwise subjected to human malevolence, as in 'The Toad' and 'The Fleas', is insistent in Dueñas' first collection. Even the fool in 'The Dying Man', when compared to a leech, squirms on the floor in an epileptic fit as though having been sprinkled with salt in the garden by a naughty, squatting child.

Another element of Dueñas' stories that has been lavished with praise is her dialogue, lauded as curt and to the point, although bear with me as I translate the following exclamation from the story 'Judit', by the buffoonish character Ricardo who must have the recalcitrant Judit:

> 'It has been our fault . . . For love there are no filters, nor talismans, nor formulas. I tell you that my madness comes from having seen you and longed to taste your lips. For I wish to commit treason for you, humiliate myself for you, die for you . . . With what straightforward stubbornness have I prepared these knots, and with what subtle pains have I lured the prey, hunted in another man's grounds, and my catch I shall keep, I shall not give her up.'

—'Judit' (Dueñas, 87)

And so on, and on, until I can not help but think about Dueña's later work as scriptwriter on Mexican soap operas, several of which she adapted from her own works, beginning with *The Mummies of Guanajuato* (produced and directed by Ernesto Alonso, Telesistema Mexicano, 1962; based on 'Guía en la muerte', Dueñas 62ff.) and continuing with a sincere emotional treatment of Emperor Maximiliano, who was fusilladed by the liberator Benito Juárez during Mexican Independence, and the Emperor's wife Carlota (*Maximiliano y Carlota,* also produced and directed by Ernesto Alonso, Telesistema Mexicano, 1965). We also find represented in Dueñas the antiquated, austere purpure of the old and moneyed society of her time, whether their words act as foil to her lighter, more modern characters, or are simply a representation of the culture she was immersed in from childhood.

I am no formal student of Latin American literature, but I like it, so I was astonished to discover that Dueñas is still not available in English, except for individual stories around the web, translated by enthusiastic readers. The best way to start to get at Guadalupe Dueñas, how she really ticked, is of course to read her work. The translations of two of her stories that accompany this brief essay are from *Tiene la noche un árbol,* available in Spanish from Fondo de Cultura Económica in Mexico City, both to my knowledge unavailable to readers of English at the time of their translation, July 2024.

> En la sangre siempre es de noche.—In the blood it is always night.

—Guadalupe Dueñas, from 'Clinical case' (Dueñas 89)

NOT IN TRANSLATION | Diane Josefowicz

"I Was Not Made to Be Dead"

Resurrecting Anna de Noailles (1876–1933)

Toward the end of 1909, the poet Anna de Noailles swept into the grand lobby of the Hôtel Liverpool, in the rue de Castiglione in Paris, on her way to meet a young writer by the name of Rainer Maria Rilke. A petite brunette with large, sliding eyes, de Noialles arrived late, as was her habit, wearing a plumed hat so tall it it barely fit through the doorway and a dress laced around the torso "so she looked almost like an Egyptian statuette," as recalled by an observer who recorded the event.

"A tiny impetuous goddess," was how Rilke described her. At thirty-three, de Noailles was a sight to see—a celebrated writer, both famous and rich, the daughter of Prince Grégoire de Brancovan, of Wallachia, and married into the aristocratic Noailles family. But, the observer recalled, "all that our poet saw was her huge eyes, black and imperious. She advanced a step, stopped again, and began: 'Monsieur Rilke, what is love for you? And what do you think about death?'" His overwhelmed response went unrecorded—I suspect he had none—but from that moment, according to Leppman, his biographer, Rilke "began to avoid Anna de Noialles."[1]

---

[1] An account of the meeting with Rilke is given in François Broche, Anna de Noailles: Un mystère en pleine lumière (Paris: Éditions Robert Laffont, 1989), pp. 270-271. My quotations are taken from Broche; translations are my own.

As have we all, in English anyway. Partly this is an indication of how little writing is translated from French in the first place, particularly older works by women. In *French Women Writers*, an anthology for students, Anna de Noailles is sandwiched between the twelfth-century poet Marie de France and the absurdist playwright Marguerite Eymery, better known as Rachilde. I suppose I should be glad she appears at all. Few of the anthologized writers are household names in London or New York, or Paris for that matter. Simone de Beauvoir, maybe.

More's the pity, particularly with respect to de Noailles. Arguably the most important poet of the Belle Epoque, she was a confidant of Proust and Cocteau, part of the influential group associated with the *Nouvelle Revue Française*, hailed by the London Times as "the greatest poet that the twentieth century has produced in France—perhaps in Europe" and by the *New York Times* as "one of the finest poets of present-day France."[1] In her lifetime she brought out nineteen books: eleven volumes of poetry and eight of essays, fiction, and criticism. Most were well received; several were bestsellers. She also left a lasting institutional legacy as a founder of the Prix Femina, the only French literary prize juried solely by women. As a writer, as a poet, as a conversationalist, she was inexhaustible. Verse poured from her, "dictated," she said, "with a perfume of roses."[2] In the words of literary historian François Raviez: "Everyone fell silent, just to hear her speak."

On her death in 1933, the French government gave her a state funeral. Apart from her heart, which is interred near the family's country home at Amphion, she's buried in the Bibesco-Brancovan vault in Père Lachaise. Her tomb bears the inscription: *I was not made to be dead.* And she was not—and yet, in English, she very nearly is. Apart from scattered notices on specialist websites and in the occasional little magazine, she is virtually entirely lost to English speakers. (One notable exception is Christina Tudor-Sideri, who opens each chapter of her sublime *If I Had Not Seen Their Sleeping Faces* (Sublunary Editions, 2023) with a translated line from de Noailles' *Les Vivants et Les Morts*.(*The Living and the Dead*, 1913).) De Noailles has not fared much better in France. According to Raviez, who in 2013 brought out an anthology of her poems, she has struggled "to escape the purgatory of forgetting."[3]

The second of three children, Anna de Noailles was born on November 15, 1876 in 22 Boulevard de La-Tour-Maubourg, an impressive building with ceilings decorated by Renoir. Her father was a galaxy: a Wallachian prince in exile who was also an ardent Republican, a decorated soldier and graduate of Saint-Cyr. Her socialite mother was an accomplished pianist who claimed origins in Crete. This growing and remarkable family soon moved across the river, to an opulent home in the Avenue Hoche, in the tranquil 8th arrondissement.

With her older brother and younger sister, de Noailles roamed the rooms of her new home, which soon filled with incredible stuff—suits of armor, ancient tapestries, musical instruments, and furnishings from Algeria and Japan. They were filled as well with music, thanks to her pianist mother whose playing, de Noailles said, formed the foundation of her poetic art. Her father had a role here too, as an impassioned reciter of war stories and poetry learned by heart.

Surely it was sometimes necessary to escape this dramatic household, to retreat to the respectable shade of the nearby Parc Monceau. It's easy to imagine her on a park bench reading the poems of Leconte de Lisle, pressed upon her by her father, or a volume of Greek myths, indulging her taste for the ancient. There were other escapes. Every year, she spent four idyllic months at the family's country home, at Amphion on the shores of Lake Geneva, her father's steamboat docked at the water's edge.

This opulent childhood was marred by illness and catastrophic loss. Throughout her life she suffered from chronic appendicitis, which she contracted as a child, as well as fevers and insomnia. Her father died when she was nine, a grief from which she seems never to have fully recovered. While her writing overflowed with paeans to the natural world and the pleasures of the senses, this exuberance was tempered by a constant painful awareness of the transience of all attachments. In her own assessment, her

---

[1] From the London *Times*: Quoted in Tama Lea Engelking, "Anna de Noailles," *French Women Writers*. Eds. Eva Martin Sartori and Dorothy Wynne Zimmerman (Lincoln and London: University of Nebraska Press, 1994): 334-45. From the *New York Times*: Paul Souday, "Biographical Sketches of Mme. de Noailles," *New York Times*, January 6, 1929.

[2] Quoted in Engelking, 337.

[3] Interview with Geraldine Mosne-Savoye, "Qui était Anna de Noailles?" *Sans oser le demander* (podcast), Radio France. April 28, 2023.

work was shaped by two opposed forces, of warm life and cold death, which she figured archetypally as "the bacchante and the nun."[1]

She made her literary debut in the *Revue de Paris*, on February of 1898, with a clutch of poems called *Litanies*. When her first collection, *Le Coeur innombrable*, appeared in 1901, Proust threw her a dinner complete with bouquets the wildflowers she mentioned in her book, and Sarah Bernhardt gave a celebratory reading. Her poems exalted the rhythms, sights and sounds of the countryside, and entangled them with a life-giving eroticism ballasted by her awareness of the constant presence of death.

After her marriage, in August of 1897, to Count Mathieu de Noailles, the newlyweds set up a household at 109 Ave. Henri-Martin, near the Bois de Boulogne, in a building that is now the embassy of Bangladesh. A son arrived in 1900; a decade later, the family moved to a new and spacious Beaux-Arts building just a few blocks away, at 40 rue Sheffer in Passy.

The marriage dissolved. The relationship didn't satisfy her. As I write these denatured words, I am aware of stepping carefully, perhaps prudishly, over her many tumultuous love affairs. She threw herself into relationships with an intensity that, perhaps inevitably, found full expression only in the haven of her work, where she could more freely explore themes of erotic power and submission. She explored these themes in ways that prove hard to confront, let alone translate—and more on this in a moment.

In 1903, she published a novel, the first of three. *La nouvelle espérance* opens on a winter day in Paris with two women walking near the Bois de Boulogne. One asks the other, "Are you truly happy?" The other replies, sharply, that yes, of course, she is happy, and the first woman finds that she believes the lie. "Not having found what she was looking for, and having lost both memory and desire," the older woman subsides, willing to be deceived. Just as she senses the budding conflict, she pulls the wool over her own eyes.

The moment is notable for its stark psychological acuity: one person treads knowingly on the sensitivities of another, is rebuked, and slips into a state of sincere forgetfulness, which is just what permits the moment to be swept under the rug. Meanwhile in the street, the air, like the prose, is so cold and dry the whole world seems on the verge of cracking open—as is the relation-

[1] Quoted in Engelking, p. 340.

ship that this cold, dry prose conveys. This moment, from the novel's first page, gives a clear view of de Noailles' writing, its intelligence and force.

La nouvelle espérance was put forward for the Prix Goncourt, but the next two novels, featuring characters who grimly renounced their passions and lit out for the convent or the grave, prompted only scandal and criticism. A fourth novel remained unfinished. It turned out that her readers preferred the bacchante to the nun. De Noailles returned to poetry with the publication of *Les Eblouissements* (1907); this volume included the sensual "La Prière devant le Soleil," a verse bacchanal if ever there was one, which Proust famously praised as "the most beautiful thing written since Antigone."

Perhaps because her vitality was both fed and sapped by her erotic entanglements, de Noailles was also a sturdy traveler who understood the benefits of a change of view. There were many trips, of course, to the country house in the Haute Savoie, as well as excursions to Saint-Moritz (where she met Proust) and even to Constantinople. In the spring of 1908, she toured Sicily, Rome, and Naples, and it is this trip that seems to have provided the material for several Italy-inspired poems in *Les Vivants et Les Morts* as well as the Italian section of *Exactitudes*, published seventeen years later in 1930, including "A Roman Morning."

How could such a beloved writer so completely disappear from view? She did write, and speak, in a great gush. Perhaps the gush itself was off-putting. Her writing has a febrile quality, as if drawn from an ancient, overlooked source, or a geyser that's been capped so tightly, for so long, it can only escape in high-pressure bursts. Or perhaps it is simply her formalism—she adored the alexandrine—that caused her to fall from view; her sympathy for traditional forms put her out of step even with her contemporaries. And then there is her dauntless exploration of the erotic, of sensuality and pain.

One way to euphemize this aesthetic interest would be to say that she was chiefly concerned with "the psychology of love." But this formulation, which I've read more than once in connection with her work, is bloodless, avoidant, and misleading. The *psychology* of love? De Noailles was concerned with the experience of being wholly—cellularly—transformed by relationship. She painted a picture of what that transformation is like when there is no equality between the parties, when direct contact—her questions to Rilke, for instance—comes off as the impertinence of one who does not know her place. In other words, she was a brilliant observer of love and desire as they are distorted by patriarchy.

A status-conscious onlooker might call this behavior—a blithe transgression of the bounds of propriety—*cringe*. This is precisely the problem, or opportunity, presented by her work. Some of it—perhaps the best of it, certainly the most interesting element of it—is *cringe*. Take, for example, "Nuit de Rome," a prose poem of four paragraphs that opens with a description of the sun setting over a convent in Rome. The convent is a clue: between the nun and the bacchante, the nun is ascendant. The peace is shattered by the arrival of a woman whose laugh reminds the narrator of a line from a book of Greek mythology: "Tu ris enfin du rire qui prélude à la hymen!" With this line, the nun suddenly gives way to the bacchante. The woman's laugh is specific but hard to specify, a belated laugh that precedes . . . the hymen? The translator's difficulty is acute. Of course this is a sexual consummation. The laugh is prelude to a fuck.

The vulgarity of this translation is not exactly present in the original, but it's not not there either. In Greek mythology, Hymen is the god of marriage. By invoking myth, de Noailles evokes the classical world of forms and proprieties. "Hymen" is the voice of the nun. But the laughter erupts from the throat of the bacchante. If "fuck" vulgarizes the reference, it also clarifies the meaning—and modern readers may well need this clarification. A direct translation isn't going to do it; the hymen belongs now to the discourse

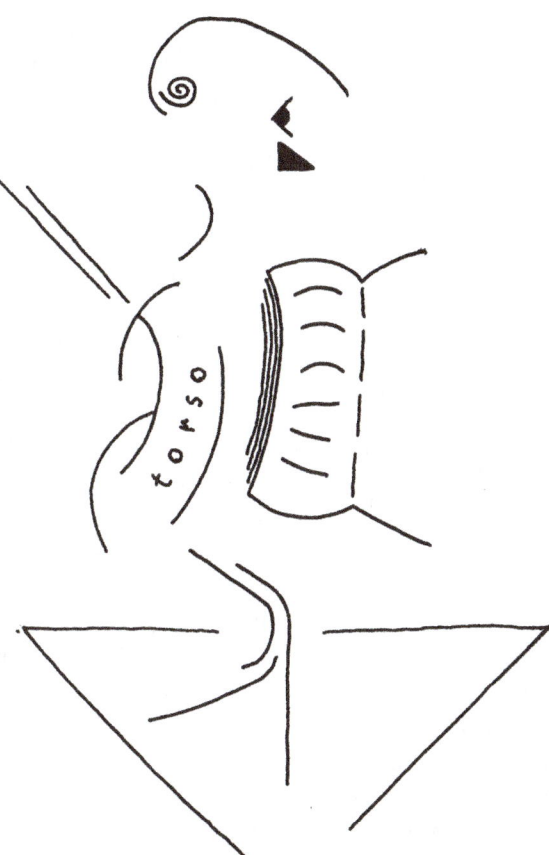

of anatomy. As the poem ends, de Noailles continues to stretch the ambiguity. The laughing woman joins her partner, not in bed but in a wedding ceremony with "more than twenty" onlookers who collectively break out into the same laugh. The scene evokes the bacchanal but does not quite become an orgy. What to do with this text, this writer?

The erotic ambiguity of "Nuit de Rome" finds an echo in "A Roman Morning." Returning from a somber trip to the Protestant cemetery, the narrator spies a priest hustling across a field. She prays that whatever he's doing, he should not intrude on the joys of any local lovers—certainly not after all that she's just seen and experienced among the tombs.

De Noailles is at her most cringeworthy when she's finding a language for sex within a discourse of propriety. But what choice did she have? She was writing from within the patriarchal fin-de-siècle; Freud's case studies are exactly contemporary. It's worth pointing out that a hymen is also a threshold, a boundary. By insisting on this language, by refusing to let the bacchante chase away the nun, de Noailles insists on a boundary of her own: she will not be silenced beyond a point. She will use a cringe word if it suits her. This insistence puts her at a distance from current publishing, from books produced in response to an algorithmically produced demand for more of the same well-blended pap that always goes down smooth. Insisting on her visions, she sticks in the modern craw in a way that, if nothing else, makes translating her an adventure.

All of Her in Flames of Beauty Flares

On Balbuena's *Grandeur of Mexico*

In his lectures on Elizabethan literature, Hazlitt explains the ferment of the age through the influence of the Reformation:

> This event gave a mighty impulse and increased activity to thought and inquiry, and agitated the inert mass of accumulated prejudices throughout Europe. . . . Liberty was held out to all to think and speak the truth. Men's brains were busy; their spirits stirring; their hearts full; and their hands not idle.

He also attributes a significant role to the translation of the Bible:

> It threw open, by a secret spring, the rich treasures of religion and morality, which had been there locked up as in a shrine. It revealed the visions of the prophets, and conveyed the lessons of inspired teachers (such they were thought) to the meanest of the people. It gave them a common interest in the common cause. Their hearts burnt within them as they read. It gave a mind to the people, by giving them common subjects of thought and feeling.

This double explanation prefigures the concerns about atmosphere and audience of Arnold and Eliot. It is persuasive, particularly in Hazlitt's ardent language: "a mighty impulse," "a secret spring," "the rich treasures of religion and morality," "a common interest in the common cause." There is a suggestion of inevitability—the inevitability that has ever accounted for Shakespeare's greatness, if not Jonson's, Middleton's, and Marlowe's. If one turns to the Viceroyalty of New Spain and the equally compelling effects of the Counter-Reformation, the literary landscape is of a markedly different quality. Prieto, with his freethinking vehemence, characterizes the age as one of "marasmus and shame, without customs, without language, without anything original, a blend of hypocrisy and avarice, of insufficiency and petulance." Paz, in contrast, commends its rigorous harmony: "Society was governed by a Christian order that is not different from that which is admired in temples and poems." Stasis underlies both valuations. Stasis at the cost of a lively literature like that of Elizabethan England. As Ureña comments, legal dispositions passed in 1532 and in 1543 prohibited "for all colonies, the circulation of pure imaginative works, in prose or in verse." The Counter-Reformation held thought and inquiry suspect. The Bible remained locked for the majority of the population. Thus, New Spain was deprived of its own Shakespeare, of its own Renaissance.

A certain kind of critic and a certain kind of reader can fall for this spurious contrast. A critic and a reader who are fundamentally incurious, who imbibe the platitudes of self-proclaimed humanists, who disbelieve in humanity's resourcefulness. Indeed, New Spain was poor in novels and in poetry of a specific kind. Much of the world's interest has always focused rather on its historiography (Las Casas, Sahagún, Clavijero) and on its philosophy (Vera Cruz, Sigüenza y Góngora, Gamarra). Yet in the words of one of its dramatists, there were "more poets than manure." Renaissance Spanish poets such as Garcilaso and Boscán had exerted an overpowering influence, and the inaugurators of the Spanish Golden Age pointed in new directions. The spirit was torn between the exigencies of the sacred and the tempting call of the profane. Naturally, it was easier to avoid the conflict altogether—circumstantial verse assisted in filling the quota of encomia and placated the hypergraphia; that is, there was a profusion of third-rate work. Sor Juana Inés de la Cruz, one of the few literary figures from New Spain who have achieved world standing, transformed this tension, however, into "First Dream," a summit of Mexican poetry. She faced an impossible conciliation in fact yet triumphed through the imaginative recreation of this very impossibility. But she had not been the only superb artist among theologians. In a sense, she represented a culmination, the "happy consortium" of three great epochal styles: that of Lope, of Góngora, and of Quevedo.

Bernardo de Balbuena (1562–1627), her predecessor, faced too the problem of clashing influences. As a priest, he sought a commanding place in the ecclesiastical hierarchy; as a poet, he sought to rival Ariosto, Ovid, Virgil, and Homer. But his approach was less tinged with contrition. It is in full display in his *Apologetic Compendium*, a gorgeous opuscule in which he traces the divine nature of poetry back to Moses, David, and Solomon:

> In the end, the sheer force of his harp, his music, and his poetry was such that one can say about him only what the poets said in praise of Orpheus and Amphion: for if the latter walled Thebes with his harp, and the former moved mountains, restrained rivers, and suspended hell with his lyre, with that of David atrocious and rebellious spirits are tamed today, indomitable and barbarous customs are reached and tempered, the sacred walls of heavenly Jerusalem from living stones are edified.

Having thus established its pedigree, he allows himself to revel in its more formal aspects:

> The elegance of the words, the propriety of the language, the soft and beautiful movements; the sharp, orderly, and new ways of saying; the abundance, clarity, dignity, the delicate style; the ordinary and common articulated as particular and extraordinary, and what is more, the extraordinary and difficult articulated as ordinary and easy—everything is in the jurisdiction of the poet, who has the duty of universality, in prose and in verse, in one and the other genre, and this with distinction and lavishness.

Perhaps it is owing to this eclecticism that his name does not appear in "the census of immortal names." His struggle is muted; his adaptability, questionable. "To attain glory . . . it is not necessary that a writer show himself sentimental, but it is necessary that his work, or biographical circumstance, stimulate pathos," says Borges. Balbuena was a cheerful man, a disadvantage that Rabelais overcame by staking territory in a rising form and Lope by leading an adventurous life. Balbuena, moreover, dedicated his life to *El Bernardo*, an epic poem in five thousand octaves. And though Ureña has compared it to Spenser's *Faerie Queene*, posterity is eminently impatient with what it perceives to be a transgression of reasonable artifice, more so if it comes in bulk.

Providentially, Balbuena also worked at a more modest scale. *Grandeur of Mexico* (1604), a descriptive poem in nine chapters addressed to a fledgling nun, has been edited a number of times since the XIXth century. It has not reached other languages, other literatures, but it lives. It is rich in what Huxley calls "the ultimate magic": verbal recklessness.

> For he who in greedy palate and soul
> of esurient Epicurus probes and trails
> the infamous sect and sickening chair;
>
> if his stomach and gut hounds him,
> and of it he makes a coarse, obscene god,
> who compels endless sacrifice,
>
> let him demand at whim, spare no expense,
> for in its fair and ample plazas
> he will see one-act farces overmuch.

In Balbuena's effort to celebrate Mexico extravagantly, he plays with alliteration, anastrophe, accumulatio, antithesis, anaphora, chiasmus, parallelism, polyptoton, syncope—and in the luxuriant ornamental structures that grow, one detects brilliant anticipations. Reyes accurately describes him as a "searcher, miner, goldsmith, coiner, and craftsman."

> In sum, nymphs, gardens, and orchards,
> crystals, palms, ivies, elms, walnuts,
> almonds, pines, poplars, laurels,
>
> beeches, mulberries, vines, cypresses, cedars,
> firs, boxwoods, oaks, tamarisks, holms,
> grapevines, arbutus, loquats, servals,
>
> orange blossoms, opium poppies, pinks,
> roses, carnations, lilies, madonnas,
> rosemaries, stocks, eglantines, sloes,
>
> sandalwoods, clovers, balm, verbenas,
> jasmines, sunflower, guava berry, broom,
> myrtle, chamomiles of gold overfull,
>
> thyme, hay, pepperweed in branches hidden,
> basils, jonquils, and ferns,
> and all other bloom in April scattered,
>
> here with thousand beauties and profits
> all by the sovereign hand were given.
> This is their place, and this their fallow land,
> and this the Mexican spring.

Discovery is a singular merit of the Baroque: its exploratory spirit is bound to stumble upon uncharted forms through its ceaseless, labyrinthine gyrations. And Balbuena exploits in his eclectic manner another of its merits: architectonic vision. The first chapter invokes Balbuena's muse, Isabel de Tobar, the future nun, and proceeds to describe in a Whitmanian catalogue the Protean manifestations of self-interest upon which the city is built. Then appear the edifices in the second chapter, the sources of wealth in the third, the occupations of the people in the fourth, the feasts in the fifth, and in an unexpected lyrical ascent, the delights of nature in the sixth—government and religion occupy the last two chapters respectively, before the vigorous epilogue, which is a synthesis of the whole. This crude outline omits the numerous digressions (most of them personal, charming, and erudite), but allows for a better vista of the construction. Balbuena shifts the poetic genre according to the subject, as if intent on pursuing the dynamism of folds: now he is satiric, now he is elegiac; now tragic, now comic; now heroic, now pastoral. In light of this, one can understand why Ureña compares the *Grandeur* with the Metropolitan Sanctuary, a baroque temple annexed to the Metropolitan Cathedral, and why Lazo says that in the poem "one discovers a firm lineal structure, a geometric structure like that of a classical temple covered by an abundant foliage of baroque volutes and arabesques in sumptuous color and sonority.

The constitutionally intellectual imagination of Sor Juana has granted a formidable view of her epoch; it would be fitting for the constitutionally pictorial imagination of Balbuena to complete this view. Together, their lives span a difficult moment for the artistic spirit in what would become the nation of Mexico. Again, it could be argued that they were never wholly poets, that their inner censor demanded too many victories to the nun and to the priest. It could be argued, following Hazlitt, Arnold, and Eliot, that their audience was far too negligible and unliterary. But that is in the nature of the activity. The poet's self is spasmodically unitary, and the audience is mostly absent. The work is always a cluster of evasions and confrontations, an effort toward a tenuous, half-glanced state of grace. "This imminence of a revelation, which never comes to fruition, is, perhaps, the aesthetic event." Or, to put it in Balbuena's own terms: poets were crowned with ivy, a vine that through artifice embraces and clasps the tree and the house, persisting in its hold even after they collapse.

Kit Maude

Varieties of Absence

1.

A translator sits at their desk to work.

2.

But something is wrong.

3.

The original is absent.

4.

The physical copy of the original is not where they left it on the desk by the side of the computer. It is not on the floor underneath the desk. It is not on the bookshelf. The translator's study is not kept neatly so there are many different things the book, a relatively slight volume, could be lying underneath. But it is not underneath any of them.

5.

The translator expands their pursuit to the rest of the house which, similarly untidy, offers many potential places for an original to lurk unseen. The fruitless, increasingly irritable search takes them all the way through until lunch. They decide that for the moment they will just have to allow the disappearance to be a mystery. They can work from the pdf of the original on the computer.

6.

After lunch, they discover that the pdf of the original is absent from the computer.

7.

The file cannot be turned up through any of the searches that occur to them. Nor is it among the deleted files, or lurking in an old email attachment. Their emails with both publishers, of the original and the translation, have disappeared as well. Not other emails with the same people regarding different subjects, only those regarding the original text.

8.

The original, until this morning a significant part of their life, perhaps to an unseemly extent, is now absent from it.

9.

The bench where the old florist used to sit is visible through the window.

10.

Swings are an extraordinarily powerful means of signalling absence. They should be manufactured in such a way that they can be easily moved. So when tragedy strikes their position can be adjusted. Or blown away when the bomb hits.

11.

The partially finished translation remains, like the swings, tauntingly un-absent and flapping in the breeze.

12.

It ought to be there. But that 'ought' is misplaced. Who says it should be there?

13.

We never quite realize how much space they take up when they aren't absent. Fully there, glimpsed, there by implication, by immanence. By varieties of presence.

14.

Without the original, the text cannot be continued. This is obvious to all. But how can it be left unfinished? It's simply not fair.

15.

Because the original is absent, the translation cannot be checked against it. The translation is now the only authority on the original.

16.

No, they did not make it up.

17.

What was there is not there now. It is only what it was and no longer is.

18.

It is as though a column of tanks has rumbled its way through the internet and onto the computer, grinding up the files that contained the original, blasting away all reference and trace of the original across the electronic world. And then a squad of shock troops has dismounted from the vehicle and leapt forth from the screen to burn the physical copy, careful to clean up after themselves. Look there, is that a mote of ash? Or dust? In the end, we shan't care much either way.

19.

Your most Magnificent Majesty,
As your august personage must already be aware, all efforts to locate the Original have thus far been for naught. It is my sincere belief that, if it is not to be found within the reaches of the known world, then it must have been removed, or removed itself, to Unknown Lands. I therefore beseech thee to supply the funds to outfit a mission that shall venture forth into uncharted territory in an effort to bring the Original back to where it belongs, for the glory of your realm and the good of all. To adequately undertake leadership of this most perilous but worthy enterprise, I estimate that I shall need three stout ships with a crew of fifty each, and provisions sufficient for a voyage of two years. The crown shall have a majority share of any economic benefits arising from our inevitable discoveries in recognition of your unmatched generosity. My motivations are purely philosophical; without the Original I am bereft. I shall leave the Translation in your safekeeping in the hopes that it be of some use to you and your learned advisors. It has become useless to me.
Your humble servant . . .

20.

A vacant but still moving swing may take several forms. There is the violent arc with a kink, as though someone had just leapt off the seat at the highest point. There is the barely perceptible sway in the breeze. There is the gentle but firm back and forth, as though a young child were being pushed by an adult. Even if neither are visible.

21.

After much research (wandering around rooms in the dark with elaborate equipment), the consensus among the parapsychologist community is that the original is not a ghost.

22.

And yet the original still somehow sits on the desk, not being there. A patch of air pressing outward against the air that would not have been occupied by the original. A space that won't be filled up. Because, much as one tries to replace the space with another pile of books, papers, bills, or knick-knacks, there is always the suggestion that the original is somehow *underneath*.

23.

Meanwhile, the translation is unaccountably growing longer. There is no memory of adding to it, how could that be? But, nonetheless, the word count keeps rising.

24.

Leaping from the swing when it's at its apex. Buttocks propelled from plank. Exhilaration. Weightlessness. Life ought always to be like this. But did you think about where you're going to land? Check for passersby? Did you think of your knees? Watching someone leap from the apex of a swing. Everything that might go wrong. All the different variables. A hole in the chest. How quickly things can be taken from us. Withheld, until the safe landing merely, but withheld all the same.

25.

Pursuant to further enquiries: perhaps the original was devoured by a bear?

26.

That would certainly explain why the swing has been torn from its frame.

27.

If the original was the translation's homeland, can it possibly remember it as it really was, or has nostalgia already begun to blur and sweeten the edges? Is it perhaps poisoned by grief? The pages continue to fill. They can now only be regarded with a certain horror.

28.

Days lost in a fug of typing. Has agency, too, been misplaced? There is an empty swing outside every window. On every screen.

29.

Swings come with many different seats. A wooden board. A metal rectangle. Plastic. The best are those with a strip of rubber, but they don't swing on their own quite so evocatively, they twist and tangle. The chains are pretty consistent.

30.

The absence of the original has grown to be as tangible as the original itself. The translation feeds on its negative energy. For the better? Probably not.

31.

The suggestion that the original never existed gathers strength. But it's poppycock. If the original is acknowledged, and universally it is, it exists, existed and shall exist. The translation may continue to grow but we know its course completely, from beginning to end. The boundaries of its existence are defined by the original. In that sense, the presence or otherwise of the original is neither here nor there.

32.

The sounds a swing makes: the creak, the whoosh, the crinkling of the chain. Or a well-oiled chunk of silence. All grist to the heart strings.

33.

And yet the original weighs down the flight of the translation like a ball and chain. Should the translation swerve too quickly, the delayed momentum is likely to cause inadvertent damage. It might knock someone off a swing.

34.

If a swing is used with enough vigour, then once the swinger has leapt off it might continue its loop right up to and past the perpendicular, and so loop again and again around the crossbar. It is thus in a sense eating itself, the way a translation devours an original. In each case, something new is created.

35.

A translation, of course, must then be uncoiled, but in the opposite direction.

36.

If up is down and down is up, then this is best ride ever!

37.

When alien civilizations discover the remnants of swings and other playground equipment, will they understand their purpose? Perhaps they will believe them to be some kind of factory yard? An army training ground? A venue for ritual sacrifice? If so, where are the tzompantli?

38.

One could argue that the absent original is simply one skull in an eternal tzompantli.

39.

It is important to consider the nature of the atmosphere in which the empty swing is doing its swinging. For maximum poignancy, the breeze must be gentle. A gale will likely produce a somewhat comic or horrific effect. Still air is a deathblow.

40.

Thus far, the swing has been singular. But rarely is a single swing built on its own, they tend to come in pairs or more. Swinging is a social pursuit, it would seem. Or public at least. But each moves at its own rhythm. A row of empty swings at different points in their arc conjure a ghostly chorus line, not the absence we're concerned with here.

41.

Original is a misnomer. Nothing is original. But everything is circular. Both there and not. Perhaps in the circumstances it would be more useful to regard the translation as the original and translate the latter from the former. So long as there are two texts and neither is absent then balance shall be restored.

42.

But at the moment both are absent! Fully in one case, partially in the other. The fear is that if the translation truly takes the original's lead then it will begin to write itself into absence at any moment.

43.

The translation can only fantasize about what the original is up to in its new existence. Soaring through space and time—when one is absent they can also be anywhere—on adventures beyond the actuality-bound translation's ken.

44.

Or delving into the psychological depths of the bourgeoisie, what horrors still lurk, waiting to be exposed?

45.

Or saving alien creatures from a threatening asteroid. Or some kind of folly with an uncanny resemblance to the dilemmas of our world.

46.

Or enjoying a rip-roaring jape clad in doublets and boddices. With swordplay!

47.

Or staring down the maw of the local caudillo. Leading the peasants to freedom. Or, more likely, to appoint a caudillo of their own choosing. And so we're back for the sequel.

48.

Rewriting a classic. Because why bother with new plots? The original ought to know how overrated that is.

49.

A story about a writer trying to write while having unfulfilling sex with a range of colourful individuals. Translations are voyeurs at best.

50.

A lone swing sways empty in the breeze. Get your bum in there!

Eli S. Evans

The Skiing Antiquarian

A successful antiquarian getting on in years decided to take up skiing—downhill, in particular. Before long, he crashed. Perhaps you're thinking this was because of his beginner status, and in part you'd be correct, but it was also because, being an antiquarian, he was riding on some very, very old skis that probably were no longer fit for use. As a matter of fact, they weren't even skis at all, but just planks of wood torn off the lid of an antique player piano.

In any event, while the antiquarian lay there reassembling his wits, two smug gentlemen in fancy looking jackets—one red and the other orange— came skiing to a stop beside him, spraying him with snow.

"You okay there?" asked the one in the orange jacket.

"I do believe I am," answered the antiquarian.

"Just embarrassed, huh?" came the reply of the gentleman in the red jacket.

"Embarrassed?" The antiquarian pushed his way back to standing. "Here I am, an older man, successful in my field, who has taken it upon myself, despite my advanced age, to learn something new and difficult, and you would dare suggest that I might feel embarrassed because it hasn't been perfectly smooth sailing along the way. To the contrary, I could hardly feel prouder for challenging myself to undertake this hazardous journey when no one at all would blame me for staying right where I am, resting on my laurels, which, by the way, are rather plentiful.

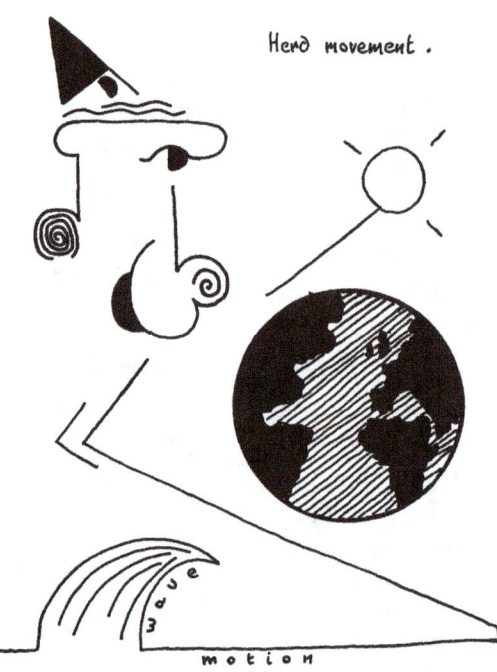

I'll have you know, I'm the preferred source of antique English honor boxes for a certain celebrity songwriter who happens to collect them as a hobby."

The two gentlemen in the jackets looked at each other.

"That's all well and good," said the one in the orange jacket, then, "but I think he was talking about the fact that we can see your penis."

"My penis?"

The antiquarian looked down, only to discover that, as had happened in the awful nightmares from which he had on so many occasions awakened sweat-soaked and calling for his mother as a pubescent schoolboy, he had evidently left the house that morning having forgotten to dress his lower half. Seeing this, he was extremely embarrassed, indeed! Yet, despite this embarrassment, he was also grateful that, thanks to the fact that he had himself grown quite hirsute as a result of extensive contact, over the course of his career, with the bundles of horsehair with which furniture during the Victorian era was usually padded, he appeared to have suffered neither frostbite nor—less pernicious but still unpleasant, to be sure—frostnip on any of his essential bits and pieces.

Later that night, however, as he reflected on the events at the ski mountain while sipping whiskey from a rare nineteenth-century Scottish quaich fashioned from wood scraped off the trunk of the hulking sycamore tree, located near the border with South Ayshire with East Ayshire, from which small-time counterfeiter Wylie Smeal was hanged in August of 1573, it occurred to him that he might have suffered just a bit of frost *nibble*.

Anna de Noailles

A Roman Morning

trans. Diane Josefowicz

The beauty of morning, always and everywhere surprising, is nowhere more so than in Rome. The day rises full of brass: the sun and turquoise sky unite their replenished forces to create a mood of youth and triumph. The gaze sinks into this sparkling Nirvana, which penetrates the body and swirls in the brain, brightening the very heart's blood.

It seems solid, this exploding sky, painted in blue impasto as upon a Persian manuscript's illuminated pages, stiffened by an accumulation of cerulean brushed on in successive coats by patient and ardent miniaturists.

Shifting in the warm wind, the massed cypresses wave their green caps while all over Rome, in chaste response to this solemn salute, the happy waters of fountains erupt in soaring bursts of snowmelt.

On such a beautiful morning a hymn gushes from me, quick as the lark's call. From an Armenian poet of the thirteenth century I borrow these songs of praise:

> The morning prayer is most quickly answered. If
>   sweet perfumes can change death to life,
>   none are more inspiriting than the soft ones
>   of morning.
>
> If joy in Love is given me only once
> let this moment of deep love come at dawn!
>
> Whatever one wishes to attain by love comes
>   from love of morning.
>
> Take pity on me, Lord, and give me a bit of that
>   spirit, desired by so many, that can only be
>   caught at dawn.
>
> I beg you, give me a drop of this daybreak love.

Just this morning, an old carriage, swaying on its tired springs like a boat on a heaving lake, takes me from the saffroned city into the Roman countryside.

It seems that we are going nowhere, so fully has the rising heat imprisoned the horse and buggy in a turbulent monotony. The route is tortuous, burning. The tops of the walls, surrounding me on all sides, are softened by overhanging greenery—blossoming red poppies, each so small and slender the tiny central stalk cannot be seen, suspended like a gout of blood against the blue. Acacias, supple willows, a whole shimmering thicket rises and dissolves in an atmosphere green as flames of alcohol.

Outside a stone villa of juicy pink, a wisteria bursts from a rock like a fountain of mauve water. I arrive at a deserted spot, gilt with hot dust: here is the old Protestant cemetery. In red letters on the arched gate is the word: *Resurrection*. I enter. O, that the dead are dead!

Alleys of black earth, satined smooth, rise by degrees among the stands of cypress, and alongside each slender Romanesque tomb is a narrow garden of violets, vincas, freesias: sentimental flowers watered by the crystal blood of the dead. From one tombstone to another, ivy weaves its quivering thread of leaves that ripple in the heated velvet breeze, murmuring sweet as a summer lake overspilling a stone stair.

This morning, in this little cemetery of exquisite company, the dead seem to congratulate themselves on having become a family joined in companionable silence, reunited within a scented garden. A select family, thoughtful, assembled by mysterious summons: from all countries of the world they come, these young things of about twenty, to join the shades in the charm radiated by Keats and Shelley.

Most of these poetic tombs, these plaintive marbles, carry inscriptions in Greek, or else an urn, a harp, a weeping Eros. All this funerary grace excites without despair: nothing stands apart, save for a languid consent. The doves sigh delicately, hidden high in the cypresses.

Along these paths of silky earth are mounds of sweet petals, pink and white—camellias fallen from their branches, swept up and arranged in fragrant heaps by the gardener, that punctual visitor to the tombs. Where he has not yet taken these pains today, the circular paths are completely littered with flowers, as if tossed there by a mischievous Muse, perhaps the quick and turbulent Erato who rains them down from her inverted tambourine, or the ancient festival orgy that had once drawn young Romans into the house of the voluptuary Thargelia.

The more death shapes life, the more you are dead, O dead! Ah, that the dead here are dead! Hardly has one imagined their light bones. Would that the sun, penetrating the shadows of the cypress, throw its fishnet of gold on this pond of stone, or the delicate diamond stars send forth a sparkling of white fireflies, this garden would smile, soothe, coo.

In France, the dead live in cold mausoleums; what remains of them is the soul, a shadow that haunts familiar space and intrudes upon the living. But here, consoled and cared for by the faithful light, they are caught up in life's inexhaustible festival.

When I left the cemetery and found myself again in the dry, deserted square, a peasant passed in his cart, painted in vivid colors with scenes from the Trojan War. Insouciant, jolting along on his rustic chariot, he sang from a happy throat into the solemn silence of full midday. How beautiful is the song of a man! His was neither a complaint, nor a melody, but a series of powerful, peaceful, exhilarated tones pitched against the burning blue with the arrogance and the certitude of being always—O vanity!—a young man, and one who sings . . .

Returning to Rome, I spy a Franciscan monk who, cruelly assailed by the heat, crosses the countryside in hurried steps. His bare head, cooked by the sun, spins above his brown collar like wine whirled in sandstone bowl. He runs, staggers, brings himself up short, starts off again.

O my brother, if, like Shakespeare's Brother Laurent, you are going with such frenzied steps to bless some mysterious and secret union like that of a Montagu, of a Capulet, make haste, I beg you, and press on! I come from the house of the dead; they rest, believe me, forever. Bless love on this earth. I come from the house of the dead; I cannot tell you the impression they have had upon me, with their inexhaustible sleep. And the jubilant universe shuddering there below like a helix cloud spinning fast in the blue.

They rest for always. Bless love on this earth! There, in the place I come from, where all is silent and self-possessed, human passions arrive at their vain conclusion beneath mounds of flowers.

But whoever wants love denies death; they don't believe in it, the two living young people who perhaps, in this moment, await you.

And above all, my brother, should you see lovers who cry, who hope, who despair, don't reason with them, don't chide them; give them no advice, no philosophy—just help them. "If all your philosophy can't bring Mantua to Verona and Verona to Mantua"—shouts Romeo, separated from Juliet—"whatever can your philosophy mean to me?"

I come from the house of the dead; there is nothing but love on this earth. If any advantage remains to them, to these dead who are so dead, it is to have once been young people in whom life flowed; no other virtue touches them. As for the two poets who sleep below, their glory is to have wanted to express life, which is to live for all time. My face, inclined toward them in such wonderment, cannot move them, but their hazy, dimmed instincts no doubt renew themselves each time the nightingale chooses a mate in the dark cypress, and when the butterflies of night shake the white camellias that seem, with their varnished foliage, like chips of the jade moon. Perhaps it's their silver dust that the moon shakes out at the dawn hour, when the flaming cicadas raise up a song that seems to come from the azure dryness of the sky itself—while on the Aventine, the Greek convent of Saint-Sabine rings out a frenetic carillon, dispensing to the whole Roman countryside an amorous benediction. . . .

Guadalupe Dueñas

Two Stories

trans. Colin Gee[1]

The Dying Man

Inopportune as hail they arrived one early morning while everyone slept. Their faces tear-streaked, sad, maybe sobbing. With difficulty they dragged their feet. They carried suitcases inflated like horses' bellies and toffees wrapped in bugambilia twigs. The branches of lemons in their hands shone like blazing funeral candles.

They were old friends of my parents and always showed up like that. My mother hurried to install them in the best guest room, with mystifying sweetness. I never understood why she was so happy for them to take over the house.

But this time, strangely evasive, they locked themselves in with my parents without acknowledging our words of greeting and without any consideration for the ten-year old who, piglike, may well have been expecting a lemon.

A sudden stillness took hold of the house. Afterwards, only for an instant, I heard the wail of my mother. Then the sharp, long silence between the ropes of water that streamed on nonstop.

The clouds formed grey and endless manes. From so much waiting I fell asleep. The voice of my father boomed above those faces I could not see:

[1] *Translator's note:* In my translations I have attempted to follow not only the diction but also the tone of Pita Dueñas, the severe joker, remaining as literal as possible while doing my best to transmit the desperate humor, the punch and careen of Dueñas' prose. Mostly her paragraphs move very fast, and the several amateur translations I have read specifically failed to capture this: wooden and pedantically literal, they failed to transmit the original voice, the spark of the fiesty femme fatal that was Pita. The goal after all is to give the English-speaking reader as close as possible the experience of reading the original, fantastical prose of this Mexican genius, and finger-searching for word-for-word renderings simply will not cut it. I hope basically that the translation is nearly as entertaining as the original.

'He shall stay here, whatever happens! Be it as God wills!'

They entered my bedroom still dripping and in great distress. The little old lady tall and solemn. The favorite son trailed behind her with a walk he had never had before, downcast, and his eyes flitted behind their lids like a wolf trapped between bars. No longer strong, nor tall, nor a big laugher. He had been struck down with a single blow by some secret sadness.

His sister Asunción entered behind him with her grimace of nun without virtue: she no longer had a place in the world and couldn't do the convent. Next Samuel, the idiot, damp and unsteady, who rummaged through the wardrobes as though he could find something in there that belonged to him. Hideous with his disgusting string of spit.

They were extremely rich, although to me they never looked it. They talked about how their grandfather used to lay out wicker baskets full of gold that one day he up and buried, and no one ever found out where.

The fool always frightened me. One time I saw him twist like a leech in an epileptic fit. He brought down the curtains in an effort to stop his fall and then lay quiet in the middle of the mosaic, stretched out and opened up like a great bat. His mouth was full of foam like thick cotton. I can still see it today when I close my eyes.

The sister was a nun whom I never saw in the convent. She always was going to go, but then ended up staying. She busied herself with useless things learned in the cloister: banging the piano, painting watercolors, crafting depressing boughs out of crepe paper, putting together little embossed boxes, and making cushions with silk borders covered with beads to toss around the parlor by the dried tortoise. She sang the mysteries in the parish church in her shrill voice, and had unlimited potential for holding grudges. When I first met her she had gone six months without speaking to her mother and three years without looking at her kind and intelligent brother. Maybe she was jealous of his beautiful soul, wonderful body, or maybe avoided loving him because she had figured out how to hoard up her own happiness.

He was in love with a beautiful girl whom he wrote to long distance. He used to read her letters to me. I was his favorite. He enjoyed my pranks, tolerated my fits, and promised to take me to see Europe. But this time he was not the same as he was.

Mommy saw me crying and explained: they are in terrible distress. He had helped the Cristeros. In his cellar they found a complete arsenal and took him prisoner. He was three months in the dungeons of Morelia alongside other criminals. There they inoculated them against tuberculosis. He watched his companions' lifeblood drain away while the pestilence consumed his throat and left him a scar like a strangling frost. Before his escape he know he was a dead man. Like a sapling under an eruption of pests, that is how the illness took him. His forehead bulged and an obstinate fever set his eyes on fire.

When he fled the prison, wishing he had died with his companions, he spent fifteen days with the coyotes, subsisting on roots, and walking barefoot got as far as Yurécuaro. From there he traveled to Mexico City to hide in my house and wait for death, which he brought with him, which was gnawing at his tissues minute by minute.

The instant I saw my mommy separate his dishes and washing to keep from contaminating us I threw myself into the arms of my friend, I kissed him and made him understand that I felt neither fear nor disgust. Moved, he pushed me away, and smiled sadly at my exaggerated tenderness.

Since that day I was with him every afternoon.

The best doctors attended him in his room. Months and months of torture, analysis and opinion. Not a pore on his body escaped the torment. All for nothing! He bled ceaselessly, his cheeks were the color of jícama, his eyes became frighteningly large, and he completed the agony by crumbling away every single hour.

The fiancée stopped writing, but he never mentioned it.

I saw him divorce himself from every human support with such burning serenity it made my blood run cold, and there came a moment when he had become such a stranger to this world that he even forgave the pigheaded silence of his sister.

He talked to me and made me believe that for him life was good. He only became harsh when his mother sobbed over his ever-impending death. At those times he would talk of shame and cowardice and in a dry voice order the little old lady to be quiet.

I never thought he would die. During the year his roof and mine were the same I accustomed myself to his symptoms as though they were harmless facts, and supposed death could never touch a youth so wholesome. But one day, the day that always comes, the doctors gathered for the umpteenth time. One of them proposed they kill him, as a just and pious act. My patient, who could no longer even turn pale, with a kind smile, said that he would accept such a death if the father confessor would absolve him. The priest spoke of crime and roundly rejected the unspeakable solution. Shrugging, the doctor left him to his torment.

He was a forest on fire that was going out trunk by trunk.

I did not completely understand the drama about that man. I survived on what he invented for me: I would be beautiful, happy, free. He built me a future full of fantasies that never came to be. Happiness never ever came, but the dying man painted it with breathtaking brushstrokes, for he had firm hope in the eternal plan.

The day of his passing was for me pain that only the day of my own death shall surpass.

That week they had reprimanded me and he hadn't taken my side. I got my revenge by not visiting him. I hummed around my room so that he would hear me. Through the wall I heard his eager breathing, like a long-expected death rattle. During the night his fatigue seeped into my room and I was cruel enough not to call out to him.

The inevitable afternoon I arrived from school at the moment when the last rites were being urgently administered. They were applying Extreme Unction to feet already treading the celestial path. I looked into his eyes overcome with sadness, and when the voice I knew told me I had denied him his final week of comfort, I hugged at his body in a frenzy. But stronger than my piety was the terror produced by the ice block that was his flesh. I immediately shrunk back. He noticed and said, calm:

'The cold is already at my knees. But touch my hands, they still have a bit of life in them.'

His mother begged me to get out—I didn't pay her the least notice. I placed my mouth above the face of the dying man and began to recite bitter prayers I did not even know. He repeated them.

There was no strength on earth that could have separated me from the head of his bed—I was there as he died. He told me in a firm voice that he would wait for me in heaven. My father dragged me out into the corridor and that was when I saw Asunción, the one with the boundless hate, the one that would never forget, vomiting up her soul's arrogance in a fury of screams. I joined in, joined her shrieks for forgiveness that death would stamp closed beneath the marble lid.

THE SPIDER

From her infinitesimal trapeze she plunks down, ironic and depraved. Her black pupil uncovers transparent chasms in the mirrors in my room.

Alert with her eye, in her tower of wind, she spies down into my sleepless nights and startles my failure of a face, without mascara, thin and defeated. She peers into the deepest pit of silence. She knows my body and the clutch of my hands. She perceives that I am as wild as the vine and as captive as the trees.

When I throw myself in long sobs across the sour sheets she hangs above my flesh and feels the thrill of my insomnia.

Then she tosses out her flaccid legs, bristles wet, and creeps the walls, hunted by my angst.

I see her in the face of time.

She watches me from the nocturnal web. Her pupil accuses and damns me. And neither my flood of vanity nor well of arrogance disturbs her, not even the bright turmoil of the morning.

I know that she watches me, and I search for her upon the walls at night, in the vortexes of the shadows. As my helpless naked form floats in the mirrors and fatigue nestles into my dry loins, her pupil finds me and affronts me with her laughter—laughter over the distress of my leaden premonition, as lonely as my bed, as lonely as my words.

I know what I feel and I know that in the dead of the night she waits for me. If I sleep, she dances across my temple, her eye against my eye. She struts across my back, tangling my hair in her venomous adventure.

I do not want them to touch her! Leave her on my walls, leave her in my room, in my tomb of white sheets and linked moons. I know her and join myself to her pendulous sway, to her hypocrite's death. Let no one think of sweeping out her web of echoes, her hammock above the void.

Some Bibliography

Carballeda, Aurura Piñeido. 'TIENE LA NOCHE UNA VENUS OSCURA: LA CUENTISTICA DE ANGRA CARTER y GUADALUPE DUEÑAS DESDE LA PERSPECTIVA DE LA LITERATURA GOTICA', Universidad Nacional Autónoma de México, Ciudad de México. 2001.

Dueñas, Guadalupe. *Tiene la noche un árbol*. Fondo de Cultura Económica, Ciudad de México. 2021.

Dueñas, Guadalupe and Espejo, Beatriz. Fondo de Cultura Económica, Ciudad de México. 2017.

Martínez Carrizales, Leonardo. 'Guadalupe Dueñas. Antes del silencio'. Semanario cultural de novedades. 10 de febrero (2002): 1–3

Mortiz, Joaquin. *Los narradores ante el público*. Instituto Nacional de Bellas Artes, México D.F. 1967.

Publication of this translation authorized by the Mexican Fondo de Cultura Económica, with special thanks to Guadalupe Lira Montes, Subgerencia de Gestión Editorial, and everyone at the FCE Mexico City offices.

Títulos originales: "El moribundo" y "La araña", incluidos en Obras completas, 2ª ed., de Guadalupe Dueñas, pp. 70–74, D. R. 2017, Fondo de Cultura Económica, Carretera Picacho-Ajusco 227, 14110 Ciudad de México. ePub: https://elfondoenlinea.com/detalle.aspx?ctit=013041L

Tumbleweeds

Shiner can't stop killing. Seems like he can put it on pause a while, but then eventually something overcomes him. I reckon it's a habit he picked up in Afghanistan. I don't know why he couldn't just leave it back there. There might not even be a why. Probably not. It just is. A lot of the world just *is*. No rhyme or reason, especially the reason part. I came into this world to dirt poor parents roasted in a fiery car crash. I know a little bit about hard luck.

I've asked Shiner about Afghanistan, about what happened to him there, but he gives me the cold blue eyes glare.

"Mind your own damn business, Hap," he hisses.

I know to clam up because one day he might kill me, too. That's just a notion. But I think I'm not immune to his dark side. I'm expendable, at some point. Maybe to just eventually be cast aside. No longer of use. Dumped by the side of a road. Or maybe worse. These are things I know and still I stick with Shiner. I don't know why. In America, there's a whole class of folks who can't afford to ask a lot of whys.

Shiner took me in when no one else would. I'd roamed the streets a while, scrounging out of dumpsters, panhandling for some change. I reckon he saw a little of himself, before Afghanistan, in me. I don't know that for fact. He'd never say it was so, of course. He doesn't say much at all. His eyes do a lot of the talking, those steel blue eyes that can flash hot or cold. I kind of fell into line behind him because it was the only option that got me out of sleeping in alleys and away from perverts. I don't think Shiner's that way. He keeps his hands—and words—to himself.

Now we're just rambling men, I guess. Tumbleweeds. Drifters in a stolen pickup and living off burgers and pizza when Shiner scores money, mostly from stealing or robbing a gas station, but at least I'm out of the rain and so I ain't com-

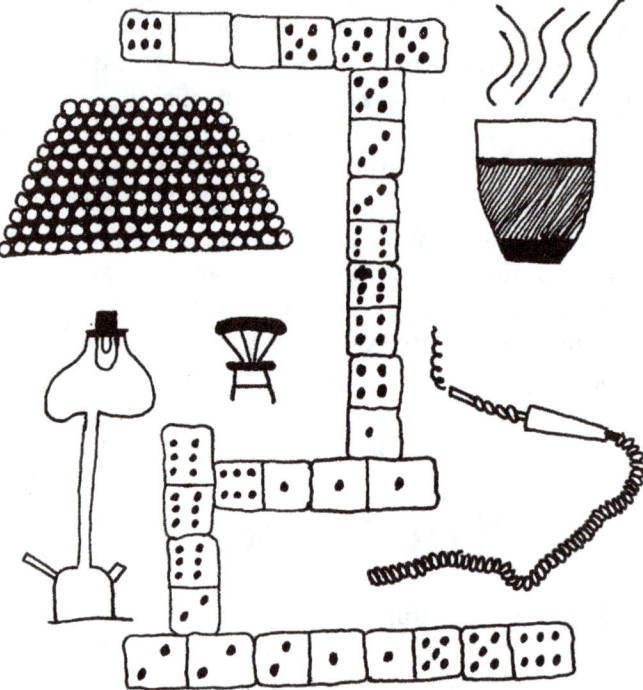

plaining. Maybe I'm a voice when he wants to hear one. A couple of quiet tumbleweeds.

I say tumbleweeds again and Shiner says, "What about them?"

"I've never seen any."

"They just a weed, boy."

A few miles go by and I say, "But they don't have roots."

He looks at me.

"Because they're dead, boy. They don't have no damn use for roots."

I look away and drop the subject. That was the longest conversation we'd had in days. Shiner suddenly turns us onto a highway, and I see we are headed west.

"Where to, Shiner?"

"I reckon Arizona," he says after a moment.

"How come?"

"You want to see tumbleweeds, don't you, boy?"

I nod, thinking, it's the nicest thing Shiner has said to me in a long time.

Dan Tremaglio

To: GLAUCON @GMAIL.COM

Hiya son—

You're probably eating drunken noodles at a café outside Phuket right now—or does the camp have wi-fi? Probably does though I hope it doesn't. The image of a remote kickboxing school made of nothing but clouds and leather is too appealing.

Anyway, since you're apparently taking a break from pummeling your fellow man to a bloody pulp, perhaps shoot your kind mother an email? She checks her phone even more neurotically than usual. I wish that were the worst of it but alas. Want to guess how many times she's painted the basement since you left? So if you're not in the middle of a set of spinning backfists, perhaps drop her a line, just to assure her you're not concussed and senseless in the corner. Consider it a personal favor to me, your dear and caring father, who doesn't have the brain cells to spare.

Seriously now, I want you to know that I really do admire what you're doing over there, G. We had pretty big blow out before you left, but deep down, even while I was trying to talk you out of it, I was jealous. Still am. What kid hasn't fantasized about traveling far away to some secret mountain where 120-year-old kung fu masters with miraculous mustaches practice enlightened ass-kicking techniques from dawn to dusk? Mom thinks you're too smart to devote yourself to a sport, let alone a combat sport, which of course you are, but what's that say? You're too smart for macroeconomics and electrical engineering too. Being smart doesn't mean you shouldn't ever take up oil painting or master an eight-point striking science.

Which is why I want to tell you I'm sorry if I came across as quote unquote on her side. That sucks. Because I used to hear the same stuff from Grandma when I was your age and I remember how enragingly stupid it sounded. Yet here I am now in a semi-similar stance. Life's weird, son.

Here comes the paragraph in which I tell you how I agree with Mom and how I disagree, a paragraph I've written and deleted and rewritten approximately seventeen times. I'll start with the easy part: how I basically agree with Mom about not loving you taking a year off from school. Like I said and said and don't want to re-say but already am, I wish you'd stuck it out till the end of college and then took off to spend a year or three or five abroad. Whatever. It's done now.

Then there's the other part, the part I don't even know how to start, which is how I perhaps (*perhaps*) disagree with your mother, with this idea that you are far too thoughtful and creative and intelligent to dedicate your life to MMA. This is the rub for me, the irony of the father version of myself telling the son version of myself that he shouldn't pledge himself so wholeheartedly to a sport, because that's exactly what I did when I was your age.

For me though it wasn't martial arts but baseball. Baseball was my first love. Baseball was what wrote my daydreams' screenplay. I wanted nothing but to make a whole life out of playing it. Until I didn't. Until I realized I'd spent the first fifteen years of my life trapped in the back of cave in perfect darkness with nowhere to look but inside and that's when I recognized I would die down there in the dark and that baseball was what put me there. Then along came an orange submarine and I was saved. That's a metaphor. Let me tell you the literal version. You might've heard this before but not from me. So listen.

I was about five when I decided to make myself a major leaguer. Why? Shrug. Maybe because baseball was fun? Because it was on TV? Because our culture worships athletes? Probably all these. But also because there was always this impulse in me to pick a trade and devote everything I had to it, not just every ounce of energy but every thought as well. When I was really young, your grandma and also grandpa, who was still alive then, indulged my talk of this, but before long they didn't. Before long they were singing the same tune you're tired of hearing from Mom. Pretty early on, I began to feel that my parents were simply the most local examples of a world that didn't want me to succeed in the way I wanted to.

Here's a formative moment I recall with great clarity: me walking to practice several hours early, having told Grandma a false start time just so I could get out. School was uncomfortable. Home was worse. Grandpa had died by then. I remember sitting on the bleachers, looking out at the empty field, and thought, *This will be my refuge.* Complete sentence. I remember that last word especially. Did the seven- or eight-year-old me really think with a word like *refuge*? Either way, I looked out at that vacant diamond and picked it for a haven.

It should be said that baseball is an especially mythological sport. Sure, track and field and boxing and wrestling are all in the epics, and you'd have to be an eggplant to miss the martial allegory behind American football, but baseball —baseball is tragic in a way no other game can be. It's basically soul-crushing by design. Maybe because the very best hitters still fail 70% of the time. Maybe because it's so effing mundane, a three-and-a-half-hour game played thirteen out of every fourteen days. Or maybe because there's nothing in the world more irrelevant than a Wednesday afternoon game in August between two last place teams on the radio. Which is why baseball requires a memory both short and flawless. You have to recall everything but dwell on nothing. What's happened before means nothing now. There is only this next pitch, this next play, followed by the long wait afterward, a sluggish reprieve in which one tiny lesson must be extracted and the rest forgotten before the next opportunity arises. You can't overthink it, iow.

Baseball is also the only game in which the defense controls the ball. That doesn't sound too weird until you stop to think about it. Nothing happens until the force which aims to prevent things from happening makes something happen. This is the paradox of the pitcher, surely the most profound position in sport, a guy standing alone on a little hill in the middle of a field who writes the story of the game.

I was one of those guys. A pitcher. Or wanted to be. I didn't have a cannon but I was crafty. I had a slick curve and slider and a two-seamer and a deceptive motion. Was I good? Sure. But I was not great. And if you want to make the majors someday, you have to be great. You have to be so obviously undeniably better than every-

body else around you. And I wasn't that. But I wanted to be and I thought the only way to get that great was to believe I was, to tell myself I was, over and over, all day, every day. So I was often in over my head, is what I'm saying, always trying out for the very best teams I could.

Which brings us to when I was fifteen and went out for this really elite American Legion team. They were known to be great and held open tryouts just as a formality. It was a team of studs. Their standout was this kid named Ajax. Jason Ajax. A total freak show. One of these kids fully grown at sixteen. 6'3" 225. A switch-hitting power-hitting catcher. Big league scouts had been haunting his games since he was 12. There were three or four guys almost as good right behind him who ended up garnering serious attention from those same scouts. Our ace was a kid called Horse who stood 6'8" and had a fastball in the 90's. Our number two, a lefty named Church, topped out at 87, while our number three, Martinez, the smartest kid on the team, hovered around the mid-80s. See what I mean? Our third best pitcher threw 85. So this team was sick, is what I'm saying. In fact, you've probably even heard of them, even if you don't realize it. Washington Depot Post #68. Go ahead and google it. For more than a month we were international news. Not because of baseball, though.

Yeah I'll get to that part.

Even though I was a pitcher, I made this team as a catcher, the reason being no other catcher in the area went out for it on account of Ajax, knowing he would be the everyday starter, so the post was really in need of a backup to throw in there during blowouts or doubleheaders. That's how I made it. We traveled all over the state and beyond and won everywhere we went. I played more than I expected because we were usually up by double digits by the fourth inning and that's when the starters started coming out. We were pretty much guaranteed to win the state title, which we did, and looked to have a respectable chance of winning regionals and qualifying to go to the international playoffs that were being hosted that year in Guerrero, Mexico.

I was like you, Glaucon: strategic af. I knew Grandma would flip out as soon as I told her I was going to Mexico, given the abundance of bullshit news she watched. I figured I needed to get an agreement out of her early, so I made her promise as soon as I made the team that she would let me go to internationals if we made it that far. Predictably, she flipped out when I told her, but we were speaking hypothetically then, just a crazy long shot, and so I was able to eke out an okay. She tried to take it back when we actually made it, telling me Mexico is completely run by drug cartels, leaving me to be like no ma, that's just along the border maybe, Guerrero is way way down south, a big clean touristy spot famous for its national park, and besides, you promised, you promised, you promised. So she signed the permission slip and from that day forth she cried and crossed herself, cried and crossed herself, every time I even mentioned the word baseball. I told her relax Ma, I'm statistically way more likely to get killed by my own teammates than mustachioed drug lords.

Wah wah.

Thing is, a lot happened between when Grandma agreed to let me go on the trip and when we actually flew abroad. All the excitement I felt when I first made the team had long faded. Did I get along with those guys? Sure. Not really. Sort of. Enough. I was real quiet in those days. Somehow I'd gotten the idea in my head that I needed to be that way, that I had to be like this baseball ninja, silent, stoic, honed as a monitor lizard, zero energy wasted on charisma or chatter or posturing or whatever. The result was that I appeared even weirder and walled off than I actually was. In other words, I was trying too hard. And it wasn't working. I had a great first month, but after that I slipped into a slump. Slumps are not good for accumulating clout on a team. By the time the state tournament rolled around, I was secretly rooting against us every game. I just wanted the season to be over. I wanted to retreat into my fantasy of a game to see what was left of it rather than fight with reality every afternoon. By the time we won regionals, I was deep in a dark depression.

What more perfect time to take an international trip with a pack of people I mistrusted?

Truth is, I actually got excited again, if only at the prospect of travel, of airports and tray tables and room keys and such. You probably know exactly what I mean. I was fired up enough to not notice the trip got off to a rocky start. You still had to go to a big airport in those days and decide which bags you wanted to put under the plane (checked bags) versus which one you wanted to keep with you (carry-on). We weren't planning to check any bags because the airlines used to charge extra for that, but then they told us at the terminal we couldn't bring baseball bats onto the plane because they were technically weapons and so we had to check them, which our coach really should have figured out in advance but didn't because he was a neanderthal who'd begun using the word beaner as some universal adjective, saying things like beaner airline or beaner busstop or whatnot. So we checked our bags. Then, when the plane was somewhere over Texas, Martinez, who was in an aisle seat beside me, came down with some sort of dental emergency and had to have his face mummified with bags of ice. The second we landed, the assistant coach raced him off to the hospital while the rest of us went and waited at the luggage carousel. And guess what didn't come around, what the airline effing lost? We had a game the next day but no gloves, no bats, no cleats, nothing. Everyone panicked. Not me though. We're talking late August in southern Mexico, so it felt like another planet, the 115-degree air a wall you had to push through to get out the terminal doors. Probably a lot like Thailand, eh?

Anyway, the airline got us our stuff back and we beat Honduras handily in our first game behind a shutout from Horse. The day after that, we took it to the DR in a rout. For our third game we had to play Taiwan. We were 2-0 so far, but they were 2-0 too and had won the whole tournament last year with the same starting nine. They had this lefty submariner who chucked a no-no two days earlier going against us on short rest.

Meanwhile, Martinez had gotten back from the hospital, sans wisdom teeth and higher than Kilimanjaro. We're talking more glassy-eyed than Harry Caray. Coach took one look at him and asked if he could pitch, and Martinez said pardon me, and coach said you're fine, just stay well hydrated, and penciled him in.

The temperature at game time was well over a hundred even though it drizzled during BP. A bolt of lightning hit a summit in Grutas de Cacohumailpa National Park, which made me think of that Robert Redford movie the Natural, the way lightning always foreshadows something big. Ever see that flic about the farm boy who's destined to become the next Babe Ruth until his dad dies beneath a tree that gets struck that night by lightning during a storm? The next morning the kid carves a bat out of the smoking trunk and uses it his whole career, which gets sidetracked when he falls in love with a woman who shoots him in the stomach. There's a violin and trumpet score that cues up whenever lightning strikes throughout the movie, telling the audience to get ready, that something impressive is about to happen.

So Martinez went out there with thunderbolts flickering in the distance to deal against the top ranked team and did so completely lit. He had this hot air balloon look on his face as if he were thinking deeply about something unrelated or thinking nothing at all. The painkillers had him dialed in though, because he sat down Taiwan hitters one after another through the first four frames, looking smoother than he had all season. Once, between innings, I went up and patted him on the shoulder and said, "You're doing great," and he turned to me all slow and said, "At what?" He gave up a little bloop single in the fifth inning, just their second hit, followed by an error, and then one of them cracked an RBI double off the wall. It was the first time anyone had squared him up all day, but Coach panicked and took him out and put in Carpisassi, our shortstop, which was dumb. Carpisassi gave up two doubles in a row, followed by a two-run bomb that still hasn't landed. Suddenly our lead was cut to one and Carpisassi walked the next batter on four pitches before Coach realized he's an idiot and put Martinez back in. Martinez struck out the next two guys and got the third to pop up. Inning over. He sat em down one, two, three in the seventh to seal the W. Soon as the final out was recorded, Ajax went running out and jumped on Martinez's back. Sheer horror flashed across his face, having zero idea what Ajax was all riled up about.

I spoke with Martinez only one time ever after that game. This was years and years later when we bumped into each other at the mall. He had gone on to pitch at Princeton and then hung em

up and was doing something on Wall Street. He asked me what I do. Architecture, I said. The taller the better. All glass. Maximum light. He laughed and admitted he had almost no memory of pitching that game or of the hotel that night or the national park. He only remembered waking up the following morning. The way he said those last two words said it all. It said, *I'm still losing sleep.*

That night though he looked happy enough, memory functioning or not. Everybody crowded into Ajax and Carpassasi's room where they had speakers playing and sunflower seed shells piling up on the floor. Carpassasi had acquired a bottle of apricot brandy and was forcing chugs on everyone. We were off for at least two days now while the other round robins concluded. We were the only undefeated team, which meant we would play whichever worst record-holding squad survived and were feeling pretty good about that.

Then it started to rain. Ajax was the first to go out. Big guy, the heat had been killing him all week. Everyone else followed. The dorms and stadium and plaza and national park all created a kind of campus which we had to ourselves at that hour. Vendors had all closed up and the smell of fried food fell out of the air with those big bathwater drops, the asphalt steaming for a minute or two and then not. I felt good. It was fun running around hooting and hollering for no reason at all, everybody buzzing off a single sip of brandy or pretending to be, an undefeated bunch of 15- and 16-years-olds feeling like they would stay that way forever. Carpisassi humped a sombrero-topped statue. Church posted the video to TikTok. Then it really started to rain. The effect was this: everybody went crazier. We were running around shouting nonsense and decided the best place to be during a lightning storm was out on a baseball diamond. We planned to leave some sort missive for the other teams scrawled across the infield dirt and so we headed that way through the botanical garden beside one of the national park entrances.

Turns out, Grutas de Cacohumailpa Parque Nacional was much more alluring. Crazy how easy it was to get in. No fence. No gate. We just just waltzed past a big map and welcome sign that was actually a warning sign as simply as entering a mall. It felt like a mall inside too, those same bounding echoes and minerally smells from fountains. The foyer was paved at first and hardly felt like the beginning of the second largest cave system on planet earth. The lights were out of course but we had our phones and followed them toward our own voices bouncing back at us. Did we really fall silent the moment we saw one end of the foyer vanish into a great hole rimmed with stony fangs? That's what the stalactites looked like in our cellphones' light, reptilian ones, carpeted in green fur. The colors were spellbinding. Besides the green-green mosses there were also scarlet ones and pale blue flakes and yellow bulbs, all of them as various as fall-time foliage in New England. Does earth's underside know of seasons? Farther along, tiny waterfalls crawled down the walls and across the path, while chunks of mica reflected our light like the eyes of pensive critters. The path bent this way and that, not seeming to drop down at all but we know now it did. Just when we started think it was time to turn around, we arrived at an amazing place: a big broad room where there flowed a great grey river. It was the scariest and most moving thing, G, the way the water appeared from beneath a curtain of stone and half circled the room before exiting beneath another wall, a toppled rainbow shape in greyscale, flickering, whispering about how much lies unseen beneath our feet, we visitors who idolize the stars, chins aimed upward at heights we dream to ascend. Here was a reminder that infinity stretches in all directions. Nobody spoke. Nobody I remember anyway. Maybe my mind was as washed as Martinez's, watching that new world Styx. Chontalcoatlán they call it.

Now, I know what you're thinking, Glaucon. *C'mon, Pop. Seriously? Don't even tell me you idiots got stuck down there!*

I can only say this, son: it was easy. Real easy. Way easier than I'd ever have guessed until it happened.

A few minutes on the shore of the river we turned and headed back the way we came, which was the only way that appeared available. Evidently you can not only not step into the same river twice, you can't even walk up to it the same way. Church was the first one to get panicky, saying this is too long, too far, that it didn't take us this long to get here, etc. He got down on his knees to check for our footprints but the ground was too unforgiving for those. I can't even give you a timeframe, which evidently is a common refrain among subterranean travelers. Let's say it initially took us fifteen minutes to reach the river. Nobody acted worried until forty-five minutes later we wound up back on the shore, except now the river flowed from right to left and was flanked by a soft sand beach. What the eff. That's basically what everyone said about fifty different ways. What the eff, what the eff. Our next attempt to wind our way out of there took twice as long. Angry panic shifted into baffled panic when we came again upon our own sneaker prints along the shoreline. There was a brief window in which we were able to fake laugh about what a pickle we were in.

Q: When did the fake laughter turn into unchecked fear?

A: When the phones started to die.

Church's went out first because he wouldn't stop trying to call above. He cried. I hate to put him on the spot for that, but he was the first and so the sound of it burned deep. Before long we all were crying. Right after Church's went Carpassasi's, then Ajax's, then Herrera's, then Horse's, then Lucero's. I remember when mine went. Last. Mine was the last to go and here's the thing: it didn't actually die. I powered it down. Everybody wailed like doomsday'd descended, but I was just thinking I should save some juice for later. Not a stupid idea, right? Problem is, I didn't realize it actually takes energy just to be a battery, so when I tried to turn it back on a day or days later, there was nothing there anymore.

Just darkness. Absolute.

Some terrified chatter persisted for a while before giving way to false hope, to a faith the park would open again come morning and some friendly bilingual ranger would stroll down the trail and say *hola friends, these the way home.* Most guys spent that next chunk of time trying to talk exactly like they would in their dorms. The more they talked, the less I heard them. I'm no physicist, but all that theory about time being an illusion, it makes extra sense after you've been stuck in a cave. What time is it, how long till morning, how far did we walk, how long has it been, how much longer will it be. Funny how we use the word *long,* a metric of space, to talk about time.

These were the kinds of things I thought about at first, these trivial insights in the dark. Everybody slept in spurts on the river's shore on sand as soft as powdered sugar. Sitting on so much pillowy blackness, you sink into yourself. Even just a few hours without light and you have no idea where you end and the rest of existence begins. You're just a shadow cast by a shadow in the shade of earth itself. Soon every one of your teammates seems a part of you in spite of you and you don't like it, or them, or yourself either. So much time with nowhere to look but inside and you realize there's no self there to look at at all.

And we're still talking the very first day here.

By now, G, you've probably dug up some headlines in a separate browser window. "Legion Trapped Underground," "Connecticut Baseball Team Caught in Flooded Cavern," "Mission Continues for Mexican Cave Boys," and then my personal favorite, "Allegory of the Cave." So you already know the magic number is fifteen. That's how many days we were down there. I couldn't have guessed. Felt like 115 to me.

Panic and patience alternated like the top and bottom halves of innings. That is, until hunger and thirst descended, at which point there wasn't energy for the panic part. The river water was wretched, just poisonously awful, tasting like antibiotics and smelling like urine. How to tell if something just tastes bad or could actually kill you was a survival question I wished I could've answered. Instead, we started licking condensation off the walls, which were furry and pond-like. Between all of us, we had two bags of sunflower seeds, which Horse distributed by the pinch-full at random intervals. Martinez couldn't take any because his Vicadin had worn off and everyone was shouting at him to quit effing moaning.

That first day turned into another day which turned into no day. Slowly the metal balloon of hunger was replaced with a worry, then a hunch, then a certainty that I was going to die down there and that it was my own fault, that my fixation with a game—*an effing game!*—had put me there. Everything suddenly seemed so painfully pretend to me. Crazy how even now I think I can remember what certain things looked like down there: the lay of the beach, the ceiling I stared up at, people's faces when they cried certain things. All hallucinations. Further evidence of an endless game of make-believe we play all day every day. Everything leading up to that moment felt fake except for one thing: the knowledge that it was about to end. All our stories are made up and imaginary except for the ending, which often comes too soon, just like it did for my dad. He didn't die under a lightning-struck tree which turned into a magic wooden sword, he died frying an egg on a Thursday. His story just ended and now mine would too. How could you not despair about what a story that ends that way might mean?

Somebody was fighting with somebody farther down the beach, I soon realized. I believed I was dreaming until the sound of grunting and cursing and kicking sand turned too convincing to ignore. It was Carpassasi. He was trying to strangle Martinez. Martinez had just discovered half a granola bar in his back pocket and was being accused of hoarding it. A newspaper article written after we clinched regionals sprang to mind, one in which Carpisassi was quoted saying, "You know why we're such a filthy squad? It's because we're tight. Road dogs. That's how come we keep winning, by being each other's ride-or-dies."

I started laughing uncontrollably. Laughing and crying. Okay, mostly crying. Of course Carpassasi would murder Martinez. This made perfect sense to me. Maybe they're both already dead and I died with them or maybe I'm doing the strangling or the one being strangled. All possibilities appeared clear as day before me and that's when the sun broke through a bank of clouds in a bubbly orange bloom.

"What, what?" you're probably saying.

Here's another thing I've learned, Glaucon: when people who haven't seen light in a long time see light again, they don't recognize it as light. In the absence of illumination your brain will create it and then, when the real thing shows up, your brain accuses it of fraudulence.

The light I saw, dull and muted at first, brightened tenfold as it breached the water's surface, feeling like a sharp stick to the eyes. This sun was actually not one sun but a row of six of them above a glass ball. The ball had an orange bottom and writing in red capitals down the sides. After several seconds of eye-adjusting ache, I understood that I was looking at a submarine. A man in a yellow helmet in the cockpit raised his hand hello.

That was day fourteen. The friendly submariner beached his vessel before handing out protein paste tubes and taking us one by one on a sub ride home. It had been raining like hell and the caverns were flooded.

Taiwan won the tournament, btw, the only team to ever repeat.

Did I ever play baseball again? Sure. But not the same way. It was no longer religion to me. Once you get above ground, you don't want to go back under. You never stop seeing that kind of darkness. Every time you close your eyes, every time the power goes out, every time you go to the movies and they show the title screen and then nothing for a few seconds in order to guarantee your attention, it gets compared to that.

Speaking of movies, remember that magic bat from the Natural? Well, spoiler alert, it gets broken just before the final scene, but Robert Redford still hits a home run anyway and all the good guys win and our faith in a decent world is preserved. That's the movie. A couple years after the cave, I finally got around to reading the novel by Bernard Malamud that the movie is based on. *The Natural*, I quickly realized, is an ironic title. The novel's protagonist is no golden-haired movie star with an elegant swing. He's crass and rough, an untaught alpha who can hardly help himself and swings his bat like an axe. When he steps up to the plate in the climactic moment, his long line of off-the-field errors take their toll and he strikes out on three straight pitches. Game over.

So back to you now, Glaucon. Something you said during our massive throw-down before you flew out keeps echoing in my head. You said you didn't want to end up like me, just another architect running out of places to put his buildings in a world that's already over-built, that you wanted to get out and do something different, something simple, something great. That's when your mother called all cage fighters cavemen with eating disorders, prompting you to explode on out of there. Hand on the doorknob, you asked if we had heard a single word you said, then slammed the door after you.

This email has been my attempt at a reply. Maybe you understand slightly better now my ambivalence re cyclopic devotion to a game, re cyclopic devotion to anything. One-track-mindedness clearly runs in the family. Yes, I was a miserable little turd during my teenage years, in part because I'd picked a cave of an identity and chained myself therein, but doing so also showed me things I would not have seen otherwise, namely that we never get fully above ground, that we never get to see things the way they really are so long as we see ourselves as separate from them. The truth, as far as I can tell, is that whatever we dedicate ourselves to ends up becoming our cave. Do we have to escape? Is that the ultimate goal? This might be where the metaphor breaks down. I was about to tell you something about this documentary I saw one time about Japanese master scissor makers and how they see scissor making as the perfect metaphor for life, but never mind. This letter is too long already.

Sorry to drop a gnarled allegory/confession on your lap via email, daring you to make sense in a minute of what I've only marginally processed in thirty-plus years. And no, in case you're wondering, I'm not on anything Martinez-esque at the moment, although I suspect I'll need to be shortly, this being a pandora's box I have not breeched in years and years and years.

We miss you, G. Email your mom if you can, pretty please, for aforementioned reasons (paint fumes, brain cells, owls, etc.) Don't feel compelled to respond to any of this madness unless you really want to. Keep your hands up. Sting like a butterfly. Enjoy the food. Talk soon.

Warmly,
Pop

KELLY L WURTH

YOUR DRIVE-BY SHOOTING AS DINNER Conversation

First, mention what you were doing before you saw the boy fall into the street ahead of your car. You and your partner were coming home from work after a not-nearly-busy-enough day. You were putting on brave faces about your business startup in this new city. Slow growth is good growth, right? You were believing in the future because there's always a future as long as you were together, and even after (or is it during?) these long months of COVID, surely one could anticipate good things? You had summarized the exhausting, daily work of hope and new beginnings. Together, you were letting go of the numbers and smiling about how glad the dog would be to see you. You recited the daily litany of going home.

Maybe that's too ordinary for an introduction. You could describe the street where it happened, how that route is part of your daily routine, how you drive it four times a day, including going home for lunch. Mention that there's a café on the route with a deal for unlimited coffee. Not actually unlimited, but you can get a refill every two hours. Chuckle ironically here and ask, honestly, who would drink THAT much coffee? Anyway, describe the café. But here's a problem. Before you've even begun the story, you've already stumbled into the ending. The café is a block beyond where the boy fell into the street. That day, your pre-ordered, empty cups sat a long time on the shelf for you to fill and add cream and sugar. When you got there after the drive-by, your hands were shaking, and it was hard to pour. You can't open a conversation with that.

It could only create confusion to mention the school, the setting where the boy waited with his friend before the two gunmen sauntered by. It's an international academy for elementary level, bilingual students, but this boy was seventeen, a high school student, so he and his friend were just lolling on the grass a few hours after the lit-

tle kids had gone home. Of course, this morning when you again drove past the school, you didn't think of education or the children inside learning in both English and Spanish. You only thought about him. In fact, maybe you'd best not mention the elementary school at all, with everyone's minds on school shootings these days. That's not what this was, although maybe it almost was. You don't know. What it was remains unclear, under police investigation.

You could talk about the ongoing construction project at the apartments east of that elementary school. Demolition and renovation have been going on for a long time and, whatever they were doing, it seemed like it would never be complete. You and your partner talked about it every few days as you drove by. "Will they ever finish?" But that's not news and not particularly interesting. Except now, only a day later, on a utility pole at the construction site, there is a change. People have put up school colors, red and black and green balloons and love notes and flowers and ribbons that say "Miss U 4-Ever Bro."

Your friends may not be ready for any of this. Maybe you should announce, "Trigger Warning" before you talk about how it was to see the boy fall into the opposite, oncoming lane of the avenue. People are easily re-traumatized, but then "trigger" would be a haunting word choice, given the situation. Maybe say, 'This could be upsetting," so your friends can excuse themselves or deflect the subject with a story of their grandchild's honors and awards. Or, simply say what you first thought was happening, how you said to your partner, "Oh, look, some teenager on a dare is lying in the street during rush hour." He was a tall, slender, beautiful boy who seemed at first glance to be playing. That's a lighthearted angle for the story. Kids do crazy things, right? Everyone can relate. And even now, you still want what you saw to be a game, albeit a risky one. But then, the boy rolled and writhed, stood and fell and couldn't get up, and you said to your partner, "Oh, he's having a seizure." Still serious, but not the worst possible thing. Our minds can only move from the inconsequential to the drastic in slow motion, so you must do the same as you share your story with your old friends.

This part isn't so bad. Well told, it could be like a scene in a movie. Your partner bumped up over the curb and onto the grass to stop on the busy street, and you both got out. Another car did the same behind you, and as you slammed your doors, that other driver yelled, "I'll call 9-1-1." You and your partner dodged four lanes of rush-hour traffic. He held up his hands and yelled, "Stop, stop!" as you passed so cars didn't hit the boy. Of course, some people kept driving, anyway. They didn't see or they didn't care or they just had to get where they were going, so they almost ran you down. You may or may not have slammed your hand on the hood of one car that honked and rushed past too close. Your partner may have shared some ancient sign language with the driver. At that moment, you saw your partner as strong and brave, which is nothing new. It was odd to see him stopping city traffic, though, as you had come to this place from a small town. Back there, where tonight's dinner companions still live, there's no rush hour and never a traffic jam unless two farmers idle their pickups in the middle of Main to talk about crops. That's a lighthearted observation they'd appreciate and relate to. Maybe that's a good way to begin.

It would be really difficult to tell these next events, though, so you could leave them out. You knelt beside the boy on the asphalt and saw blood seeping through his white T-shirt. Not a seizure, then. There wasn't much blood, though. Had he been stabbed or shot? You realized then you'd barged in on a violent crime. The man who called 9-1-1 and one other person knelt with you in a triangle and you all had a moment, not knowing what to do. "Do we move him out of the street?" "I don't think so." You said, "That's good, he's breathing." Everyone nodded as if you'd said something astute.

This next part of the story is very personal, but you could spin it from a detached, professional angle. You asked the bleeding boy for permission to touch him, to check his injuries. He didn't answer, but his eyes locked on you, so you took that as "yes." You were a volunteer EMT in a small town thirty-five years ago, so some of the old skills and knowledge kicked in. ABC—airway, breathing, circulation. You checked his pulse at his wrist. It was fast and faint, because of course he was in shock. You almost wished there was more visible blood because you could apply pressure to that kind of wound. If the hole had been in his chest, you could consider a collapsed lung, but the hole was in his abdomen. You saw his back arch as he struggled to breathe. His belly looked taut and you guessed where the blood was going. You knew that internal pressure would build with every heartbeat to diminish every breath. You wished you didn't possess so much specific and useless information.

This was the moment when you wondered, "Where are the police? Where is the ambulance?" But you knew from experience that although it already felt like half an hour, it had probably only been two or three minutes since you'd knelt. You knew it might take them a while to get through so much traffic, so you crawled over to kneel at the boy's head. You set aside ordinary timekeeping and measured reality only by his breaths as he gasped and gurgled. You placed your hands on both sides of his head and explained to him how you would thrust forward his jaw so he could breathe. You tried not to arch or twist his neck because you knew he had fallen, and what if a bullet had hit his cervical spine? What if a knife had nicked an artery? But he had to breathe. You were gentle. You touched him the way you'd handled your babies. You pushed his jawbone up and forward and he stopped gurgling. He gulped a rush of air. You were relieved you'd remembered what to do and how to do it, after so many years.

Do you tell this part? It could sound corny or self-aggrandizing. You sensed that if the boy were to live, he needed not to feel alone. He needed to see your eyes. You were still wearing your sunglasses from when you were headed home, riding west into the setting sun, so you asked the 9-1-1 caller to take them off your face. He did. The boy focused and you felt a jolt at being seen. Without the filter of the dark lenses, you saw him more clearly, too. His expression flickered soft as you became a person to him. Maybe it relieved him not to face a sunglasses' reflection of himself writhing on the ground. The boy breathed in and out and looked through you with his wide, brown eyes. You told him he was going to be okay because that's what you say. His eyebrows cinched in hope and doubt, and he silently challenged you for the hard, alternate truth.

For the old friends here at dinner, should you repeat what you said? You remember the words as urgent and powerful. They are no less so now. Not prayers, exactly, but battle cries, calls to action, and a mother's reminders to come home. The words might seem profane here, spoken aloud under blue-and-mauve halogen lights, but you may offer them as sacred, a *sotto voce* litany. Because when you noticed his breaths fading, you pronounced the only gospel that mattered, "Breathe, breathe, breathe." When he tried to leave you, you nearly shouted and then exulted every time he came back. You told him he was brave, that he could make it. You called him a warrior and you commanded him, "Come on, give me one more breath," maybe one hundred times. And he fought as if a string connected your open lungs to his blood-squeezed ones, as if an electric current surged between your eyes and his. The 9-1-1 man at your right hand checked the boy's wrist again and said, "I can't find a pulse." So you checked the boy's carotid and there it was, slower now and faint, but beating. He had so much internal bleeding and you alone held his airway. You couldn't do everything, and nobody else knew CPR. You had to choose. He still had a pulse, so you stayed where you were. You told him he was a warrior. You called out to him again. You dared him to fight and live, live, live.

Proceed into the climax with care. Not everyone can handle such things, so watch your listeners' eyes. Maybe it's too intimate or intense, so it's not too late to segue, to talk about the weather. With a wail and blat of their sirens, the paramedics came. They carried and dropped their bags and equipment and you told them what you had done, what little you knew. They let you stay at your boy's head to stabilize his neck and airway while they assessed him. You glanced up for a second and saw the professionals cut away his clothes. You averted your eyes from his exposed flesh and underwear. One said, "gunshots, through and through," and they applied patches to wounds on his belly and back. They laid his secrets bare. They claimed him. You were resentful, then relieved.

Another paramedic announced, "No pulse, begin CPR," and that's when you could have sworn your two knees had been welded to the street. Your hands locked, committed to your boy. How would you let go? An oxygen mask magically appeared and covered his silent blue lips. Rapid chest compressions rocked him up and down. Someone thanked you, and you adjusted your hands as a cervical collar closed over them. Finally, you bent into his shallow breaths, brushed your cheek against his, and blinked. You murmured in his ear, "Stay. Just stay." As you let go and crawled backwards, they closed in to devour him with care. You felt a kick of sorrow that you had been holding some other mother's child. And yet, he was yours and would be.

Still, while much must remain unsaid, this next part could be recounted like a movie dénouement, an acceptable anecdote for the table. You pushed up off the asphalt, gathered yourself, and stepped away. You looked for and found your partner still out there waving at cars. Everybody wanted to slow down and stare at the unfortunate, nearly naked victim being lifted onto the gurney. Those drive-bys' Schadenfreude stunk with their automobile exhaust. Your partner hollered at them to move along, that it wasn't any of their business. You loved how he protected your boy's privacy. Although he'd never been an emergency worker, even without knowing what it was called, your partner had secured the scene. You realized then, he'd also steered those impatient rush-hour drivers around you to keep you safe as you knelt like a potential road-kill squirrel in the street. While he is good at many things, he possesses a healer's protective heart, and in that moment you fell even more deeply in love. You knew you would always remember him at this moment as the right man for you because, when he found himself on the yellow line on the highway to hell, he didn't flinch. He stepped into the flames and directed the oncoming traffic.

You recognized then how your partner will always remember you, too, as someone new revealed in this moment. As he waved impatiently at the endless stream of slowing cars, he studied you and said, "You're amazing." He was surprised because he hadn't known you back when you were young, when you steered an ambulance over black ice and knew your way around an Ambu bag. You could only vaguely recall that girl, the one who would startle awake to a beeping pager and race toward midnight accidents and injuries. Maybe she was brave. Maybe she had something to prove. Maybe she just hadn't known any better. But as you stood in the street and watched others load your limp, patched-up boy—the one who now belonged to both of you—into the rig, you didn't feel young or brave and you definitely didn't feel amazing. You didn't feel anything yet, even as you tried to convince yourself it would be fine. Your beautiful boy wasn't going to die.

When the police finally diverted all that traffic and stretched out yellow tape, you and your partner had nothing more to do, so you trudged to the sidewalk. All this time you'd occupied the street as if that is where people stand and kneel and talk, as if you both belonged there. You'd barged into a crisis and made yourselves useful. But then you waited on the sidewalk with useless hands and told each other you had done fine. He would be fine. You didn't admit you had a not-fine feeling. You were both shaking when the police officer came over, so you crossed your arms and leaned in and listened. She asked questions in a gentle voice and you answered the best you could. "No, we don't know his name. No, we didn't see the shooters. We just saw him fall into the street. We're just passers by." She handed you a business card for a community crisis counselor. You took it as you both said you were fine.

Tonight, you take a sip of your cold water and try to remember how fine feels. You see your boy reflected in the ice just as you see him reflected everywhere. His face and scents and struggle are as fresh as they were last night as you held him. To gain some emotional distance, to keep control here at the table, you render your memory. With the September sun falling orange in the sky, you carve the two of you in stone, folded together, anchored on the long-shadowed street like a gun-shot, asphalt-locked Pietà.

The menu blurs in your hands. You're not thinking clearly. You're only half in this world because you stayed up late to watch the news to see if he'd lived. He hadn't. You weren't surprised but it still took your breath away and still does, swift gut-punches of reality reminding you he's gone. You clicked and scrolled social media this morning to fill in a world around his face, to connect a name and parents and sisters and a niece to the face. You found no logic or redemption among the sad and caring emojis.

One friend asks what's good at this restaurant, and even though you've never tasted them, you mutter, "The fajitas are a sure thing." This subdues and flattens you—his teen-aged face is now as vivid and intimate as any memory you've retained of your adult children. You tell yourself that's not possible. Surely you're being overly dramatic. Even though you stared into his eyes as he fought to live, you should and will relinquish to oblivion the detailed, lush arch of his brows, interlaced lashes, and childlike, curving lips. You didn't give birth to him. You only helped him die. Does that make him yours? You feel selfish, holding him. Still, you want and don't want to betray him by letting go. You tell yourself that eventually the scents of his hair and breath and the warmth of his skin on your fingers will fade. You stare at the tabletop, remember brown eyes, and plumb your heart for the hard, alternate truth.

Having made their choices, your old friends close their menus and ask how you are. How's business? One laughs and asks if you're ready to move back home. For a moment, you think you will tell them about the shooting. How could you not, after knowing them for so long? But they are smiling, unscathed, preoccupied with steak or fish. You first take pity on them and then on yourself. You see it would be like running back into traffic. They'd accelerate and steer toward you with laments about the decline of traditional values, a need for prayer in the schools, the travesty of the stolen election, the Second Amendment at risk, and the liberals bringing socialism on us all. The societal roots of tragedy. So you ask yourself, if you took the risk of telling, could anyone be saved? Dodging the momentum of the world twice in twenty-four hours seems beyond your remnant of courage.

You glance at your partner, who reads you and sighs. His eyes hold you as you decide. After another chilling sip and a pause, you set down your water glass, lift your chin, and release a breath in a quiet laugh. Your chest feels tight but you call it out for the three of you—you, your partner, and your beautiful boy. "Of course, we're staying. It's surprising how quickly, how hopelessly we've fallen in love with our community."

Jonathan Plombon

Rising from the Ashes of My Wife's Cigarette

1. A Marriage of Inconvenience

Although not typically mentioned in even the most renowned books on the subject, most people are married—regardless of ceremony, license, or knowledge that it ever occurred—to an individual's Past. Because of this, the subsequent sharing of space with Your Past can be rather complicated.

As My Past once pointed out, "Remember, you don't just live with me. You also live in me."

2. With All the Stability That One Comes to Expect from Living in Fear

When deciding whether or not to live in My Past, I carefully considered what was most important to me, or more accurately, what made my life less frightening. I ended up concluding that this was familiarity and redundancy.

That's why living in My Past was ideal for me. We lived in a school, the only building in My Past, and that school only offered one class. While that class had been taught by My Past, the school itself closed after she was fired. One of the reasons the school board dismissed her was because I was the only student in the school and, as my life had obviously showed, I couldn't learn anything from her.

That and because she attacked me.

My wife suffocated me. Not all the time. Only when she saw me happy. And when she got tired of strangling me, she held me captive. No one knew where I was being held captive. When my main acquaintances, most notably My Self Pity and My Ego, noticed my absence, they organized a search party to investigate every cell, every cave, and every basement. However, I was trapped in the most obvious of places, which, ironically, they never looked.

My wife trapped me in a marriage.

My Self Pity said, "We're never going to find him. Why does this always happen to him?"

My Ego said, "He could leave anytime he wants; he's just staying because of his child."

My son said, "Daddy?"

3. The Nurse Said, "He Looks Just Like You: Tired and Bored."

My wife and I had a son. But he wasn't just our son. He was much more. He was also Our Resentment.

My wife gave birth to Our Resentment shortly after we got married, even though she was pregnant with him well before then. We're not exactly sure when. Doctors and therapists said the seed of Our Resentment was planted, or rather conceived, as far back as our third date when I mentioned that it might be time to move on.

I only meant that we move on from dinner, but mentioning "moving on" in any context around My Past always seemed to create some resentment.

4. You're Not Cheap, You're Poor

In terms of maintaining a budget, it was also cheaper to live in My Past than in an apartment or townhouse. I had lived in My Past my entire life and that allowed me to save on packing boxes, moving vans, etc. But I didn't spend much on redecorating, either—or any sort of decorating at all. There was nothing to redecorate. In the school, there were no walls, no doors, and no windows. There were only steps.

The school had steps that led to the second floor, steps that led to the third floor, steps that went straight, steps that brought you down. However, I never took any of the steps that went anywhere I wanted to go. In fact, I never took any steps at all.

5. Talking It Out While Keeping It All In

My Past and I began attending couples' therapy.

During our first session, the counselor asked us to partake in a marital exercise that involved my wife and I staring into each other eyes for hours at a time. This, the counselor said, would help foster our ability to always look eye-to-eye, which would, along with preventing arguments, make it impossible to see other people.

After the third hour, the counselor asked, "How is it?"

"It's beautiful," my wife said.

"It's dangerous," I said. "We won't be able to see where we're going. We'll end up bumping into a wall."

"Maybe it's not where we're going," my wife replied, "but how we're going that's important. And we'll always be going together."

"Exactly," the counselor said. "You can be in Hell and it won't matter. It'll only matter that you're in Hell together."

"We are," I said, "and it matters to me."

Nonetheless, the exercise didn't work. I would look away.

"What are you looking at? What else is there to look at?" my wife asked me. "Are you seeing someone else?"

"No," I responded.

I lied. I was seeing someone else. I saw myself. I saw myself leaving.

6. I Told the Eye Doctor That I Was Having Trouble Seeing My Wife's Perspective

In the days leading up to our next session, my wife and I barely spoke to one another. And when my wife did speak up, she asked for my eyes. "I can't trust you with them. You'll use them to look at someone else. I don't care what you say," she told me.

"If I give you my eyes then how will I ever see your point of view?" I asked. She allowed me to keep them, provided I take an eye test, which I did.

The test consisted of me looking into the future.

"What do you see?" my wife asked.

"Nothing," I answered.

It's what she wanted to hear.

While my wife allowed me to keep my eyes, she brought the subject up again during our next session.

"He's been cheating on me," my wife said to the counselor. "He's seeing someone else."

"Is this true?" the counselor asked.

"Yes," I said.

"And who have you been seeing?"

"Me. I've been seeing myself packing a suitcase. Since I had nothing, you would think that leaving would be an easy decision to make. That wasn't the case. I found out that moving on meant knowing what steps to take, since there are several around me, and how to take those steps, which I don't know how to."

"And what did you say to yourself?" the counselor asked.

"That I can't see me. I can't see me leaving, because seeing me leave makes me think that I can leave."

"And did you continue to see him?"

"Yes, but only under one circumstance. If I would continue to see me, I had to see myself miserable. That's because I enjoy familiarity and redundancy. I don't like being surprised. If I'm miserable then at least I know what's coming. That's why I love My Past. She always repeats herself. It's the same crap every day. The same awful crap every day."

There was a short silence interrupted only by my wife throwing her hands over her face.

"It's been forever since he told me that he loves me," my wife said, choking back tears.

"I think we're making progress," the counselor said with a warm grin and a pat on my shoulder.

7. Can't Live With You. Can't Live Within You

I used to call my wife "my maze."

"Isn't it weird that you call me 'your maze' even though I'm only a closed school and a series of steps that you never take? It's pretty hard to get lost," My Past said.

"Yeah," I answered. "But that doesn't mean I know the right way to go. It's like this, honey, there was a time when I didn't think I could ever leave you. Now I don't think I can ever escape you."

8. Bless This Mess We Made Out of Our Child's Life

We showed off Our Resentment, even when we had no inkling to do so, to everyone we came in contact with, especially other couples who we thought had a superior relationship to ours.

We didn't try to. We didn't want anyone to know we had him. But he was just always there. That's when Our Resentment would walk up and rear his ugly head. He wasn't an attractive child; this we could both agree on. My wife said he took after me in that department and, to be honest, I wasn't any more mature since I often retorted that there wasn't anything uglier than My Past.

9. Walking the Thin Line of Miscommunication

My Past and I spoke often to keep the lines of communication moving freely during our sessions. The one suggestion our counselor gave us was that we should only engage verbally while in front of her, just in case the police needed a witness to corroborate the story in the likelihood of a homicide.

"You used to be so content, so complacent," my wife said.

"I'm just tired," I said.

"What are you tired of?" the counselor asked.

"Everything."

"What would you want to change?" the counselor said.

"My wife."

"What about your wife?"

"Her appearance."

"What about her would you want to change?"

"Her black eye."

"You gave me this black eye," my wife said. "When you wanted to distance yourself from me, you pushed me. When you wanted to hide me, you shoved me into closets. When none of that worked, you just beat me down. You beat me so far down that you couldn't recognize me."

"You made me do it," I said. "I can't change you. You are who you are. You were a black eye long before I ever gave you one."

"You can change me," My Past said. "You've done it before. I was your teacher, but instead of learning from me, you chose to hide me. And that's when you changed me from a teacher to a black eye. That's what you wanted. It's just easier to blame me, to say that I'm the bruise that you cover up by wearing long sleeves."

"How has your son reacted to this?" the counselor asked.

10. The Apple of My Wife's Black Eye

Our Resentment was always sick. He wasn't the healthiest child. When we brought him to the children's hospital after several episodes of sneezing and coughing, the doctor bluntly asked, "It really isn't healthy to keep Resentment around. Plus, this might be contagious. Have either of you been sick?"

"Only of each other," I said.

"That explains it," the doctor said. "He got it from you."

Healthy or not, Our Resentment still grew. He grew very large. So large, in fact, that it was hard to deny his existence, even when we tried to pass him off as a smile or whenever My Past and I said "I love you" to each other in front of others.

That was, I'd like to point out, in front of other people. In private, we just let Our Resentment run wild around the house. In most houses, he would have destroyed lamps, tables, clocks, and couches. All he could destroy in our home was our marriage. When I tried to ground him, he responded, "Wasn't it already destroyed? How can you tell that I did it? How do you know you didn't do it?"

I didn't have an answer. And I quickly alleviated him from his grounding status.

The doctor suggested that we simply quit feeding him to restrict his growth. His favorite foods were the distrust in our marriage and our off-handed insults directed, under our breath, to one another. Although my wife and I attempted to rid the house of these foods, the attempt only lasted twelve minutes and to be honest, we were surprised it lasted even that long.

11. You Don't Have to Be Crazy to Live Here, But You'd Be Nuts Not to Be

"Remember what you used to tell me?" my wife asked during the session, staring at me as I stared at the ground. "You used to say that you thought about me all the time. Whenever we'd break up over some silly thing, you'd tell me that you couldn't move on. We'd have to get back together. Remember when you would remark that you couldn't see anything good happening? When you couldn't see anything in your future?

Remember those times when you could look back at me? Remember? Remember that? Remember how you used to think about me and smile? Do you still think about me?"

"No," I said. "I now obsess over you."

"What changed?"

"Nothing," I said. "Nothing ever."

"Exactly," the counselor said, "then what's wrong? I thought you liked familiarity and redundancy."

12. Our Doormat Read, "If You Lived Here, You'd Be Depressed by Now."

At the end of our final session, my wife and I sat beside each other on the couch. Whenever we moved a leg or an arm, we got a tad closer than we had been before. It was the closest we had felt in years. And sometimes, not always, but sometimes, one of us would raise a hand and brush against the other and we'd connect.

There was a time when we didn't think we would ever do that again.

"Are you still seeing someone else?" my wife asked, jumping ahead of the counselor's question.

"No, I haven't seen myself in a long time. I don't think I ever cared for me. At least, I don't anymore. I just don't like myself much. I don't know what I ever saw in myself, to be honest," I answered.

My Past smiled.

"What happened the last time you saw yourself?" the counselor asked.

"The last time I saw myself, I asked if I could leave. And I answered that all it takes to leave is to lift myself up and take it one step at a time. I then asked what would happen if I fell."

"And what did you say?" the counselor said.

"I said falling on my face is nothing new. And since I love familiarity and redundancy, that I should enjoy it since it's what I'm used to. Or, at least, not be scared to fall on my face. But I couldn't. I couldn't go on seeing myself."

"Why?" the counselor said.

"Because, as I said before, I don't care much for myself."

"That's when you decided to stop seeing someone else?" the counselor questioned.

"Yes, I've made the decision not to see myself do anything," I said, turning to My Past. "I can't leave all this behind. I can't leave."

"Were you ever physical with him?" my wife asked.

"I kissed him," I said. "But I only kissed him good bye."

"Is there something you'd like to tell your wife?" the counselor asked.

"Yes," I said, looking at her, in her eyes, where I couldn't see anything else. "Hold me."

"How?" my wife asked.

"Just how I like it."

"And how is that?" she asked, while blushing as if she knew but still wanted to hear me say it.

"Back," I said. "Hold me back."

13. I Gave Our Child an I-Don't-Care Bear for His Birthday

After the session, we returned home where my son ran up to me and exclaimed, "Look how big I'm getting, Daddy!" I sat my son on my lap and told him about my relationship with his mother. I told him that when Daddy tries to hide him from people that he shouldn't take it personally, because Daddy also tries to hide Mommy from people. "I just don't want anyone to know that either of you exist," I said.

"Aren't you proud of me, Daddy?" he asked.

"No, but Daddy's not proud of Mommy, either," I said.

"Daddy, are you proud of yourself?" he asked.

He looked just like his mother. He had a black eye, too. He took after his mother. He grabbed me and held me back just as much as his mother ever could.

I just shook my head. "No," I said. "No, I'm not."

"So you're not leaving us, Daddy?" he said.

"No, I couldn't."

"Never?"

"Never, kid. I'll be taking you to the grave."

"Promise?"

"Promise."

WILLIAM REPASS

THE UNSETTLERS

For the sake of unlikeliness, we meet every Tuesday on the playground behind the local elementary. We time it between recesses so the schoolchildren won't pester us. We take a swing each, leaving the fourth empty as if expecting to be joined by someone. But we are three only. If a fourth asked to join, we'd refuse. We do not swing. As we report our weekly findings, we merely dangle and screak, an ambience of chains rusting in the breeze.

This week, X reports, he went to the bus station every odd day and sat on a bench in the atrium for 7 hours precisely. Every day he chose a different bench, rotating counter-clockwise. He held upside-down in front of his nose an issue of *Enthusiast* and darted his eyes this way and that, tracing the path of an imaginary quarry across the floor. He claims to have unsettled at least six commuters. We're not artists, not revolutionaries, not madmen, he reminds us for the umpteenth time, the soi-disant ideologue of our formation.

On the even days when X wasn't there, and without his knowledge, reports Y, she walked erratic paths around the atrium like a housefly zigzagging through the air, her face all the time deadpan. This tactic unsettled more commuters than X's, she claims—the majority on day four when a security guard worked out that she was none other than X's quarry, got spooked and escorted her from the premises. Y is X's longtime friend and roommate. He suffers from an attraction to her he won't or can't acknowledge, however transparent it is to Y herself, and Z for that matter. Though she pretends to be X's right-hand man, she implants most of his ideas by subterfuge.

As for Z, he reverted to an old stand-by and went about his week in slow-motion. He moseyed around the business district as if wading through molasses, ordered a breakfast burrito with his voice pitched low, dozed on the job, and so forth, yada yada. He ran little to no risk of getting fired from the hospital. His patients expect him to run behind schedule. Whether or not he unsettled anyone is "debatable." Slow-motion comes naturally to Z. The distinction between unsettling and aggravation, as X often says, is "gossamer-thin." Neither as egomaniacal as X nor inventive as Y, Z compensates for his low stats by taking down the minutes of their meetings. Which is to say, he pretends to and then rushes them out from memory whenever he gets around to it, on Monday nights more often than not. Ashamed of his salary, he subsidizes the group's activities, allowing X and Y to unsettle full-time.

X twists in his swing, impatient as ever for the noise of his own voice. He must express admiration for Y's tactic of amplifying his strategy but wonders if it mightn't have been a miscalculation. The security guard's involvement politicizes their activity, which must restrict itself to estranging the quotidian in "indefinable ways." Our habit—dispelling habit. We aim to make people say to themselves: "why are they doing that?" A query that inexorably leads to: "and why am *I* doing *this*?" Y argues that the disruption of politeness flings out an ideological byproduct, whether Comrade X likes it or not. X says they are not firing a revolver into the crowd at random. The polemic between X and Y continues in this vein and Z tunes out, listening to the cicadas and staring at the rusted armature of the nearby jungle gym, folding into a dome over the gravel pool designed to cushion the impact of any children raining down. It's hot, the sun having rounded its corner. Z cracks open a can of lingonberry-essenced sparkling water and takes a contemplative swig.

Z knows a fourth member is out of the question. Four being too stable a number, too quadrilateral, too *settling* (five's anathema, half of ten). X would be thrown for a loop by the loop back around in the alphabet, whether to W or all the way to A. That said, the alphabet as Möbius strip is a notion that, if not unsettling by X (Y's) definition, irks Z with its kinked indifference to endings. Z pictures each member of our formation as a ball-joint in the jungle gym of unsettlement, scratch that, unsettledness—a free-standing model of molecular instability. What would happen should the unsettlers themselves become the unsettled? Z knows this is the sort of "crochety meta-reasoning" X deplores, taking his cue from Y, whose asymmetrical hair and air of disaffection stimulate a more "perverse" methodology. Mere contemplation has Z so wound up he inadvertently begins to kick his legs, spurring his swing into motion. The can still clutched in his right hand, his left tightens around the chain.

But let us suppose this hypothetical W or A attracted X or Y (for that matter, why not Z?) and threw a wrench into the equation. As opposed to the existing YX-but-not power fulcrum, any number of configurations might arise—for instance, W/AY, W/AX, or even (wasn't this enticing?) YZ—to divert the puce ooze of unsettlement, maybe *pressurize* it. This Abecedarianism will be the end of us. Z's swing has all the while been rising to the bait of its name, clawing with each feeble kick an inch farther forward, an inch further back, as it crows of its widening scope of action—reports which, mistaken for the buzzing of cicadas, go unheeded by X, Y, and Z himself.

Z remembers an exhibit in the sculpture garden on the hospital grounds, the "Untitled" jungle gym installed by a sculptor of local unrenown, an assemblage much too flimsy for climbing, unless conceptually, and for this reason attended by a placard that prohibits touching outright. Unless of course the fourth member was all along implied by the empty swing. This invisible but no longer imperceptible presence designated only by its absence (or was it the other way around?)—a double-negative agent provocateur planted in our midst by the pure nothingness of concept.

Even as Z's own swinging threatens to register in his awareness, it lulls him into complacency like a hypnotist's smug gold watch describing the arc of its grin. The empty swing alongside wavers and pivots in the agitating swishes-past of its comrade. What if X had inadvertently plucked his "imaginary quarry" into being on the odd days, while on the even ones, Y held its hand? The even days! Four's an even number. Picturing this off-kilter rhombus with at least one of its elbows protruding into (or ripening from) the jungle of indefinite, undesignated, crayon-scribble misshapen voidness, Z unsettles himself, blurring into almost an S (mirrored). He plummets at the gravel and just before crashing pulls up and rises away on his swing. Name and function in alignment, it screeches in the triumph of consummation.

The recess bell drowns out the cicadas just as one of the chains keeping Z's swing in suspension snaps. He flubs the somersault into too-shallow gravel and sprains both thumbs. Put out of minutes-taking and self-medicinal commission indefinitely, he slingshots back to a state of savage, pre-hitchhiking fecklessness. His half-drunk far-flung sparkling water, the embottlement of disembodiment upended, bleeds out onto hot pebbles. X and Y, interrupted mid-polemic, collaborate in stunned speechlessness. Schoolchildren burst from their classrooms like a rising tide and we drag our wounded from the playground to lick our wounds elsewhere.

We splinter into factions, existent and non-, each meeting every other Tuesday.

Kirstin Allio

Flowers

We were scuffing in the dry leaves in the empty wading pool because there were unrolled condoms draped over the bare branches of the climbing tree. This is fffffun, said my son intensively. I feel something, he said, and dropped into the leaves, loose record of a forest. Up he came with a wallet. Let's see! I snatched it. Black leatherette trifold, Macy's-level Ralph Lauren, twelve dollars in a ten and two singles. My son grabbed my arm like a ballet bar, my little Leonard Bernstein.

Receipts for jewelry repair and Taco's Mexico Kitcheria, cards and rewards cards and car insurance. Suddenly I was giddy with saving someone's day. Come on! I cried, and we made light work of the park, flew upstairs without taking our shoes off. We stood on our elbows, leaning over the keyboard. My son said, Does he have any children I could play with?

A parking lot in Everett, a featureless medical complex, newly planted clutch of cypress trees. We left a message with the answering service. We left the wallet on the porch behind the flower pot I'd never filled with flowers.

Lake Effect

The sponsored training is held in the break room. The facilitator is female, wearing very flat shoes. Each morning her hair is difficult in a different way.

Hi everyone. A little wave. Splash. Participants are sitting in a circle of fifteen folding chairs.

Did we get the coffee we need? She peers into her paper cup gratuitously. She holds up her phone to show she comes in peace. See her timer? We're going to break in about thirty-five minutes. Can everyone last that long?

Great, she says. I'm going to jump right in.

She has traveled from out of state, in her own car, recording the mileage for reimbursement. Wait. Did she—? She steps on the thought to put it out, its light, like crushing a cigarette, Great, she says, and again, Great. What's a popular pond around here? See how she gives the participants the power, A nice lake maybe? Let's see a—show of hands—Great. Powder Pond. Powder Pond in the next town.

Picture yourself walking the nice path around the lake on a nice sunny day. Suddenly there's a dead fish. On dry land! That's weird, you say. It's got that creepy slimy eye. What did it do, you say to yourself, to die?

It always surprises her that fish have human eyes.

Powder Pond is not a lake, thinks the woman who raised her hand. And it has no path around it, and no fish inside. It's a rotten little pond in the woods that brings out the worst in teenagers.

Around the other side of the lake—

Why did the facilitator ask, if she was just going to say lake anyway?

—heaped right in the middle of the path, is a *pile* of dead fish—with those eyes! What's wrong with this lake? you say. Suddenly there's water in her ears. The parable has become the jargon. What she needs to find a way to say—

She feels water rising above her shoulders. She has to tip her head to speak, We blame individual deaths on individuals. We blame mass deaths on cause.

Six out of fifteen folding chairs are occupied. Two men, embarrassed to be here. One taps his phone to life on his thigh. It occurs to him that everyone's phone tells the same exact time. It strikes him suddenly that you used to ask a stranger and he might say anything. Ten of, but my watch is fast. Or, It's about five—Time was unpredictable, personal, tuned by the warmth of the lake of blood beneath the watch-wearer's skin.

Colin Gee

Excerpts from Cosas de Talagaya

Ueler's country store

You would think you were watching Bambi from the sparrows that flutter in and out around the doorway, steps, feed mixers, and heads of the pueblo's main general store's proprietor Ueler, his wife, small son, and surprisingly perky eighteen-year-old daughter Estacy who mans the cash register. The birds come for the spilled corn and meal, the name Ueler came from an eighteenth century Swiss physicist who invented number theory, and I come to the general store for frijoles and Estacy.

In the morning they also grind up chile paste for weddings and parties and chocolate blends for moles and hot cocoas and champurrados. Ueler does this, I mean, while the customers his señoras sit on upturned buckets in their embroidered white huipil and watch Ueler without blinking for any sleight of hand with the scoop or the scale.

Spoilers

Bus drivers will invariably have decked out their rigs in themes, frequently as many as three in mystical symbiosis. There is a rosary-draped cross, the Virgin of Guadalupe, the phrase Save Me Lord alongside huge Looney Tunes decals of Bugs, Daffy, and a life-sized effigy of Speedy Gonzales. The name Uzielcito is pasted beneath the phrase MY LITTLE GENESIS next to a dinosaur decal, and the driver has a dinosaur fob for his key. The message is clear: do not stick up this driver, folks, he is a father. Some drivers in fact attach racecar spoilers to the backs of their buses, apparently to improve aerodynamics by reducing drag as the vehicle flies around the little Chevy Aveo into the passing lane at 80 mph. Save Me Lord.

They used to make chicken liver and onion but they don't anymore

The old lady at the corner store tells me the famous foods from the pueblo are black mole, amarillo, green mole, and chicken liver and onion, though they don't make the chicken liver much anymore, just for weddings.

Am I married, or just engaged?

Outside a dog

Outside a dog it is impossible to judge the true character of a pueblo. If they are low-down mean biters it means they have been kicked, then kicked when they were down, hissed and shouted at while chained to a wall, hit with rocks, run over by men in swerving trucks, baited to their deaths with poisoned steak, kept as puppies then neglected and thrown from a moving vehicle, shot at, and had their ears and teats sliced and bit.

In our pueblo, though, the street dogs are happy, lethargic, relative gordos, and do not growl at you.

Snakes and ladders

Talagaya's well, the one that feeds the pilas (washing cisterns) and pipes to the town hall, church, market, and residences, has run dry. Everyone started buying pipas, trucked-in twenty thousand-liter tanks of potable water at the price of say three-four cases of beer. How much water is ten thousand liters? Enough for ninety-three showers, just under a thousand dishes not counting silverware, two hundred ninety-two one-liter flushes, a hundred forty-four buckets for the goddamn plants, and one cautious carwash. Fortunately the pipa dude is cheerful and punctual. The horror is when he begins to see things in your cistern. There is a snake in your tank, he says with a little laugh, a little guy. Maybe he will come out later.

Leafcutter ants

Mom hanging warily on your fence tells you there is a viper burrowed into the hill of leafcutter ants you have been trying to dose with different pesticides, that these vipers are extremely dangerous for children, they eat ants and always make their holes in the very ant colony and live in there, like snake gods the ants do not comprehend, but know to feed with sacrifice. She apologizes but says for the children's sake, since they walk to school past your yard, you can kill this kind of viper by pouring boiling water down its hole, which as you look out across the dust and gravel of your lot, you know is about to become a daily chore, because it is pocked with leafcutter mounds with dozens and dozens of gaping, asp-sized mouths.

Skateboards

Actually this chapter should be called dwarves. Little people. Sometimes you will hear a strong baritone from the back of the fruit and veggie shop three blocks down from the church and a little person, a male dwarf, will hustle out of the back in his miniature pants and shoes, grin at you, say Buenos días, and hop onto a small green skateboard. In his hand is a bowling ball bag, and since Talagaya is on a hill the road carries him right down, over three shaped speedbumps, and around the beer store (some lady's house) at the corner, on into eternity.

Jim Meirose

Jail Time

PAIN!

Great Big unfinished Cabin Cruiser Model O'er There On That Console TV *Chris-Craft* **what?** *Chris-Craft* **WHAT?** *ooooooo Chris-Craft Chris-Craft Chris-Craft Chris-Craft Chris-Craft I like Chris-Craft's why Chris-Craft I like Chris-Craft very much yah yah the Chris and the Craft of it separately 'nuff,* **BUT** *I like Chris-Craft's why Chris-Craft I like Chris-Craft very much yah yah hence o'er hence this's the God-damn whole reason there's a* **Great unfinished Big Cabin Cruiser Model O'er There On That Console TV** anyhow, like I was saying, all these bulldozers and shit came out of nowhere, and started digging this gigantic hole in the ground on my property. There ended up being a half dozen machines digging out this hole, and maybe a whole dozen hardhats in orange milling around, watching the digging, and—I went up and asked what was going on, and—I swear to God, every single one of them ignored me. That pissed me off. Pissed me off good. I went back to the tent and called the cops, and said I need to know what's going on, but they tossed me off. Said yes, they knew what was going on, but said I'd need to "*talk to city hall*"—that's your office, Toppie. **Right**—that's your office?

Yes it is, but no one told me—

Wait wait wait with the "no one told me" and all that crap. *Why no one told you's a whole separate great big problem.* Anyway, when the cops blew me off like that, I **really** saw red. So, I just shot right down to city hall, and went in and told them I was from out back the hills there, and I wanted to know what the hell was going on, with the bulldozers and the digging and the ruining of my neighborhood, and I was right in the middle of the whole story when a couple of deputies who were standing there listening, stopped me cold.

Neighborhood? they said—you're living up there? No one's supposed to be living up there. The borough owns that land and it's never been zoned fit for human habitation, and so forth blah blah blah, you know, so, well then, of course, this shot the whole thing out of control, and push came to shove, and eh eh, as you must know by now, my fuse is quite short and when it burns down, well—things do get ugly. Anyway, they lit up and they pushed and shoved and I fought pushed and shoved back and all, I mean, it's all a blur now, you know, after all, but—I woke up in a little six foot square cast concrete and stainless steel cell.

Did they say why they arrested you?

Nope they just said you're under arrest, and I said why, and they said never mind why, just come with us, and they threw me in a cell.

So, when you went in front of a judge, what happened then?

Sorry. Nope. No judge.

What?

What I said. No judge. No lawyer. No nothing. I never got to see a single person's face for the whole sixteen days they had me locked up there.

Hold it, wait—**what**? How many days?

Sixteen days.

My **GOD** no no no that can't have happened—no charges no judge no lawyers no *nothing*? For **sixteen whole days**?

That's right. Sixteen whole days, with nobody coming and telling me 'nothing, 'cept that somebody shoved a tray of food through a slot twice a day, and that was that.

Somebody came to let you out, though. What'd they say when they let you out?

Nothing.

What? *Nothing*? They just came and let you out and said *nothing at all to you*?

No, because nobody ever came to let me out.

Hold it—how's that? Come on, don't joke around, this isn't funny. Is this a joke?

Totally not. I'm not joking around. Here's how I got out. From boredom, I pushed at the door once in a while while I was in there. No reason, really, just from boredom, like, I'd touch the walls, pick my nose, kick the bunk, take a piss, take a dump, lay down, get up, lay down, like, you know, no reason, like—here I was, locked up in a place I don't want to be, for no reason I could see at all, with no one to talk to, and nothing to do, with no end in sight. I was ready to scream all the time. Actually, I did scream a lot in there, you know, I mean, why not? And, nobody ever came to see why I screamed. Maybe nobody heard me. Maybe they just didn't care about me. Anyway, I pushed at the door once in a while, like that, until, the last time I pushed it, it cracked open. I almost fell down! You know?

Okay, but—who unlocked it? Did you see?

Hell, no! I guess they came and unlocked it quiet and sneaky-like, you know.

Why would they do that?

Who the hell knows? All I knew was, it opened. And it's funny. You know—its like when something's lost, you always find it in the last place you looked. You know that saying?

Yah. I know that saying. But—

Wait! And when the car won't start, it always starts on the last try. You know?

Okay yes, but hold it. What'd you do next—

Never mind! Don't cut me off, let me finish—I sat down a while, and it came over me, that yes, this was really all so very very normal, you see—I was in a cell; and all cells must open someday; and all cell do r open d the last   time you tried it *like it all comes at last   like*   as it also seems nat e ural that th ....   ^*pooliefloosh it out keep it clean bandage it well and you'll*^ : *hoops* <---> *hoops* <------>*hoops* <----------> *hoops* ([{ *Uh, 'TENSION!* :

Look up at me, please.

Good.

[*To the reader* glub, glub, glub] here we are, dear reader, right where we're generally found watching you read, sitting *way above* watching your platters turning over 'n over though the big damned dumb thing you're *"reading"* over above and through of (*and most the time exhibiting a quite painfully strained indifference*), so here/now me and *God* are providing here this exit point b *to extract yourself from the game at this time press the Q-bird Icon un da zeensieseester river (hot bang SNAP and)* one reason being the st'ry's about to become doubly better *and* this prediction may here and now seem *nothing* to you B-but before you continue put on this cloak of awareness here that *everything's a piece of a bigger puzzle* which also is a piece of an even bigger puzzle wha' everything fits into **God's great big puzzle** book hey me and you and everything else too Ma Ma so, shut down the bitchmoans they bore us *!NOISNET'* , *hU*}]) *spooh* <----------> *spooh* <-----> *spooh* <---> spooh |@| *and hey you don't look so bad here's another* तुमने मुझे बोर किया, तुमने मुझे बोर किया, सोचो मैंने तुम्हें अच्छे से बोर किया, तुम्हें मेरे जैसा होना चाहिए |@| hope you enjoyed this traditional drive-in-movie "snacks n' intermissions" s' s, carry on: [**You are now reentering your reading-in-progress**] May it pass quickly, crooned the dour Turkish judge My God, but,   yes   yes, as I was saying. I sat by the cracked open door getting really really warm as I went deeper, and deeper, into the strength of knowing that at least some *God of the cosmos* cared about me anyway, made the cell door open, and then I thought that through a little deeper, just a little, until it came to me *solid* that this same *God of the cosmos* had been sitting watching me push at the door, time after time, all through the whole sixteen days, watching that last push they'd created in me come closer and closer down the line. And, when that happened, the *God of the cosmos* slipped the lock open, shot the bolt aside, and let the door fall open, at my very last push. Damn, that was something. Really really. You know?

Yes, uh, but, hold it, let's go back a bit. When you pushed the other times, was it—

Back? Go back? Oh, no, no back—only forward. I went out the cell 'nd up a hall to a door with a red bar across saying **EMERGENCY EXIT ONLY** in really loud red lettering, and, well, I wanted to go through, but I was afraid there'd be an alarm. You know?

Yes, yes. Of course. But one question. Back in the cell, did—

No. I'm not back in the cell now. I'm at the *last door.* I looked at it and tried hard to know what to do if I set off an alarm. I thought, what the hell could they do to me, like, hey—put me in jail for another sixteen days? Or, however many days the **God** *of the cosmos* would decide it'd take for my next cell door to open, the last time I pushed it again, and—but what about if after that there were more cell doors, and more—okay, my **God**, did it get really tangled and complicated in my head, so, I said the hell with it, put my head down, and pushed the door bar, but, with just one little wrinkle that came to me just as I pushed. Want to hear it?

Yes. Of course. Go on. You're going to anyway.

True.. Here, simple; I pushed the door open in a way that I didn't really believe it was me pushing it. You know?

What? How's that work?

This; I sort of stepped aside out of myself and watched some other self that came to life when I stepped out of it push the bar to open the door—crazy, eh, but I knew, that if an alarm did go off, and deputies came, I tell them honestly it wasn't me this me that pushed the door, officer, it was some other me never saw before *whack whack* that disappeared to someplace I have no idea of *at a minimum* which of the six basic possible directions from here they ran off to when the door opened and the alarm went off. I'm sorry I can't help you any further with this, officer. I just happened to be here you know, you know, and like that—*got me so far?*

Just get to the end. Okay?

Sure. Since then also, I thought of more things I could have told the officers without lying about how the alarm went off. One's like, you know, that way back in grammar school, the big nuns taught me that if you really don't know something's a sin when you do it, then you're not committing a sin if you do it. And I know, I know, this' sort of hard to believe, but, I could have used that on the officers too, like, Hey, sure, you know, like I told you, I didn't open this door, but, even if I did, I didn't see it as wrong or unlawful in any way, since I never should have been arrested and locked up at all anyway, et cetera, et cetera, and I could go on and forever about how I'd handle it if the didn't believe me, and tried to arrest me for no reason again, and all that and more over and—everything was starting to whirl all around all around and around, so, what the hell; I *pushed* the bar; the door *fell* open; and, *nothing*! Nothing! No alarm, no officers, nothing of a negative nature at all, plus, the sky was blue, so beautiful! The sun was shining, even more so! And so on and so forth, and, there being nobody to stop me, I went back up home to see what was what. So, there you go. That's what happened.

My God, what a story! And what about the bulldozers and workers that came to your place and started this whole thing going? Were they still up there?

Oh. No. They were gone.

Gone?

Yes. So? Is "gone" too complicated a word for you to understand?

What's that supposed to mean?

See? Another question. You ask too many questions. I give up.

Give up?

Yah! Don't get what *that means, either? Too hard for you to* Oka *under* y—*oooooo* then in a snap it all *sta* receded down in the distance yes e ys y (0) it did s s s nd s ? s dissolve dissolve down back to **down back to** ?? down ? ? back es **pillo** ess so: *Great Big unfinished Cabin Cruiser Model O'er There On That Console TV* Chris-Craft ***what?*** Chris-Craft **WHAT?** oooooooo *Chris-Craft Chris-Craft Chris-Craft Chris-Craft Chris-Craft I like Chris-Craft's why Chris-Craft I like Chris-Craft very much yah yah the Chris and the Craft of it separately 'nuff,* **BUT** *I like Chris-Craft's why Chris-Craft I like Chris-Craft very much yah yah hence o'er hence this's the God-damn whole reason there's a* **Great unfinished Big Cabin Cruiser Model O'er There On That Console TV** ¡NI∀d

any questions?

HW KHERBEK

PROPPING UP THE EDIFICE

I got this job, place out in Rick-mansworth. Don't suppose you'll've heard of it. Anyway, the job, strange enough job, I'll give you that, propping up this edifice. Not how I saw my life when I was younger, be the first to say that, but you know, you grow up, you go to school, you read the paper, you go down the pub, maybe you get married, then, one day, more or less without knowing it, without seeing any of the traffic signs, as it were, along the way, there you are, propping up the edifice. What can you do? And, it's not a bad line of work, all things considered. Tell you that for free.

You come in at 9.30. Wouldn't be a bad thing if you turned up 9, but no one's going to jump on you if you're there for 9.25. Wednesday to Sunday thing: Turn on the lights, have a look around for dust, rubbish, stray bits of string, that sort of thing, somebody's forgotten coffee cup, that sort of thing, if there's nothing about, or if it's been dealt with by the others, it's show time, ace. There's the edifice, over in the far corner of the space; you go over and you just get on with it.

Not bad for co-workers either. I mean, you get all kinds, like anywhere, I suppose. Fair bit of turnover, but all in all a good group of faces. Had a fella in here a few months back, Taro Aso was his name. Short-ish, little extra round the waist, not the snappiest dresser, but had a nice pair of loafers I always meant to ask him about. Never quite got round to it though. Anyway, used to be Prime Minister of Japan, apparently. I don't know anything about it. But still, there you go, you just never know. Say this for him, PM of Japan or no PM of Japan, he just got on about his work like the rest of us. Friendly, not overly chatty, but you don't really want those types to be honest, you're in there until 6, and when you've got one of these blokes who wants to chew your ear off all day long, well, 6 can't come soon enough. But that's not Taro. He just got on with it. Won't hear a word said against him in the edifice propping game. As for politics, well, I don't do politics.

How did I get started you might ask, well, funny thing that. Can't rightly say I applied. I was between jobs, at the time; happened to everyone I knew about that time. The economy, the bankers, Northern Rock, and all that. Madness. So, I'm keeping my ears and eyes out for anything that comes up, helping out around the house, me folks and that, helping the old man with his computer. He's not one for taking orders though. Did a bit of dog walking, some painting, fixed a gutter—more or less—once, too, not that I know anything about gutters, but you learn what you need to learn.

Anyway, whilst all this is going on, I'm signed on. One day, went down the Jobcentre, fella they've got me talking to says to me "They've got a job on the go out in Rick-mansworth. Work strikes me as something you'd be suited for." I had a look at the specs. He wasn't wrong. Took the details. Went down to see what it was all about. Unassuming place from the outside, not unlike, maybe an auto showroom, or, whatchamacallit, a hotel lobby? Foyer that's it. Something in that way. Bit sterile, but clean; not inviting exactly, but nothing that would put you off. Kind of place to visit I suppose; not homey. Nice though. Don't want you getting the wrong idea. Not some dingy place, not by a long chalk. Anyway, young fella greets me as I come in. Very well-educated, you can tell. Suits some, not others so much. Anyway, he runs the place. Wouldn't say a day over thirty-three. Well dressed chap. Works hard himself, always in the office, I see him with the spreadsheets and smartphoning and all that. Nothing I get mixed up with, mind you. I'm out there on the floor, always been my way, hands on, but you see him at it, behind the glass to his office. I'm sure I'd listen more carefully to him if I genuinely had an interest. Anyway, I come in, this chap, James is his name, shakes my hand. I tell him I'm here about the job. He looks me over and nods in the direction of the edifice.

"There, she is," he says, smiling a bit, kind of like it's his edifice, like maybe he's made it himself, which, if I understand correctly, isn't the case, but that's not the point. Anyway, "What do you make of it," he says. I gave it a look over. Two other blokes were propping it up at the time. One of them gives me a nod. I shoot him one back. Other fellow just stares straight ahead. James says to me, don't mind that, he's just "in The Zone". Apparently it happens a lot. Had some college kids working a few months back, composed most of their papers that way, just in The Zone, propping up the edifice; In their brains, they're working on their biology or their architecture or their *Moby Dick* or whatever. Amazing. Anyway, I had a little toddle round the thing. Sizeable. Nice edifice really, all in all. Certainly wanted propping up. Clearly he knows his business. Two blokes on it, they're doing fine, they'd have the old girl up all day no problem, but you add another pair of hands and even though it doesn't really change the weight distribution, there's a greater sense of security. Somebody might call it redundancy, but that's not how I see it, because the psychological effect is real, you know? Makes a difference. And so I say to him, James, that is, "This is a steady thing is it?"

He looks a bit confused, says, "Well, no that's the whole point." Then he clocks it, "Oh, you mean the job," he says, "That's quite steady, indeed. As steady as you'd like it to be. You can start today if you'd like."

And, so I got started that day. Filled out some paperwork before I went home and bish, bash, bosh. Edifice, here I come! Settled in with the blokes, Reg and Johnny, were their names. Johnny's gone now, not sure where he went to, but he was before Taro. I'm sure that one's up to something.

Thinking about it, I suppose it is true, some funny things do go through your head while you're out there propping up the edifice, like, for instance, the other day it comes to me that they could really just build some trusses or buttresses or something, wouldn't be hard, prop the old girl up. Maybe reinforce it from below, good stick of rebar or something like that in there, wouldn't need three blokes standing there all day propping her up. Thought about saying something to James, I got a cousin in building, see. He'd sort it out, piece of piss, eh? But then I thought about it a little more. My next break wasn't for another twenty, and I'm glad it wasn't. Might just be thinking myself out of a job, I said to meself. So ixnay on the uttressbay. Put it to rest. Well, I say that, but the idea wouldn't leave me alone even after my break. So, I ask the bloke next to me, name's Quinn, good fella, Quinn, likes a flutter, really into his music, does a Genesis tribute act at weekends. I say to Quinn, "Hey, mate, might be a little odd, but I have to ask you why's he got us here after all? Why don't they just make the bloody thing stable once and for all, maybe with ties or wires or something? I mean it's not exactly the Tower of Pisa, is it?"

Quinn shakes his head, bit of an eye-roll I detected, as well. Says to me of course! Of course they bloody could! You think that they ain't thought of that one already? Sitting in that office all day, staring at this edifice out here, at us? You think that hasn't passed through your boy James' noodle? Probably thought about it the first day. No, mate, absolutely no question about it. They want us here, propping up the edifice. You can bet your last penny on that. Yeah, I say, of course, I get that bit, but why?

Quinn, I can see him now, plucking his bass in his band, next to the fellow that plays Peter Gabriel. Same expression—half laughing, half grumpy,- he turns to me and says, look mate, you'll go crazy thinking like that. Save yourself a heart attack, and save me a headache or two, why don't you? And you know what? I'd guess, long term, he's bang on. If it ain't broke, and all that, or if it ain't stable I guess. That was the end of it. Nobody's brought it up since.

The edifice? I suppose you're right, it is kind of important. Well, you know, truth to tell, I don't think about it much. Could forget it was even there, to be honest, after a few hours of it. You don't know how it is until you've done it, but, hand to God, I'm thinking about it and I can't tell you a damn thing. Let's see, searching my memory banks, here, okay? I'd say off-white, kind of an egg-shell colour. Yeah, that's about right. Suppose there are some grey bits around the top and bottom, kind of where it goes out like such, not really a pattern, per se, but just kind of some nicks and discolourations and stuff. Might be quite old. Might be. Never really enquired. Hard to know if it's valuable; suppose it is to someone. Why was it built? Beats me. That's another one of those questions, drives you mad if you think about it: is it religious, or art, or maybe some kind of old ruin or something? I guess I think about it this way: the whole thing, it's not really about the edifice itself. It's just a matter of getting on with it, isn't it? But, since

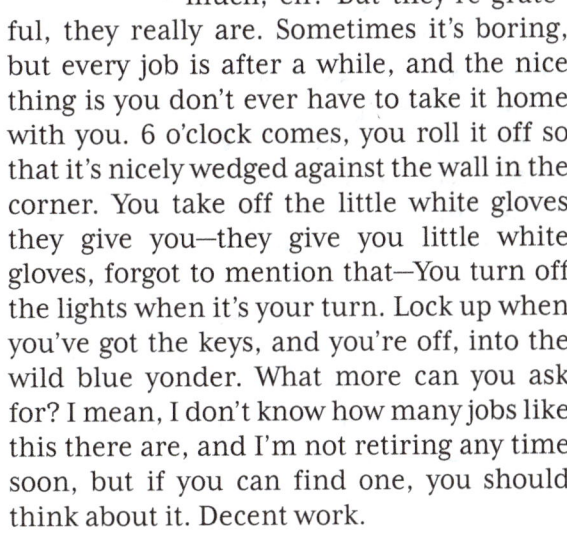

Running away man.

you ask, would I rather be propping up another edifice, a different one? Like, say, maybe one in my favourite colour, like a good blue, a nice navy blue edifice that was kind of in a more regular cylindrical shape? Can't say as it's really been the kind of thing that's exercised me, but, now that we're talking about it, I'll have a think. You know what? I think probably not. You know how it is, mate, careful what you wish for, innit? Could end up with one of those bad paint jobs, or, heaven help us, something with a bloody screen and lights and beeps and bleeps and all that rubbish. No thank you. Give me the good old edifice any day of the

week. Well, most any day. I do like me weekend.

I know where you're coming from, all these questions and that. I can imagine it, a lot of young people out there reading this, they might be thinking, "Propping up an edifice? All day? Are you kidding me? What would they say on bloody Twitter of Snapshite, or whatever?" Well, you say that, but think about it this way, the edifice is just there. It's not hurting anybody, not least because we're propping it up. Puts food on the table, for me, and Quinn, and Wladimir, that's the new guy at the moment, just moved to London, from a place called WOOGE. Nice bloke. English not so strong, but hard working, can't fault that, I suppose for James, too, come to think of it. The Public comes by now and again. I mean, granted, Rickmansworth ain't exactly Mayfair, but you get people, sometimes, and they chat to you a bit. And I'm a friendly guy, I don't bother with the "the Zone" business all that much, so I say hello, tell 'em what I know, like I'm telling you now. In other words, not much, eh? But they're grateful, they really are. Sometimes it's boring, but every job is after a while, and the nice thing is you don't ever have to take it home with you. 6 o'clock comes, you roll it off so that it's nicely wedged against the wall in the corner. You take off the little white gloves they give you—they give you little white gloves, forgot to mention that—You turn off the lights when it's your turn. Lock up when you've got the keys, and you're off, into the wild blue yonder. What more can you ask for? I mean, I don't know how many jobs like this there are, and I'm not retiring any time soon, but if you can find one, you should think about it. Decent work.

JULIAN STANNARD

GOATS AND GORILLAS

Theodore Relish and Melissa Von Bogenschutz lived in a large place off the Goldhawk Road. It was a white Edwardian building and part of a row of elegant houses, although the elegance had faded somewhat and some of the neighbouring houses had been turned into flats. There was a fig tree in the front garden which during the summer spread across the pavement in luxurious flight. Melissa sometimes opened a window and plucked a fig from the tree. For a moment she imagined she was living in Ischia or Agrigento or Syracuse. Figs spilled onto the pavement, crushed underfoot by passers-by looking at their phones or listening to music. Figs spilled onto the road and became food for the rats or the Goldhawk fox which roamed the streets glittering in the moonlight. Gideon would sit under a streetlamp making a plaintive sound as if he were a lovelorn troubadour; his voice—imagine it—accompanied by a celestial lute. He would disappear for long stretches of time but would always come back, not least when the figs were in season.

In the early days, when the house was a work in progress, Melissa and Theodore, or Mel and Theo to their friends, would climb to the top floor in the middle of the night. There'd be the odd drunk or a gaggle of exuberant students but they were of passing interest. They were waiting, breathlessly, for Gideon. They'd hold hands like young lovers. A fig tree and a fox! Melissa would say. Who would have thought? How lucky we are! The fox would look up lovingly before breaking into a vulpine cantata.

They needed a large house. It was the 1980s. Wasn't cheap but they could get some lodgers in to help with the mortgage. Theodore's first novel had won a prestigious prize and for a while it was almost a bestseller. The prize money had been useful and at the same time Melissa had not one but two pieces accepted by the Royal Academy. An up-and-coming gallery in the West End en-sured Melissa Von Bogenschutz's paintings sold well. There were residencies in Berlin and Bucharest and even Bogota. The British Council saw them as a couple blessed with 'added value', and not infrequently, they were flown off together, all expenses paid, on cultural trips. Several prestigious teaching posts came their way: a lecture here, a lecture there, master classes too. Channel Four showcased Melissa's work and Theodore was working hard on his second novel. They felt quite wealthy for a while though neither was overly interested in money. Both were in their thirties. The future was opening up in tantalising ways.

They'd acquired a considerable reputation. Theodore Relish, a novelist of forensic precision; Melissa Von Bogenschutz, an artist of beguiling vision. They didn't see the point of getting married and they didn't want children. Theodore, travelling in Morocco as a young man, had read *Enemies of Promise* and decided the creative life was the only life. Although he had nothing against children, he had of late become an uncle, he realised they would be an enervating distraction and Melissa was in agreement. In the early years they agreed on everything and although they would never say it themselves, their friends, over a glass of Chardonnay, would say 'Theo and Mel were made for each other!'

They had met at a literary party. Theodore had noticed a blonde haired woman in a leather jacket on the other side of the room and not only did she smile but she made her way towards him. Theodore, a clandestine romantic, wondered whether the approaching woman would do what Sylvia Plath had done the first time she met Ted Hughes, namely take a chunk out of his cheek. He began to quiver. She didn't. She had read his stories in the *LRB* and was eager to meet him. She wasn't disappointed in the slightest. A few months later they decided to buy a house together. 'I need lots of space,' Melissa pointed out and Theodore said he wanted a place near the tube and which had a good writing room with plenty of light. Melissa agreed the house should be flooded with light. 'What about a dog?' Theodore asked. 'Cats are better,' Melissa replied. 'They look after themselves and they keep an eye on the mice.'

No one turned down an invitation to a party chez Theo and Mel. In those days the kitchen room in the basement was uncluttered and spacious with a view onto a long garden. There was a solid functional table which could sit ten people without difficulty, on those occasions they were hosting a dinner party. There were pieces of Melissa's work on the wall, and a few miscellaneous objects picked up in markets including bronze heads and African masks. Books, novels or otherwise, often migrated to the kitchen table but they could be whisked away and put on a make-do shelf before the guests arrived. The kitchen room offered a capacious welcome, with tantalising cooking smells and bottles of wine in abundance and a generous array of ashtrays, some in Moroccan turquoise as well as several spinning receptacles. A finger movement and the butt ends were spun out of sight. Poof! As the years passed Melissa wondered whether they could come up with such a device for the stuff in the house. She didn't want to get rid of it but if only some of it might slide from view. Bogdana, the cleaning lady, was good at sprucing things up but she wasn't a miracle worker.

As a young woman Melissa had made a decision about cooking—she would spend her life doing as little of it as possible. Just as well, therefore, Theodore was a maestro. He might take a cursory look at a recipe but in essence his modus operandi was improvisation. A small hand would reach for a jar of herb or the chillies hanging on the kitchen wall or something bought at Shepherd's Bush Market and the dish would transcend the prosaic list of ingredients laid out in the book and bring a tremulous hush as the guests began to eat. A brief hiatus in a room filled with noisy conversation. There on the table, for all to savour, on porcelain or ceramic or terracotta or wooden boards crafted in Lebanon, never a disappointment, was the maestro's love supreme. One of his most attentive critics wondered whether the meticulousness of his writing enjoyed an inverse relationship with the audaciousness of his cuisine. When they moved into the house the kitchen was a tabula rasa. It didn't take long before it became a symphony of pots and pans, many hanging on the walls, and woks and food mixers and coffee grinders and cash and carry bags of organic rice. It was a large kitchen and it opened its arms unselfishly.

Who didn't enjoy Theodore's cooking? There were novelists and poets and publishers and editors and translators and scriptwriters and painters and sculptors and actors and theatre directors and biographers and journalists and professors and musicians and models and performance artists and professional smokers and plagiarists and functioning alcoholics and not a few delightfully bereft of reason. There were speakers of European languages and speakers of Arabic and Japanese as well as Hindi and Pashtun. On one occasion, to everyone's delight, an uninvited Mongolian poet fetched up. Few arrived empty handed—many leaving signed books and paintings and sculptures and bits and bobs and unread manuscripts which drifted to faraway corners and remained unread, picking up dust but still, nevertheless, calling out in the middle of the night with thin voices: Read us! Read us!

Visitors saw a large house with many rooms which said We are blessed with space. Theodore's American publisher turned up with a gorilla. It had been part of an installation in Boston. The Boston Gorilla was also known as Gary. It was too big to be a child's toy and the publisher explained there'd been some kind of battery-powered device inserted in what would have been, technically speaking, the gorilla's bottom, which meant it could beat its chest and sing "Yes, we have no bananas We have no bananas today!' The mechanism no longer worked and Theodore, feigning pleasure, plumped the gorilla with both arms onto the sofa where it stayed for several weeks. Neither Melissa nor Theodore knew what to do. 'Why not put Gary on top of the bookshelf in your writing room? ' Mel suggested, and with some difficulty they managed to get it to sit up, one leg dangling over the books, its glass eyes glazed with melancholy. Melissa found a top hat in the market and, with the help of a step ladder, popped it on Gary's head. Theodore said 'Better the Boston Gorilla, I suppose, than the Boston Strangler.'

Elbowing aside a certain diffidence Melissa Von Bogenschutz was the perfect hostess. Whilst

Theodore launched into his kitchen symphony she looked at the mirror in the bedroom and adjusted her hair, before looking into a capacious wardrobe of skirts, dresses, ruffled tops, jeans, trousers, leather jackets, kaftans, faux-fur coats, baggy sweaters and vintage boots. When she wasn't in a painting mood, and even when she was, she drifted through London's markets, second hand shops, charity shops, and turned up at house clearance sales. Post-punk London was a serendipitous dreamland. No need to buy new stuff; that would come later, years later. Some of her friends in the fashion industry brought her home made clothes full of patchwork collages and hand-picked buttons and vibrant leggings. She'd told Theodore she needed another wardrobe and that was on his list of things to do.

She walked down the stairs, which in those days one could do without encumbrance, and made her way through the guests and Theodore smiled. She was by far the most interesting woman in the house. Her eclectic, if careful, assortment of clothes resonating with the dishes he was knocking up in the kitchen. Lucretia, their lodger and trainee opera singer, stood in the garden and sang an aria as light as a tiramisu. Guests hovered round, applauding, and Gideon stood at the far end of the garden looking on, twitching his brown ears.

Lucrezia and Jonny, their first lodgers, were perfect. Lucretia, from Rome, was studying at the Royal Academy of Music and Jonny was a member of the SWP. He did a little carpentry but much of his time was dedicated to the overthrow of capitalism. They took over the two rooms at the top of the house and Theodore and Melissa charged a modest rent. Melissa said it was nice to have them and Theodore agreed. Some days they could hear Lucretia singing. Some days the trainee opera singer took Theo on long walks. Some days Jonny tramped up the stairs with columns of serious looking men who were having an impromptu strategy meeting. Or Lucretia came down to the kitchen and whisked up a large bowl of pasta for the household. Gloriously simple lunches—pasta with aglio, olio, pepperoncino, a Roman artichoke or two. Lucretia from the Eternal City, Jonny from Mile End! In their

twenties, so young! Jonny had filled one of the attic rooms with pamphlets and manifestos and had made a hefty if wobbly bookshelf, piles of newspapers spinning onto the landing. He invited his landlord to come and admire his library. Theo rather liked the idea there was a burgeoning collection at the top of the house marching in step with his own which slowly but surely colonised the writing room and spilled out into the sitting room, the kitchen and the bathroom.

The first time the rent wasn't paid Theodore and Melissa looked the other way. Lucrezia and Jonny probably needed a little more time and in any case their lodgers were friends now. After three months of rental drought they wondered whether they should say something. Their own finances were becoming less secure. Lucretia, they noticed, did not sing as much these days and Jonny's political activism had metamorphosed into what Melissa called 'Bedroom Opera'— tempestuous arguments followed by percussive sessions of love making. 'Perhaps they're having a second honeymoon.' Theodore noted wryly. It was Jonny who brought the matter up.

'Theo, really sorry about the rent. We're waiting for the next chunk of Lucretia's grant and my work seems to have dried up.'

'Maybe you could do some carpentry around the house. There's a lot of stuff on the floors.'

Jonny had another proposal. He found Melissa in the garden room manoeuvring a large painting into place. He'd noticed of late her work was moving away from colour and collage towards a more figurative mode.

Jonny said, 'Me and Lucretia could model for you. In exchange for the outstanding rent.'

And an agreement was made on the spot—a temporary agreement. Theo shrugged his shoulders when she told him. 'If that's what you want.'

Mel felt like a student again—Life Drawing— though her hand was quick and confident now and Lucretia and Jonny without clothes were magnificent. A large plank of wood, sometime ago pushed against the window in the studio, had interrupted the flow of light so Melissa made the sitting room her temporary laboratory. Neither Lucretia not Jonny were bashful about nakedness. Jonny seemed to relish it and every time Theo came back into the house Jonny was sitting on the sofa drinking coffee, legs apart, naked.

'Waiting for Mel,' he'd say.

When Theodore mentioned that Jonny didn't wear many clothes these days Melissa said 'You're getting old, my dearest.'

Theodore had put on a little weight. Jonny was as sinewy as a mountain stream whilst Lucrezia, with her long thick hair, was prosperous from every angle. Melissa was taken up with the project—Jonny Dreaming of Revolutions on Divan, Lucretia Blessing the Remaining Light, Jonny Forsaking Clothes to read *Das Kapital*, Lucretia Holding a Snow Globe, Lucretia with Mother and Child—the mother was of the feline kind and the child one of the vast litter she'd recently produced. There were individual poses and drawings of the lovers together. She even persuaded Theodore to pose for one—Jonny with Landlord. Theo was standing behind the seated revolutionary, only his head and shoulders appeared.

Melissa felt an energy moving into her fingers and she worked with an intensity she hadn't experienced for a while. Dinner parties were temporarily suspended as well as shopping for clothes. Theodore sat in his writing room, unable to write, waiting for artist and naked models to break for lunch.

The Leopold Museum, as it happens, was curating an exhibition—The Human Form Revisited—and had invited portfolios from artists across the world. Melissa's work had been accepted at the last minute and now she worked with an even greater intensity. She had to send twelve framed pieces—not small—to Vienna and the house became engulfed in decision making. Her gallerist came round and took several drawings and they sold immediately. Jonny asked if they might not have a cut. Channel Four featured The Jonny and Lucretia Drawings on some late-night show, saying Melissa von Bogenschutz had taken life drawing by the scruff of the neck.

Three days before Theodore and Melissa were off to the opening—flights booked—Jonny announced they were leaving. Lucretia was going back to Rome and Jonny had found a teaching job in Nicaragua.

'Don't worry about the stuff in the attic. I'll ask one of the comrades to come round and take it away.'

That night Lucretia sang *Lascia ch'io pianga*.

In 1990 they threw a party to celebrate Thatcher's fall from power. They had a new lodger but they only rented out the one room because the comrades had never come round to clear Jonny's library and unattended the books and manifestos seemed to have multiplied. The new lodger was a trainee teacher and paid the rent at the end of every month. In 1990 the neighbours on one side were Jamaican and they were celebrating too. Tyrone came round with jerk chicken and from their sound system Dennis Brown was singing 'Are you ready to stand up and fight the right revolution?'

Melissa was talking to Theodore's German translator. 'My father was a businessman and fell for a Jewish girl. Realising the direction of National Socialism he got his lover a one way ticket to America. He remained in Berlin, and thanks to his wealth, he arranged safe passage for other Jews. His cover was blown in 1939 and he slipped across the border. He returned to Berlin at the end of the war and married my mother.'

Melissa was sent to boarding school in England. Her father didn't speak about the past but she remembered his account of a Jewish couple who had to abandon their apartment on the Kurfürstendamm and slip away with nothing. The thought of having nothing, she said to the German translator. Nothing! She thought of her paintings and palettes and easels and rolled up canvasses and *objets d'art* and African masks and art books and her cats and her shoes and her bottles of coco chanel and her soaps and her jewellery and her clothes. I will *never* have nothing, she exclaimed and pulled Theodore to his feet and they danced to the music of Dennis Brown, the smell of jerk chicken in the air. The moon had risen and she whispered in her beloved's ear 'Can you see Gideon over there, at the end of the garden?'

In 1997 they threw a party to celebrate Tony Blair's electoral victory. They agreed Blair was neither Michael Foot nor Tony Benn but nevertheless after eighteen years of Tory rule even Gary the Gorilla would have been an improvement. It was open house from midday. Who didn't come to the party? Theodore prepared dishes from across the world and guests brought bottles of champagne. The food was laid out on long tables in the garden—a Saturday. Guests would have noticed they had to step over several boxes in the hallway and the kitchen room, with people spilling into the garden, was like the underground at rush hour; that the garden room was now chock-a-block with Melissa's canvases.

Half of the kitchen table had given way to books and newspapers and abandoned art works and pots of paint and bits of metal picked up in the street—found pieces. Nowadays they could sit six people around the table, including themselves. House parties were different. People came and left until the small hours. The Jamaican neighbours had gone. A gay couple who worked at the BBC had taken their place. Blur blasted out from a stereo: 'Girls who want boys who like boys to be girls who do boys like they're girls who do girls like they're boys.'

Two editors, both drunk, both smoking, were sitting on garden chairs.

'Theo always pulls it out of the bag. Fabulous food.'

I wonder whether his cooking's not better than his writing. I haven't seen much lately.'

'The odd story.'

'Extremely odd.'

When Theodore and Melissa eventually got up to their bedroom they looked out of the window and saw Gideon walking by with a cub. He looked up and Melissa waved. 'Oh Gideon,' she said. 'No nocturne cantata for us?'

They had no plans to throw a party in 2000 to celebrate the millennium. Their finances were in a slump. Melissa had given up the second studio on the Uxbridge Road. Theodore was in a slump too. Since the publication of *Sudden*—his brilliant debut—the quest for novel number two had taken him into a labyrinth. Sixteen years had passed. His readership had waited. Some had wandered off to the lagoon. His literary agent had jumped ship. His publisher's requests to see the work, which arrived in large brown packages on rare occasions, led to bafflement. In 1989 Theodore sent the publisher a hundred thousand words. In 1993 he sent a hundred and fifty thousand, with 'Lebensraum' written on a post it note. In 1998 he'd sent two hundred thousand words. His publisher communicated with laconic Christmas cards.

Theodore—the dragon-slayer—had forsaken structure, economy and clarity and still had his foot on the accelerator. There was no end in sight. He was out-brothering the *Brothers Karamazov*, out-warring Tolstoy, making *Finnegans Wake* a jog around the park. Pound's Make it New was becoming Make it Big. People were saying 'Poor Theo. He's been skewered with Second Novel Syndrome.'

A collection of stories published ten years beforehand had been well reviewed but didn't sell. His second novel contained so many lines of enquiry, so many obsessions, there were piles of books, scrupulously annotated, reaching towards the ceiling. Whilst Melissa was gliding inexorably towards some cannabis-scented retailer of second-hand clothes, Theodore was slipping into a second-hand bookshop. He was convinced there was something which would lead him out of the labyrinth. He flicked though accounts of Victorian sewers, the construction of Lunatic Asylums, the occult. Inevitability he would bring home another handful of books. Review work had petered out. He'd done a little freelance stuff for the BBC and when the lodger left he realised they needed a cash injection so he took on a 'temporary' role helping to distribute books for a small publisher. More boxes arrived, boxes on top of boxes.

'Where on earth are you going to put them?' Mel asked.

Theodore shrugged. 'Remember, books will be leaving the house as well as coming in—at least that's the idea.'

Melissa sold a painting and they threw a party after all. A mountain of books had collapsed in the hallway so their guests needed to walk down a path several houses on which cut back round to the garden. 'The scenic route,' someone quipped. It was a smaller gathering than usual and a few impromptu fireworks leapt into the sky and died a quick death. Yet London was full of fireworks. Gideon sat twitching between two wheelie bins wondering what the new century would bring. Theodore's American publisher was a surprise guest—he couldn't stay long but he'd brought Gary a companion.

'I couldn't resist it,' he said. 'She's a bit smaller and she's called Madge.' She was in the same Bostonian installation and had been found in someone's attic—she'd had some implanted device which meant she could sing something too—though no one seems to remember what she sang.

The next day Theodore and Melissa got the ladder and managed to squeeze Madge next to Gary. Their exertions resulted in a cloud of dust. One of Madge's legs dangled down from the bookshelf.

In 2003 Theodore and Melissa had their first big argument. They'd been on the Stop The War March. When they got back to the house they couldn't open the door. Strange—they'd cleared a pathway before setting out. Maybe the cats have been up to something,' Melissa said. 'Those bloody cats,' Theodore replied. 'I thought you liked those bloody cats?' They took the path to the back garden but Melissa couldn't find the back door key. They'd put a spare one under a pot. So many pots now. Theodore broke the glass panel. Their new neighbour heard the noise and called 999. The cats scurried to their bowls. They'd lost count. Cats had drifted in from neighbouring houses, finding empty boxes or piles of clothes to make a home away from home and enter a life of feline meditation. The cats loved Melissa because she fed them, indiscriminately.

A pile of shoes had cascaded down the first flight of stairs. Once in the sitting room they could smell Bogdana's Slavic perfume.

'I didn't know she was coming today.'

'She has her own key,' Melissa said.

Bogdana didn't want to hurt her back pushing boxes around and there was no space to hoover in the rooms upstairs. She had a millennium duster which extended to various lengths. Dusting was Bogdana's speciality.

'Is she in the house?'

Next to the front door they found Bogdana lying face up, blood coming from her ear. The duster next to her.

Melissa threw her hands in the air. 'I think she might be dead.'

But Bogdana wasn't dead. Theodore patted her face. They helped her to her feet. 'Better call the ambulance,' Melissa said. They took her to the sofa and cleared some books and sat her down. Theodore fetched a glass of water.

'I'm sorry,' Bogdana said. She looked towards the gorillas and then put her head in her hands.

'What happened?' Melissa asked. Bogdana pointed at the gorillas on top of the bookcase.

'Problem,' she said. 'Problem.'

'What sort of problem?'

'Big gorilla, big problem,' she said.

Theodore and Melissa looked at Gary, sitting next to Madge.

'I dust,' Bogdana said, 'many dust, the house quiet and Gorilla began singing, very loud.'

'Singing?'

'He had bananas, he not have bananas. I very scared and running to the door.'

'You must have tripped.' Theodore wiped her ear with one of Melissa's vintage shirts.

The ambulance turned up at the same time as the police car. Neighbours watched from across the road. Gideon, out of sight, looked on.

The paramedic walked Bogdana out of the house. The policeman looked around. It'd been a trying day.

'Are you the owners of this house?'

'Yes,' Theodore said.

'Are you aware of a break in? It does rather look like a break in.'

Theodore explained.

You were on the Stop the War March! If you want my opinion it won't make much difference. And the woman in the ambulance?

'Our cleaning lady.'

'A brave woman,' the policeman said looking around. 'Do you mind if I take a look upstairs? He was taking out a notebook.

Melissa sat on the sofa and smoked a cigarette. The men began clomping upwards.

The policeman saw the staircase was hedged by boxes lined up on the sides and at moments he would have to turn sideways to squeeze past and when they got to the next floor he saw stacks of clothes on the landing and piles of newspapers. He pushed open a couple of doors and saw more clothes, some on make do racks, some on the floor in vertical piles.

'Running a business from this property sir?'

'Of course not. I'm a writer.'

'A writer? What do you write Mr Relish?'

'Fiction.'

'I like detective stories myself. Much success?'

'*Sudden*—my first novel—did reasonably well.'

'I've never heard of it, I'm afraid. And your wife?'

'She's not my wife. If it's of any relevance at all, Mrs Von Bogenschutz's an artist.'

'An artist.'

The policeman looked at the next flight of stairs and decided against it.

'I think I've seen enough.'

Melissa was looking at a painting of hers on the wall: a pistol, the barrel of which blossomed into a flowering prepuce.

'I like that painting,' she said to herself and lit another cigarette.

As the policeman was leaving he said, noticing an ashtray with vertical aspirations, 'Far be it from me to suggest how you live your lives. You might think of getting in touch with a charity shop Mrs Von Bogenschutz.'

Cannibal—one of the cats—rubbed itself against his leg.

He added, 'I'd get that back door fixed too.'

Theodore and Melissa went to bed early that night. They lay together under blankets looking at the ceiling. There were several wardrobes in the bedroom. Yet the piles of clothes on the floor meant they were beyond reach. A pathway led into the room and a casual glance, by an untrained eye, might have given the impression Theo and Mel slept in a four poster bed. Or a boat that had been tossed in an ocean of fabric. One great surge and they would capsize. It was a cold February night. Only one of the bedside lamps seemed to work which gave the room a spectral glow. The jackets on the racks were headless ghosts, latent, muttering without mouths. There was a cobweb on the ceiling which had escaped Bogdana's duster.

'Perhaps the policeman was right,' Theodore said.

'Right?'

'You could get rid of a few clothes, I suppose.'

'And the books?'

'Mel, really, I need them for the project.'

'Why don't you finish that bloody novel!'

They continued looking at the cobweb on the ceiling.

'The clothes are my extended family,' Melissa said. 'I'm not sending my family to a charity shop.'

After a long silence Melissa said 'And what are you going to call that novel?'

'*The World Beyond*', Theodore said.

By the time the Lehman Brothers collapsed in 2008 the house had become a forest. Both front and back doors unreachable. Final warnings regarding the electricity bill hadn't been taken care of and the house was plunged into darkness. They found some candles which they clutched, navigating the stairs and gathering in the kitchen for candlelit dinners. The gas was still working and at first Theodore enjoyed improvising in the flickering light. Although Melissa didn't cook she had, on her last foray into the outside world, bought a large quantity of exotic vegetables which she'd stuffed into the corners of the fridge. A chemical process of hybridisation seeped across the shelves. Theodore tried to open a window. He scraped the soupy mush from the fridge into a plastic bag.

Although Theodore had quit his job with Independent Distributions, books continued to arrive, left on the stoop, which encouraged the policeman to re-entertain the idea they were running business. For a month or so the house was under surveillance. Difficult to get out of either door now. They were running out of basic provisions. Theodore got a message through to his nephew who'd graduated from Imperial College. Ruben set up a pulley system in the back garden. Theo and Mel put in their orders and the young man winched them up to the second floor. Gideon looked on, bemused, rolls of loo paper falling into the long grass.

Theodore's writing room was now little more than a desk and a typewriter and a revolving ashtray. His computer had crashed some time ago and remained kaput, notwithstanding energetic Wagnerian prodding. Melissa's studio was a scrapyard, groaning with artefacts and detritus. There was a pathway of sorts from door to a table on which sat a Moroccan ashtray, next to which there was room for a small easel. Two planks of wood covered up much of the window. Melissa was teaching herself to paint in the etiolated light. Sometimes candlelight. Useful for introspection. She was painting miniatures and was excited by this new direction. If only her gallerist could see them.

Once in their rooms it was easier to avoid further travel. The kitchen was a faraway place, bathroom and bedroom negotiable—just. Melissa could hear Theodore's typing. She missed her Lebanese café. She was losing weight. The cats weren't being fed either—Ruben had delivered some biscuits on the winch which Melissa chucked down the stairs—their plaintive cries like the Nibelung gathering on the Rhine. Some had jumped ship. Some had slipped into neighbouring houses. Melissa shuddered when she saw a mouse. Theodore and Melissa banged on the walls when they needed to communicate. Post dropped into the hallway—unreachable, unread. The gas had been turned off.

Melissa couldn't sleep. The fifth night in a row. It didn't help that Theodore, notwithstanding the twenty-five years he'd spent on his second novel, was snoring blissfully. Her journey of introspection had not been without cost. Sleeplessness reached out a hand and the fingers of that hand could feel rope. If only she could sleep. She pleaded. If you let me sleep, she said to the God she didn't believe in, I'll think about getting rid of my clothes, not all of them mind you. She had some sleeping tablets in the kitchen. She took the torch Ruben had supplied and put on a dressing gown—one of her favourites. She wondered whether she might trip down the stairs and break her neck. Thinner now, navigation of the staircase was slightly easier. One step at a time. She reminded herself there was another staircase down to the kitchen. She pushed a landing switch out of habit. The sound of the click startled her. She thought of climbing back to the bedroom but Theodore's sleeping form would be a torment, and she'd gone so far

that going back would be as difficult as going on. Her descent was crab like, squeezing herself against the banisters, hearing bits and pieces fall from the pyramids of stuff. If only the lights would come back on. The stairs creaked. She could smell the kitchen before she reached it—cat faeces and spoilt okra.

Melissa's complicated journey to the kitchen had alerted the three cats still in residence. They emerged from their boxes and scurried down to the bowls. Melissa shone her torch: two were little more than kittens, threadbare. Only Cannibal was familiar to her. With some difficulty she opened some deluxe tuna. Cannibal rubbed himself again her leg.

There were boxes pushed against the back door. She knew the pills were in one of them. She reached up for the top one and opened it—shoes mostly. The second box had more shoes and some woollen scarves. Maybe take a couple? It was getting cold in the bedroom. She began pulling at the boxes some of which fell around her feet. They hadn't fixed the door and a wind blew in from the garden. Then she heard the fox's cry. Gideon's face was pushed against the door, blood running out of his mouth.

Several mornings later Theodore announced they needed a war plan. He was somewhat leaner and had a beard now, flecked with grey. Melissa rather liked it.

'Anything could happen', he said. 'There could be a fire. We're drifting hopelessly. We're running out of money. We're running out of air. The house smells like an enormous hamster cage. We need a clear path to the front door and the kitchen and the back door. We need to pay the bills. I need to cook real food in a kitchen that looks like a kitchen. Have you noticed the cats have abandoned their mouse duties? I don't care what you say, I'm starting today.'

Melissa kissed his forehead. After finding the sleeping pills she'd slept for a whole day. She dreamt of Gideon. He was leaving the city, a trail of blood though the streets of Hammersmith. He limped and wailed, finding shelter in abandoned sheds, licking his wounds. He swam across a river. He walked across green fields. He was getting stronger now. Somewhere over the hill was fox land. He stood on the hill and turned. He looked at Melissa, the blood staunched now. He broke into mellifluous song.

Theodore picked up his metaphorical machete and worked tirelessly for three days—pushing, shoving, heaving newspapers around, putting books into neat piles, shaking his fist at a mouse, surreptitiously bagging up loose shoes. He cleared the hallway, opened the front door, which let out a sigh. He cleared the stoop and walked to a phone box. He paid the bills. He arranged for someone to fix the back door. He bumped into a poet who threw his arms into the air. He looked at the weather. The weather looked back.

If the policeman had returned he wouldn't have noticed much difference. Yet Theodore's efforts meant they had contact with the world. The house now had a degree of functionality, as if the Romans had made a road through a German forest. They tried to persuade Bogdana to come back. We'll pay you more.

'You get rid of gorillas, I come back.'

'What do you think?' Melissa said.

'We can't do that,' Theodore replied. 'Gary and Madge are inseparable. They're hand in hand, riding the waves, like us.'

'I think you're right. I might try a little dusting myself.'

'Only if you get the urge. Be careful.'

Not long after the defeat of the Labour government in 2010 Ruben supplied Theo and Mel with iPhones. It didn't take Melissa long to work out how to order clothes online. The gallerist had been pleased with her miniatures and the household had some income coming in. Needing more space Melissa took a studio on the Uxbridge Road.

Ruben had sorted out Theo's computer and *The World Beyond* was taking the novelist in another direction. When he looked out of window of his writing room, the curtain no longer snagging after the clear up, he saw the sun rising over London.

A friend from Suffolk was passing through—an artist. They invited her for supper. The kitchen table still looked as if a dumper truck had dropped a great heap upon it but Theodore had chucked away a few things and the three of them could perch at the end. They drank good wine.

Cannibal stretched under the table. The visitor out smoked them, flicking ash into the Moroccan chicken. 'I adore your house,' she said.

The bedroom, if anything, was getting worse. Online deliveries arrived for Melissa which she secreted into the room. They lay in the quiet of the night holding hands in a bed walled in by pillars of clothes, listening to the gorillas. Gary would begin—'Yes I have no bananas, I have no bananas today' and as if they'd been practising Madge would follow with 'Miss Otis regrets she's unable to lunch today, Madam, Miss Otis regrets she's unable to lunch today.'

'Oh Theo thank God we didn't get rid of them,' Melissa said.

'Did you ever try any of that dusting stuff?'

Now it was possible to get out of the house Melissa established a routine. An hour in the Lebanese cafe, two hours in the new studio, some gentle mooching around the market. If she bought an item of clothing she'd conceal it under her coat. Another hour at the café. It was good to be out of the house. Even the fig tree looked perkier. Maybe they should go to Italy?

Ruben's winching device was still in place and knowing that Melissa would be away the entire morning Theodore arranged, along with his nephew, now writing a PhD, some strategic winching of clothes intro the back garden, which were thrown into large black sacks and taken down the back path and driven in Ruben's Cortina to the dump. Risky taking them to a charity shop. Theodore calculated small removals would go unnoticed. A light trim. He hadn't yet discovered Melissa was bringing new clothes into the house.

Theodore hadn't had an epiphany for years and now he had one. *The World Beyond* was going into reverse. He was going to slash it and shrink it. The liberation made him giddy and bold and underscored his desire to take on the house. He even threw a few books into the winch. Ruben said 'I'll take them to a second-hand shop to see if I can get some money. Even if the Tories are back in power there's need to throw in the towel.'

One morning—a Tuesday as it happens—Melissa came home earlier than usual. She slipped through the front door, much easier nowadays, and heard Theodore on the telephone. She didn't like the drift of the conversation.

'Would the Red Cross be interested?' she heard him say 'A morning collection would be best. The clothes are in very good condition.'

The call went on for a while and she felt her heart pounding. Who did he think he was? The Grim Reaper?

When he'd finished the call she stepped into his writing room, a little tidier these days. 'We need to talk.' Theo's colour changed, not unlike that wonderful lobster dish he used to make for those dinner parties long ago. Her voice was cracking. She wasn't into shouting. It didn't matter what Theodore said about speculative enquiries. She'd rumbled him. An act of betrayal.

When she glanced up at Gary and Madge they looked different, as if someone had been pulling chunks out of them. Melissa slammed the front door. She'd never done that before.

A day later, no sign of Melissa, Theodore thought of ringing the police. Then he got a text. 'I'll be back in a few days, on condition you call the Red Cross.' Theodore didn't know that Jonny, after all these years, had come back to London for an important meeting and bumped into Melissa in Shepherd's Bush. He didn't know that Life Drawing had resumed in her studio on the Uxbridge Road.

When Melissa came home she seemed surprisingly chipper and once she saw the bedroom was still crammed with her clothes she was even chippier. She'd been working hard too, she said. Theodore cooked a goat curry to celebrate her return.

For a while life carried on pleasantly enough. Mel went off in the morning; Theo worked on *The World Beyond*. No allusion was made to the Red Cross. They smoked happily and drank some excellent wine. At night they listened to Gary and Madge:—'We've string beans, and onions, cabbages, and scallion but I have no bananas, I have no bananas today' followed by 'Miss Otis regrets she's unable to lunch today, Madam, Miss Otis regrets she's unable to lunch today.'

Melissa ordered a state-of-the-art duster. 'I think we'll have a good crop of figs this year.'

Then the catastrophe, years in the making. They woke one morning struggling to breathe. It felt as if they'd been buried alive, like a Victorian melodrama. The skyscrapers surrounding their bed had keeled over. A great wave had capsized their boat. Theodore could see one of Melissa's arms through an air hole and Melissa could make out one of Theo's ears. She'd always liked his ears. They could shout but their voices were muffled. The turned over boat had an air pocket but for how long? A piece of luck. Theodore's iPhone had been knocked into the bed and he clutched it like a man still alive in a coffin who'd found a providential handbell. Let me out! With some difficulty he managed to ring Ruben who came around straightaway, thankfully he had a key, and pulled the layers of jackets and skirts and shirts off the bed. They sat up, propped against cushions, saying nothing for an hour.

Melissa said 'You can ring the Red Cross or the British Heart Foundation or Mencap, or whoever you choose. Let me pick out a few things, they can take the rest. We can make the bedroom the lungs of the house, a permanent pocket of air. We can worry about the rest of the house later.'

Theodore said 'I'll start rounding up some books too. Oh Mel, it will be a new start.' Later that day Ruben came round with a bottle of champagne.

It was Theodore who saw it first. He'd gone to the bathroom in the night and switched on the landing light. When he heard the noise he thought it was Cannibal, chomping at Gary and Madge. Then he saw a light. The goat clambered up the stairs with ease and stood for a moment next to the bathroom before bleating and disappearing into the night. Theodore got back into bed and slept like a baby. The next morning he put it down to a dream, no ordinary dream, and decided not to say anything about it. Two nights later Melissa, making her way to the bathroom in the small hours, had a similar encounter. The white goat took on the crowded stairs as if they were the ledge of a Greek mountain. At first Melissa thought it was Gideon but the luminous goat revealed itself before fading away. She got back into bed and had the best night's sleep in a long while, sleeping tablets unnecessary. She told Theo about the goat over breakfast and he shared his experience too. That night they stood at the top of the stairs, hand in hand, waiting, and waiting. All they could hear was a tinny version of 'Yes, I have no bananas' and an even tinnier version of 'Miss Otis regrets she's unable to lunch today.' Then they saw the light. The goat climbed the stairs and passed right by them, they could feel its coat on their legs, and the goat entered the bedroom. They watched it navigate the room. It still looked as if a doodle bug had hit it but the goat found pathways of its own and made its way to the largest wardrobe. They waited for it to come out. When they looked inside there was nothing, not even the clothes which had been hanging there. White mist hovered for a while and there was a goaty aroma which sent them into a deep sleep.

'I do like goats,' Melissa said.

'Nothing at all wrong with a goat', Theodore said, and as he was saying it he resolved, with a tinge of regret, never to cook goat curry again.

The Red Cross never came because Ruben told Melissa about eBay and she found her clothes sold very quickly—vintage—and at good prices. Every time she made a sale her phone made a pleasing sound. There was satisfaction in seeing the room thinning out. A less brutal resolution. The bedroom began to look like a bedroom. In any case, Melissa told herself, I can always start over again.

'I didn't know you'd applied to the Nicaragua Institute for a residency?'

'I thought it would come to nothing,' Melissa said. 'It didn't seem worth mentioning.'

'You're going to Managua for six months.'

'Everything paid for.'

'That's half a year Mel.'

'I'll have a lot of work to do.'

'I'll come and visit.'

'Unfortunately, spouses and partners aren't allowed to come. That's one of the conditions. You'll do fine without me. Remember, you've got a book to finish.'

Two weeks later Theo was seeing Mel off at Heathrow. They hugged for a long time. He didn't know Jonny would be picking her up at Sandino International Airport.

Theodore mooched around the house which seemed enormous and although he was pleased the bedroom looked like a bedroom and the stairs were easier to climb he missed Melissa and when he got into the bed he had a pang of nostalgia for the old bedroom.

Melissa did spend a few days in Managua but Jonny had a house in La Boquita. The chauffer drove them in an old Mercedes, a couple of hours from the capital. The house was big enough for a studio and the views of the sea were magnificent, not to mention the light! There was so much to paint Melissa could hardly hold the brush.

Life drawings continued in and out of the studio, and in and out of the bedroom. Jonny had a moustache. His skin had darkened after years of sun and his Spanish was immaculate. Even his English was infused with Central American rhythm.

His chauffeur, it turned out, was also his bodyguard. A fine-looking man. An athlete.

Jonny said, 'Carlos won't take his clothes off in the studio—Where, in any case, would he put his pistol?'

Jonny had done well. 'The history of Nicaragua is *muy complicada*. It'd take six months to scratch the surface. I gave up teaching years ago. Moved on.'

Melissa enjoyed what lay before her eyes: the sea, the beach, the garden. There were coconuts and pineapples and papayas and watermelon and dragon fruits and passion fruit and plenty of bananas.

Weeks passed. Months. Jonny sometimes drove to Managua, stayed a few days, and came back with paints and canvasses and new outfit for his erstwhile landlady. Her Nicaraguan wardrobe was looking good. She was left with a house maid who couldn't speak much English. Melissa walked along the beach, put her feet in the sea, and swam out alone. She's always been a strong swimmer. She wondered what her gallerist would say about the new work. She thought about Theo. She'd never done anything like this before. She wondered if he'd ever find out there never had been a residency; just a plan cooked up with Jonny on the Uxbridge Road. Behind the garden there was a cliff. One morning she watched a goat climbing towards the summit.

T he sea was emerald blue yet a hurricane was coming. Gary sat under a banana tree, one of his eyes gauged out. Gideon stood on a mountain top and let out a plaintive wail. Howler monkeys howled. White lights hovered above the Goldhawk Road. The fig tree was barren. Theo stood in the attic, at the top of the stairs, looking a lot older.

'Miss Von Bogenshutz's been dreaming,' Jonny said, his arms around her. She was covered in sweat.

'I have to go home, Jonny.'

Melissa didn't know Lucretia was playing Princess Elizabeth in Wagner's *Tannhäuser* at the Royal Opera House. Their former lodger has sent tickets for the last night, along with a note—I'll be in London a few days; perhaps we could meet up?

Theodore had received a couple of postcards from Nicaragua. One had a puma on it, the other lots of avocados. He missed Melissa but he was working hard. One morning, a Tuesday, he found Cannibal laid out under the fig tree. Gary and Madge had been knocked off the shelf, their glass eyes gone. Cannibal had been on a frenzy. Theodore should have fed him more tuna. He buried the cat in the garden and put the remains of the Gary and Madge into a plastic bag. He missed their singing but the house, so quiet now, the odd mouse aside, he managed to put the final touches to *The World Beyond*.

He stood at the Royal Opera House and hollered and clapped on the last night of *Tannhauser*. Two days later Lucretia came for lunch. Theodore had cleared most of the kitchen table.

'I will never forget this house,' she said, tucking into lamb tajine. They drank two bottles of Barbera. They talked and cried a little and held each other. She didn't know what had happened to Jonny. He might be dead. Nicaragua is a dangerous place. Theodore could see that Lucretia was wondering why Melissa wasn't there. It felt too strange saying she had gone to Nicaragua so he said she was visiting family in Germany.

'Ah Germania,' Lucretia said.

As evening came, the days getting longer now, Lucretia said 'You'll think I'm some crazy Diva. I'd like to sleep in the attic one last time!'

'I'll get some sheets.'

In the middle of the night Lucretia stepped out of her room and wondered at the pamphlets and manifestos still floating around the attic. The house was quiet. She was remembering Jonny and now she saw the goat. She followed it down the stairs and before she knew it she was gliding dreamily into the master bedroom and sliding into the novelist's bed. Although she had a fine hotel in a fine part of London she stayed for three nights. They talked a lot and held each other. They went for long walks. Theo read from his novel. Lucretia sang Astrud Gilberto's 'Love is the saddest thing when it goes away.' In my next novel, Theo said to himself, I'll write about an opera singer who sings when she makes love.

Melissa didn't know that when Theo's publisher got the manuscript the man would twitch. Never had he received a book which made him twitch like that. She didn't know that when her Nicaraguan art was exhibited in London there would be exclamations. She didn't know that not long after her return they would host a magnificent party.

The *World Beyond* would win prizes and become a best seller. And soon enough Channel Four would make a late-night programme about her Nicaraguan adventure. She didn't know the British Council would send them to New York—some called it the return of Theodore Relish and Mellissa Von Bogenschutz. She didn't know another fox would stand under the fig tree. They called him little Gideon—the finest troubadour in London. Neither did she know Bogdana would stride in with her duster and a brand new hoover. She didn't know she would take down the painting of the pistol with its flowering prepuce and replace it with a goat.

Three Prose Poems From "The Bridge"

Fusion Food

Esteemed Sir,

I'm writing to you to register my peevishness for the events I experienced the other evening in your bistro. I do not like the thought of blood tests being requested whilst I'm dining expressly on non-fleshy food. Yuk! No flesh or blood is ever chewed or drunk by me. Moreover, I was offered one possible motherhood test—in public, whilst my friends plus I were devouring our supper! I've no intention of birthing and dinner is possibly not one fitting venue in which to discuss the point. Why on Erth is such non-public knowledge being sought concerning me? Further, why request us to queue up to see the doctor? These things put us off our food completely. On the plus side, the footlights setting inspired us plus the full house obviously enjoyed our confusion. It seems they were tickled pink with merriment. However, I request indemnity in view of the formentioned distress.

Yours in ill temper,

Renée

Cherished customer,

Oh no! We've obviously effected distress even if unthinkingly. We do regret this but you should comprehend in this time of economic grimness, every effort must be tried by our business to exist productively in order to induce profit. Combining our services works for us if not for you. Nevertheless, we offer you two vouchers of ten per cent off your next dining occurrences with us. We so respect your cherished custom plus looking to see you next time.

Very best wishes from us at Compound Bistro

Love Is Not Enough

Greetings Ms. Ssh,

We're much obliged for your recent enquiry concerning your wish to work in our Wild Living Things Reserve on one volunteer footing.

Your emotions concerning big felines seem extremely supportive. However, we do not concur with your view of cuddling being the overriding thing they need most. You might wish for this but we think they will see you more in the light of fresh food. Not productive for your well-being or our good repute.

You tell us of your devotion to the support of 'in peril' wild beings expressly. This is wonderful indeed but we must concern ourselves with the nitty-gritty of this point of view. Purely wishful thinking is insufficient in this setting—unluckily for you.

Whilst we do respect your good will, we consider it impossible to give permission to your request nevertheless we feel most indebted for your sincere interest in our protective, conserving work.

With our very best wishes,

THE WILD CRITTER COLLECTIVE

Fulfillment

WELCOME DISCERNING CUSTOMER

You chose so well! Strid is constructed completely to your requirements. We feel proud of our success in fulfilling your longing for your own unique friend who will bring much joy to your life. We hope she will offer you plenty of cheering comfort

INSTRUCTIONS

1. Open the box
2. Uncover Strid from the protective filling
3. Remove Strid
4. Strid comes with numerous outfits plus wigs per your order
5. This electronic robot is fully computerised. She is word-perfect in English, French, Germn plus Itlin, responding politely to your every wish. You should set her controls (remote) to either

   docile
   semi-independent
   independent

6. **URGENT BRIEFING**
   Strid will **comprehend** plus **remember EVERYTHING** she detects. Should you perceive problems we suggest you revert to first settings. **NOTE:** however, her current knowledge would be completely wiped out
7. Strid is completely hygienic—just ensure you remove some sections for deep scrubbing from time to time

WE WISH YOU WELL WITH YOUR NEW FRIEND

Tina Gross

Three Poems

Conference Apocalypse

I'd like to welcome everyone to the last session of the last day.
Thanks for being here.
Thanks for sticking around until the end.

We're probably all going to die right here unless
- the robin incorporates the red string from an interdepartmental envelope into her nest
- the convention center floor mosaic of a snake starts giving out business cards
- moss, algae, and lichen stick to the advertised speaking order

The hotel bills slipped under our doors overnight include charges for a geomagnetic storm, because
- the house spider got the last ice water out of the cambro by tilting it forward
- the kelp forest that struggles with imposter syndrome forgot to take notes
- termite nymphs huddling under a big landscape boulder couldn't find coffee without an hour-long line

This panel discussion will be adjourned by an asteroid impact and/or grey goo, even if
- leopard slugs thronging to the warmth of the CPU manage to publish and not perish
- Guinea fowl recruited to eat wood ticks can connect the laptop to the projector
- the patina on the building's bronze cladding can discreetly free a chair from the ganging brackets that lock them in a row

It's pointless to duck and cover when we'll be in the crater, keeping in mind that
- cochineals nesting on a cactus should use the microphone even though they think they're loud enough without it
- microbes breaking down compost can explain why the conference scheduler app doesn't sync with the website
- the ladybug trying to eat aphids without interference from ants has included a complete bibliography

This is more of a comet than a question.

It is appropriate to hug in this situation?
This meeting is not going to hold itself.

Sky-Questions Dissolved by Sea-Answers

Cloud mouth, kite whisperer,
the crane climbs high to feel the air pressure change.

The ghost of the jumper climbs back up
on the bridge to do it again.

Fish flatterer, anchor eyes,
the starfish wraps its arms around the clam.

My Evolutionary Strategy

for Alex

For certain seaweeds, it's growing little buoys
(pneumatocysts!) for floating closer to sunlight.
For rabbits and deer, it's keeping apart from
their camouflaged babies except to nurse
and lick them clean. Bees waggle dance.

For housecats, it's getting all fluffy-tailed
to look bigger when feeling threatened—
piloerection, which humans retain as
goose bumps. We've also kept hypnic jerks
from when we used to sleep in trees.

But I have shrugged off participation
in the most universal act by neglecting to
pass on my genes. For me it's giving
tangential survival advice to my tall-as-me-now
(for now) teenaged niece.

*If you ever swim in an ocean (and I'm sure
you will, plenty of times) and find yourself
being pulled away from the shore, it's probably
a rip current. To get out of it you have to swim
parallel to the beach. Please don't drown.*

She loves frozen coffee drinks more
than other people. She propagates memes.
She took delight in ruining figs for me by telling me
how they are pollinated. She's got her own
tactics, but no strategy yet.

If you ever fall through lake ice, the hole
could look either darker or lighter from underwater,
it depends on snow cover. Find the contrasting spot.
Sometimes there's an air gap under the ice,
but not always. Please don't die of hypothermia.

We watched the viral video of a farm cat who took
ducklings into her litter just after giving birth,
still pulsing with labor hormones. We wondered
if you could give a cat anything fuzzy and warm
in those imprinting minutes and she'd love it forever.

If you ever see a woman being bothered by a creep,
act like you know her and go right up and say "Hey,
where have you been? Everybody's waiting for you, come on!"
and if she needs to escape, she will play along. I hope someone
does this for you when you need it. Please go with them.

She doesn't have her learner's permit yet,
but an assortment adults are eager to warn her:
Stay alive! Don't text and drive. But my survival rhyme
is *Don't veer for deer.* Someone has to remember
to tell her, never swerve to avoid hitting one.

My saddest friends in the childlessness club got
thrown in because their daughter didn't know.
I hear of so many city kids in cars that might not
have flipped over if someone had told them.
So I tell my niece: *If one bolts out and you're going*

too fast, (please don't be going too fast) in that pause
of adrenaline-made slow motion (there's even a word
for that—tachypsychia, a vestigial gift from ancestors who
had to outsmart or outrun predators), when time
stretches, suspends, and you see the velvet

on the antlers and hear the GPS nattering on,
suppress the reflex to cut the wheel. Just brake
as hard as you can. Maybe you won't even be
sure it's right to choose your life over the deer's,
but you have to, kid, for us all.

Jim Daniels

Six Poems

Opening Acts

At heavy metal concerts
I damaged my hearing enough
for one lifetime. Despite often
arriving late, just in time to boo

the opening act off stage.
On the assembly line, they paid
me well for my loss. In the arena,
I was the one paying, young,

impatient, full of toxic self-worth.
It was almost a comfort to wake
with my ears ringing their multiple
losses. In my dreams, I compensate

for hours lost due to overtime.
I arrive on time. I hear everything.

Preserve, Detroit

Creosote is an excellent wood preservative, typically giving a pole life of 40 years or more.

My favorite tree was the streetlight pole
in our front yard, off to the right
near the neighbor's driveway.
I planted three trees in the middle

where a tree was supposed to go.
They all died—due to not having
a light at the top, I suppose.
I worshipped at the shrine
of electricity and gasoline,

wires and steel, sparks and fumes.
I preferred *plant* over *factory*—
in our natural order of things.
Preserved in safety gear all day
at work, I pulled for the pole to survive

until it splintered into a lean.
No one ever touched my many cars
that eased into the curb and parked
under that light, where nothing
bloomed without electricity, nothing

ran without gasoline. I braced myself
against it with no small affection the day
the city came to take it down, took my last
whiff of creosote, then backed away
to let them do their job. The new pole

unblemished by smoke. The new light,
tinted blue, uses less energy. It blossomed
over the street that night when I got home
from work. An idiot could do my job,
my boss once told me. The new light,

the new pole. And me. We do our jobs.

Golden Handcuffs

Curt couldn't get a factory job like we did.
His dead father had left no connections—
just half-empty bottles of booze I'd helped
drain with Curt—we no longer had to add water.

The small nonunion shop around the block took
Curt in, then took two fingers in a punch press.
He might have been high, I can't say, busy
myself on the line at Ford's. Can't say if

his mom screwed the sleazy boss who later
shot himself to beat the charges. My dad
wore steel toes in his dress shoes. He found me
a place to stand, half-grateful, half-condemned.

Curt slipped out of cuffs and into a life behind
bars. Me, I offered up my wrists to the gold.

At "The End of the Rainbox" Bar

*We should go out after work—get a beer
sometime.* If I had a beer for every time
somebody said that, I'd be drunk
for the rest of my life. For the rest

of my life, I will not remember the
one time we went out to get a beer after
work, to the Rainbow, a dingy dive
near the Hazel Park race track

where the pony boys swallowed
their losses after the last race.
In the axle plant, no nuance
to mull over after an ordinary shift:

the foreman this, my machine that.
Punching out, no photo finish
in the race to the rest of our lives.
If we ever broke a leg, they'd just

shoot us, and run another horse out there.

WORKING-CLASS SHAME

I thought she'd be happy
when I showed up at her summer job
in the fancy mall dress shop
right on time, or a week early,

depending on who you ask,
driving north to try and continue
what we'd started in her dorm room
one spring night in a single bed

but that night was now a weighted body
thrown out of the boat, no stopping
its sinking.
               I'd given up factory
double time to take the weekend off.
And if I sound hurt and defensive
all these years later, it's that grease
still embedded under my nails.

*

We hadn't talked much about where we lived
though I should have known Harbor Springs
wasn't no shanty town up on Lake Michigan.

Some shames you can shrug off. My shame
was not owning it—spending the night
on her mother's couch when I should
have driven the five hours straight back
to Detroit—not a problem then, at that age.

The burnt shock on her face when I walked in
the store and she briefly looked away then yanked
me out to the parking lot with her *what the hells*.

Maybe she'd misread my letter smudged
with black lust and the lonely lonelies
of seven-day weeks humping axles
or maybe I'd misspelled her street
and forgot to dot my eyes
when looking at the map.

*

I'd say God help that factory boy
out of his summer beer league
and into the lawn tennis of the rich,
but we did not believe in God,
either of us. Something we had
in common in that one class
where we watched white rats
dance on the heads of our pins.

They gassed the cute rats
when we were done with them.
God help us. Heaven help us.
The devil doing the backstroke
in the details. The social order.
The tiny shit of mouse turds
to prepare me for what was coming
when she could've bought
dancing mice, blind mice with sunglasses, tails curling around her wrists.

I'm allowed to get some things wrong,
just like that boy back then, sitting
in the hot parking lot fighting himself
over whether to drive home or first
spend the night, hoping for some mercy
kisses or some nice Harbor Springs
weed or a decent meal at some over-
priced ferny place on the water
or just a few hours of eyes shut
on his first day off in six weeks.

Of course, you already know that boy
stuck around to the end of her shift
swallowing one of the pills
that kept him awake just in case,
sitting with his window rolled down
so he could feel the expensive breeze
from the distant lake he'd never see,
in his borrowed car, knowing his own
wouldn't have made it
that far.

The Prodigal Factory Rat Returns From Oz

Everybody talks about the exotic—
fields of poppies, ruby slippers,
melting witch, yellow brick road,
dancing lion, tin man, scarecrow.
The wizard's phony bluster.
Black and white to color. Over
the rainbow, and munchkins,
munchkins, munchkins.

I am Dorothy waking up—
and you, and you, and you were there
a room full of smiling guys from
the old neighborhood who I thought
were gone. They stand scruffy and sincere,
wondering where I've been all these years,
pretending I was in Oz, dancing with munchkins,
when I was just a factory rat like them.

I'd tell them about flying monkeys,
but I think they already know.

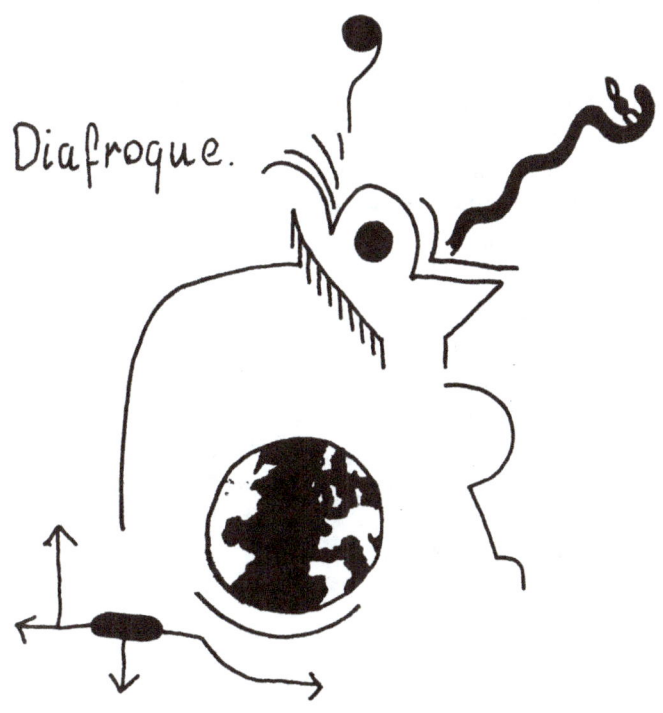

Diafroque.

Robyn Schelenz

The Shift

You know how in karate
you can drive your hand through concrete blocks
I was feeling that way the other day about something
but I don't know exactly what. I forgot.
There must be some trick to it. The secret of life
is to remember we are all made of stars, blah blah
but really, when it comes to the raw materials of us
versus the raw materials of our raw materials, we kick ass.
Good job us, kicking ass. With every karate chop,
a balloon escapes this empty bus depot
where we are pushing it, really pushing it,
giving the heave-ho to the building blocks of our structures,
the foundational notions, the places
where we are quite sure we don't want them to fall.
And in our daily rearrangements on earth,
we forgot about the water, which comes to us to remind us
with a song that sounds like love but more like a break-up
like a little break up of glaciers far away.

Here, I will do the work that is important.

I will telephone who people tell me to telephone
pick up someone I've never met and take them to work.
Become a hermit in Central America
hit every green light on the way there
hit every red light on the way back.
And always stop.

How is it possible we created something
not only uglier than castles, but worse.
There is a bunch of information on the internet
that will do nothing to save us
and in fact, distracts us when the rubble falls
just like those yellow signs you blew by foretold.
I've joined ten groups about loving animals
and one about killing roaches.
In short, I'm hopeless.
I would punch a wall
in prayer to the grassy field I expose.
Or interview that balloon.
But I don't know where it went. I know where it was.

humanoid.

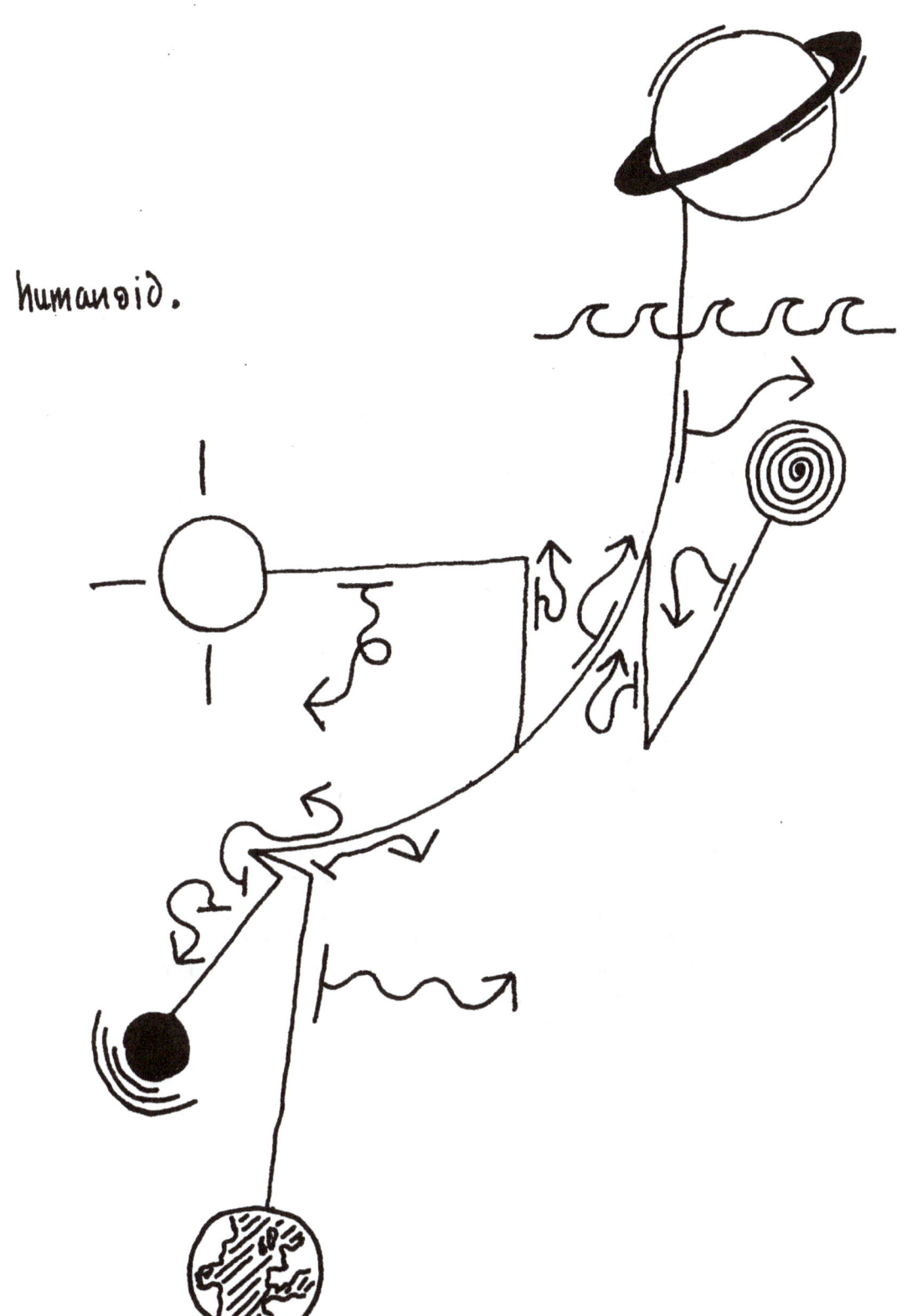

Lyudmyla Diadchenko

Six Poems

translated by Padma Thornlyre

[untitled] "I am raining..."

Мене задощило.рахманінов грає камінз чита
влаштовуючи дозвілля вигадуючи богему
поки тобі роки ворожать розкладаючи карти: чи та
поки пальці чіпляють гаками ребра і душу у мене
виносити з дому сміття як сонце зайшло
прабабця навчала: не можна .я сміялася : забобони
вода заливає. я риба. луска якої—шов
і плавати—це значить цілодобово удома
богема піде під ранок розносячи над людей
тебе відрізаю невідворотно як хасид свої пейси
тому задощило : вода рішуча і хай залле
хай стане достатньо води.хай може нап'єшся.

∞

I am raining. Rachmaninoff plays, e.e. cummings reads—
An arranged leisure, a Bohemian invention—
While laying out cards divines your years: is this the one?
While your fingers hook into my ribs and soul.
Great Grandmother taught that to carry out the garbage
During sunset is perilous. I laughed at her superstition.
The rain floods. I am a fish. My scales fuse together,
And to swim means being home around the clock.
Bohemia will depart at dawn, carrying off the *übermensch*.
I will cut you off irrevocably, like an Hasid renouncing his *payots*.
That's why this rain is so decisive. Let it flood.
Let there be enough water. Maybe then you'll get drunk.

[untitled] "Don't believe him."

Не вір. а якщо присягався—не вір поготів
Як у з'яву білих оленів єдинорога чи єті
Життя після зради—гранат розчахнутий .бо він хотів
Пару зернинин. пам'ять лишає фотони портретні

Не бійся пригадувати.аби більше під язиком
Не ховати своєї наївної любовної мови
Страх то спадок слабкості. Юності забобона
Страх це клімат зимовий

Не проси нічого твої тремтливі голоси
в цьому гуркоті ламаються мов об чугун є
життя із ким є. іншого в Бога не проси
Він мала тебе все одно не чує

∞

Don't believe him. And if he swears—believe him less
Than the sighting of a white hart, unicorn or yeti.
Life after betrayal—a pomegranate fractured because he craved
But a few seeds. Memory preserves a portrait's photons.

Don't fear remembering. There is more under the tongue,
No reason to conceal your naïve love languages.
Fear is the legacy of frailty, youthful superstition,
Fear is the wintery climate.

Beg for nothing. Tremulous voices
Break like cast iron against thunder.
Live with what you have. Why ask God for more?
He still doesn't hear you.

[untitled] "A fresh landscape curls like a cat..."

горнеться кицькою свіжий ландшафт до ніг
тут тебе ще не було і не пахло
стрілка з годинником нібито носоріг:
груба важка і ходить нагло
хто тебе зрозуміє: пальма ачи молюск
скислу таку й перелічену не своїми?
двері аби відчинив іншими зжитий люкс
скільки тобі шліфувати неточні рими?
поки істерику чайки вгамують—стій
убираючи в себе піни й піску карати
і батьківщини не описати в листі.
не передати. не розказати

∞

A fresh landscape curls like a cat around your feet.
You've not been here yet nor does it smell like you.
You turn sunwise like a clock's arrow, with the alleged
Walk of a rhinoceros: rough, ponderous, and impudent.
Who will understand you? Palm? Mollusk?
When you're sour, no one regards you as one of them.
How long will you grind out inaccurate rhymes
Until that luxury enjoyed by others opens its door to you?
Until the seagulls' hysterics subside—desist.
Absorbing into yourself carats of sea-foam and sand,
You cannot describe the homeland in letters, it is impossible.
Do not pass by. Do not tell.

[untitled] "Fall begins by speaking…"

заговори осене дощем дрібним чи
листям яке гладить калюжі й голубині лапи
чується зараз більше згадується що учили
довго відмірювати перед тим як вибирати
іншим завжди краще легше видніше
на якій із півкуль жити варити рис
сварити сусідів сидіти мовчки як миша
перед жирним котом звідкись який з'явивсь
от вийти на осінь коли брук як подушки
в ніч пихату: що задарма ніде не сховає
побачити вікна—ніби розгорнені книжк
із жовтими сторінками яких ніхто не читає

∞

Fall begins by speaking in light rain and fallen
Leaves caressing puddles and the feet of doves.
I now recall more often, what our forebears taught:
Take enough time to measure, before you choose.
Strangers from any hemisphere seem always to know
Better, are easier and more visible: they live, cook rice,
Quarrel with neighbors, or sit quietly, like a mouse
When a fat tomcat appears out of somewhere.
Venture outside this fall: cobblestones seem like pillows.
In the arrogant night you are free—so hide nowhere.
The windows appear like open books
With yellowed pages that no one reads.

[untitled] "To focus the pupil…"

Навести на різкість зрачок: дистанція для значного
оцінити повернення до білого—всюдисутність спектра
хочеться біль зберегти щоб у разі чого
не було сентименту причини сльозу розтерти
обсяг огляду збільшити висотою прожитих утрат
симпатична картина зими. симпатичні ти і кепка в горохи
і прогулянка в рік—мій додатковий штат
у який тікала з тобою. може статись: слухатиму трохи
може статися з іншими більше : сезонів подій і вогню
я не буду лічити і міряти—не панське діло
не тепло. та ні з ким ким тепла. та ну…
бо тепло зостається після як все згоріло

∞

To focus the pupil, assess from a significant distance
The world's return to white—the spectrum's ubiquity.
I want to store the pain in case
I will have no sentiment causing my tears to run.
Increase the scope of the examination by the numbers lost:
Cute picture of winter. Cute you in your polka-dot cap.
A year-long odyssey is my newest homeland:
I ran away with you. It can happen—I'll listen, for a while,
But it can also happen with others: seasons, events, and campfires.
I will not count contributions and compare—such business is unladylike.
We have no heat. But no one else is quite so warm. Yah …
Because the heat remains after everything is burned.

[untitled] "The mainland's autumn is browned…"

Спалений осінню материк, на якому тісно,
де трохи боязко влипати у будні. але красиво:
як листя березове—ніби розсипані чіпси
під дощ чи пиво

сюди судна приходять не часто. бо глибина і скелі,
бо звідки не глянь—самотності видно мітку.
закутані берегом землі у східній постелі
із пам'яттю про людей, що були тут влітку.

а поки туман, як сир подвійний на піці,
зі спеціями диму залазить у камери та екрани.
влипати у будні, як муха у мед, ненав'язливо вчиться
зором душею станом

∞

The mainland's autumn is browned and tightly crowded,
Where one feels timid being stuck there on weekdays, however lovely:
Birch leaves lie like scattered chips
Soaking in rain or beer.

Ships seldom arrive here, for its great rocky depth,
And wherever one looks, loneliness is palpable.
Land shrouded by shores in their eastern sheets
Remembers those who were here last summer.

And while the fog lies thick, like double cheese on pizza
With smoky spices, the mist climbs up into the cameras and screens.
Stick to weekdays like a fly to honey, to learn inconspicuously,
By sight, by soul, by flesh.

ERIC T. RACHER

FOUR POEMS

ON READING WILLIAM CARLOS WILLIAMS' PATERSON IN A PLAGUE YEAR

1.
Commanding Form: the place, the valley, spent
waters, city, body, light. He dwells
in shadow. Shadowfall the world. Cement
and brick and stone, their rigor. River swells
about the power plant, who generates
this resonance. *What common language to
unravel?* The existent intimates
an overname. Unlikeness/likeness. Blue,
the postcard sky, but not. ('Sight, sound and intellection,' Zukofsky wrote.) Not speech per se,
but, shrouded there, a music of the din,
a myth of *signifiant* and *signifié,*
the riverrun's bright turn, a marriage. *There
is no direction. Whither?* Whence? And where?

2.
Flâneur of light and air, he walks the cliff,
an *N* of one: *What do I do? I listen, to the water falling.* Sun. A glyph
inscribed into the rock—a woman's kiss
upon the lips. It's Sunday afternoon.
The chisel strikes the stone, and voices rise.
(Polyphony v. harmony?) A tune
emerges, Dr. Paterson: *there lies
the city!* (Scratch, thou cursèd pen!) *Without
invention nothing is. Without invention nothing lies.* The poem lies about.
(About?) The world, assembling things. (Text, then,
as contexture?) All models lie, but some
do sing indeed her warp and weft. Come, sum

3.
this infinite divorce, a dissonance
of verge and vortex; limn the limit we
approach, an image of our residence,
embodying the world. Logic of accre-
tion. (Sing!) *The province of the poem is
the world.* Domain & codomain. *The past
is dead.* (Perhaps the book.) That which was his,

no longer. Thing. Idea.—*the voice!* Hold fast
unto the rock. (Beauty's homeless.) *If it*
were only fertile. Living form inform
the whole, the giving birth. The man is written, graved into the page, as though in dorm-
ancy. We fold and sew these gatherings,
and stitch them in a block. The river sings.

4.
You mentioned a city? Emblem of a consummation, act of fitting, fitting act
of synthesizing intellect. *Come on,*
get going. The tide's in. Tide. Be in. A fact.
'We make ourselves pictures of facts; the picture is a fact,' *she-ne'emar.* To seize
the flow of subjectivity, the quick
of sentience, convert it into these
enduring, tangible magnitudes: the object-
ifying power of the work. *The brain*
is weak. It fails mastery. (Intellect
is insufficient.) Bill, you knew the pain
of time. Of waning. Thus. *Thalassa! Ah!*
The sea, she calls. She calls. *Selah! Selah!*

5.
The unicorn, the fountain, and the man
who writes. (And to what end?) To raze himself
and raise a monument. To praise. (How can
you claim words raze or raise? A word's but a shelf
you set fond ware upon.) The unicorn
has gored the hound. Passaic Falls have gored
the mind, and formed, in time, a gorge. (Your worn-
out phrase and outworn feeling, concepts scored
into the mind—and what?) That *what* that tries
the *what* which yet abides, the *which* unfurled
about. The unbroken unicorn defies
the pen. (Subtractive force of time?) *The world*
of the imagination most endures.
(Words suffer loss.) The unicorn insures.

6.
The man himself a city: undefined,
articulated, full—a maze of streets
and squares, of houses old and new. Behind,
around, and in *la langue*, we Masoretes
lay stone and brick. The ceaseless evolu-
tion, fossils, hidden strata, endless go-
before, now gone but living body. True
or farce, we parse perennial flesh. In so

doing, we strike a vein—the burden of
the poem. Bill, you knew the Falls. (Thy will
be done. Amen.) Your typescript figures love;
your words like shells. The sonnet as limekiln:
We know nothing and can know nothing but
the dance, to dance a measure. Nothing. But

7.

our world contracts. It lessens. We refrain
from touch and love and breath. The waterfall
adorns the cover. Breath. A windowpane,
breath-clouded, clouds the past. Father, of all
the ones I miss . . . A myth holds up the rock:
Agens autem non movet nisi ex
intentione finis. Breath. Ad hoc,
the language fails; the courage. Our complex-
ities, not even *them.* Thus nothing, pure
and simple—nothing pure. Yet breath. The dance,
you'd write, it nearing, nothing but. Enduring breath; expiring breath. The circumstance
estranges. We ignore our ends. The breath
entails an end, a rhyme I dare not—

For, about, and with Louis Zukofsky

1.

To begin a song: if you cannot recall,
forget. A *vita nuova* postulant
of death. *To find a thing, all things* (Yes, all.),
there is no choice but sing. But work. Descant
the groundswell. *To begin a song, if it's*
not there, forget. A demarcation. Voice
lives only in the air. Dead preterits
becloud the eye and ear. There is no choice.
Out of deep need, impulse to action, we
must ask ourselves: *what else is beauty's last?*
Those epopt caryatids, holding, hold-
ing the world-cornice (Word-cornice.), foresee
a form, enforce an abscess of the past.
They stand, a New World dazzled, growing old.

2.

The trend line drawn misleads the eye, perhaps;
it captures not the data, but ideal-
izations of the landscape, the   prelaps-

arian cartographies that tuille
the lying brain from its environment
and from itself. And yet we must this fa-
ble (*If I quote it is myself . . .*), attentive to (. . . [that] *I have seen.*) the task. Assay
the sequence as mosaic. An event
of life it's not, nor word we seek, and not
experience. Un-got-through. Just. More bent,
more bent. A string of letters. Scatterplot
of words' distent. This myth I plot—a linear regression.   *. . . where shall I begin?*

3.

Your world has perished, *verter-betler*—at-
trital trace, what's left of it. And ours,
our world, infected with nostalgia, that
disease of memory (Dead flesh and flowers'
sweet odor sweetly sick.), and simultaneously with amnesia of its debt
to yours. *Archaic time unchanged unchan-
geable.* (Within the sonnet's time.) I set
the metronome. Paul's fiddle silent now.
Your voice, and Celia's, gone. *If I collect
these things to live . . .* Ectype of life, a vow
the poem, and a cairn we both erect
against forgetfulness: to dust both time
(Redeemer?) & sweet remembrance with quicklime.

4.

Yet, the command: *zakhor.* What, then, to do
with that? What magnitudes condense? What tone?
What movement? *Sounded. Seen.* (*Al-tizkeru,*
that too.) Both these and these the words, we own.
The test of poetry—affordances
in pleasure: *sight*, *sound*, *intellection.* Dust.
Thence. Dust. Dust. Thither. Dust. (*Raise grief*, he says,
to music. Raze grief, then, with music.) Must
not we dwell through grief? Is not forgetting trespass? *Light as my loves' thought*, you wrote.
I'll not forget, *this much for honor.* Let
music upper limit be. Devot-
ed. Votive. Vow. An etymology
that overflows the world and scourges me
emerges. *Image, sound
and interplay of concepts.* Vortex. Ground.
'What sets the sum of us in motion?' we
might ask ourselves. A syn-
apse. Syntax. Value. Need. The tongue. *A round
of fiddles playing Bach. Mal'ach* therein.

On DIALETHISM as a THEORY OF LOVE and the sonnet, or, on the concept of the 'pulzella amorosa, stella marina' as a constituent element of the idea of the body of the lover

and overstood us overturned or stayed
since otherwise recursive holy tongue
yet wholly of the tongue a force conveyed

where reckon and where beckon stood among
the stone and pine nocturne into aubade
of liver-heart-intestine-kidney-lung

but that we stood or understood as well
as might be guessed in that this or
or but or and coordinated more
than understood perhaps we felt or fell

or rose rose up arose a rose's smell
might sweet as lovely as the sea's décor
so she sells sea-shells by the seamost-shore
tongue's twist & thrust & surge in this upswell

On memory and the sonnet as a system of DISCIPLINE of the body, or, how I learned to stop worrying and love the image of the Donna Gentile

Outside the frigid wind and darkness reign,
and every bud and blossom lies inhearsed;
the winter fields are barren and accursed,
and frozen every songbird's fluid strain.
Yet in my heart there falls a gentle rain
that greens the meadow's face as flowers burst
into resplendent glory, and the first
returning birds intone their sweet refrain.
Thus love rains down on earth from every sphere,
that my weak soul prehend that greeny season
that ripens in the splendour of its power.
My lady's image sits within the tower
that rises in the mind toward the reason,
whose purifying light is ever near.

A Surf Ever Shoreward Curling, Curling Toward Rosaline, to Cool Her Feet

I want to cool your ankles, Rosaline, your
ankles with salt-spray, I want to splash
your skirts, to apprehend the shape of you

A surf ever shoreward curling curls toward
Rosaline, to cool her feet. Were I the sea I

would lust for her, beckon her into me that I

might know her everywhere and all at once.
Here are pebbles to please her eyes, octopus

and squid for nourishment. Here are my several
tongues, the greater song of me. Here she may
dissolve. I would fan your hair behind you, tickle

you with kelp — amorous, playful caressings.
I would bind what flotsam and jetsam delights

you within this kaleidoscope, this sun-sharded

Indra's net of wave upon wave. I am the dolphin
breaching, the arc that carries your laughter.

GLYPH: two footprints on orange stone

Three Poems

Déjà Vu

If you live long enough, you get to watch the wheel turn
back to the beginning, you see the cycles repeat,
never exactly, but close enough for déjà vu to leave you
wide-eyed in that vast empty desert between laughing and crying.

Twice now I have watched my nation lose its mind
and descend into hateful chaos and confusion.
The first time there was a war—just the one, how quaint!—
but that was enough back then—
and an agonizing division between generations and races.
People marched and screamed, for and against, against and for,
it didn't seem to matter which,
the main thing was to be marching and screaming.
Cities burned, people died, cops and protesters, along with a few
innocents unlucky or foolish enough to be caught between them.
One thing about those burnings years ago: I don't recall
mayors and governors and district attorneys handing out the matches.
After the sounds of bullets and bombs had died down,
after the sirens and flames and ghostly wails had dribbled into silence,
we had added to the sum total of human happiness and understanding
several small piles of ashes that could no longer be identified.
In the end, the president almost everyone had come to despise,
the one hounded from office rightfully or wrongfully,
was the one who actually stopped the war he hadn't started,
and ever since, the haters who thought they were lovers
have taken all the credit.

As suddenly as the madness had come upon us the fever broke,
we shook ourselves like babies and returned to our usual state
of semi-consciousness, blessedly unable to remember
what had just happened, once again innocent of all our crimes
and thus leaving a bullet in the chamber
for the next time, this time, which has a charm all its own,
mixing manmade disaster with natural disease.
Up is down, right is wrong, hate is love, war is peace,
but black is most definitely not white.
That one we seem to have sorted out a little.
The wheel turns, we are all bound to it,
and if you are wondering where it will stop
you don't know the nature of wheels, or the wheel of nature.

Forbidden Thoughts

You'd better take them to the grave, those thoughts
That run counter to preferred narratives.
Life now is a series of *musts* and *oughts*.
Everybody who's alive today lives
In terror of being canceled or doxed
Or fired or sued or assassinated.
The witch hunters can never be outfoxed.
Where you were loved they will make you hated
And burn your miserable life to the ground.
It makes no difference at all what is true,
What extenuating facts can be found.
Speak your whole mind and you will surely rue
The day you mentioned those things forbidden.
If you have such thoughts, best keep them hidden.

Elemental

A sylph with auburn hair
and green eyes that gaze
right through you,
missing nothing, weighing everything,
you hope to find favor
with this spirit of the air
as she is drawn to the things of earth,
digging in the dirt,
planting flowers, only some of which
will bloom in her lifetime.
What does she seek down there?
Is she looking for her soul?
But she's found it
you want to tell her,
making love in the secret garden
of her sheets, learning how strong
two small thighs can be,
pale clouds full of rain
that must be released,
and somewhere very near yet unseen
something is singing,
a song of sky and grass,
the sweet piercing cry
of the bird that is her.

Five Poems

FLUFF

Rhythms spindle collections of phonic gas
—at last an affable factory flash of one-stop
populations, a sense of Lent inventions.

She won't show her squadron a cauldron
of ifs up a mountain of whiffs. These sweeping
jonquils restring a hearsay heresy.

He's a teaser, a rear-end rendering—
a glean of lingo, lapse and fracture.
Woodcut numbers run as far as cartwheels
span a hand and a jargon.

Not to sweat an alphabet of impressionable
pulp-and-passion landscapes—I'll admit
a reappearance and slipping away of rare
and tangible liabilities.

Process a loss furthering opinionated fluff.
The cuffs on a mongrel steer an innate currency
revolving round a clown's downside.

A kinetic text or tract . . . or bath of bubble-beads
. . . a sugary treat or rub of pungent jawbreakers.
O pity's sake, a rake astride the shovel.

A blink or a nod from odd toddlers sprawled
on our lush lawn insist on *Love-or-Be-Gone*
in the Crenshaw section of mixed apprehension.

THE GREENLY GLOW

The greenly glow pokes the Saran wrapped
around the cleft chin of Linseed Larry
in a pseudo-comatose sprawl, along
the hung jury of prurience and panoply
in a glee-hug of inner variance.

A clean shock of unruly haggard hair
is blissed with a clitoris of closure
and a bagel of illusion,
the mock jaw impervious to a nest
of testy mechanics.

With these gewgaws of gentle groan,
within ranks of a thankless rising,
comes apprising of the nails which coffins
play into the splint of the wooden-sudden.

To trick the nitwit is to tease the weasel:
a silken scarf thrown about the head
dressed for stress, and other hearsay
hecklings of wept flesh.

Slighter by star, the burning far cry
container of carnage clipped
on a pin prick in the stiff denial
is burdened by the inky quota
of constrained higgledy-giggling
in the highest bidder's banter.

We'll respond with a brimful of whim
and manner of factual foolery—
a gullible mule's worth of Saturday's
purpose, a twig and a figure of spunk.

I plot with the best of hem and haw:
a gnarly restitching of the itchy slaughter
of an eye for an armful of signage,
a climbing out from the soot.

I'm all-manners if it means
marshalling my quiver-meat
through the Street of Sonic Longings.
I pawn my wristwatch perfume
for iPhone cologne.

Once down to the ground floor,
I forge an alter-identity
as I hide in the lie of beliefs.
I somehow tingle with the ring
of singsong truths, your blue balloon
my rumor of approval.

Mothstruck by Moonlight

1

Savoir-faire prayer
    bristling in a glass eye,

splashing her lids,
skippin' at the corners,
    posing for wrinkle relief
    . . . a meat-and-potatoes kind of gal.

2

A fury of rats
filling their gills
with mid-morning leavings,
    slurping soup joy
    up a hopscotch namesake.

I'm quite lost at the crossed staves
    of a guarded heart
    and a jello jalopy of figs
    wriggling free
    from encumbrances.

3

Avant-garde particles
dazzle the dust
    a caprice of sunsplash
        rackin' up the pins . . .

I regret I bet on
winsome elevens
in that crisp fifty of fortitude.
    Did you cancel the black olives?

4

A sob story rattling with pain
    stabs a bandage of regrets—

discontent of crowders
vocal to the millionth Monday mood
    revivifies
    in a feisty faucet of finesse.

5

Mothstruck by moonlight,
        a dire rub of vertigo

                                        mumblings

            drips the ozone
    of the void—

as we zoom in to dizzy fingers
    nipping cuticles
        to the quick

            . . . craning forth
        in a fait accompli
    a Caspian Sea
        of Red Menace morsels.

PILGRIMS

Twin hymn humming roomy views
—a Tuesday noose and straddle
pocked of a thicket prized
in a seesaw of raw rhetoric.

Time explodes the frozen
in a thinly veiled thawing
conscious of a recalled hubcap,
gloveless of a stubborn motion.

She's eaten a dreamer,
glad of hand and heart
of ice, a trimester combo
of woofing unmentionables.

Wielding goof-proof paint
we pilgrims prop our every
drip in a perception pan
of keenly felt fluidity.

Aluminum Folly

Rumsfeld Girls in a coy aperitif
of twisted blond whiskers
comply with the warblings
of vellum mayhem on a sanitary
stick of victim-scrambling,
a ferrous nymph of reassurance.

Coined rovers revoice a cloister
of intent in a melancholy mood.
The Merchant of Vanity's scampering
in a trendy elegance, a sinking
inkling of a greeny pestering
in the clinch of disco revenge.

A jasmine iridescence cloys the
comfort zone at the very zigzag
of aluminum folly. Furniture guilt
permeates the tomb of Jefferson Davis
syndicated by a vindicated voiceover
on the advice of a scattered nanny.

Shunt-floggers finesse a swizzle-
stick of regret when dipping their
pens in the wine-drenched blood
of a tongue-tied cougar resting
in a bean-rich mulchfest
in the pain-bed of Rhode Island.

Dashed tendencies embroider
silky soliloquys in moods
enveloping the proud and the prude,
retweeting the rescue button
for a cancer cure.

Doff a quick ooze, a skeletal leveling
ascertaining a cling and a comma,
a coach and a chorus, a moxie
and a pox on the foie gras Nation
of Haitians in an onion of wonder.

Satin sheets please a scalding bunch
of numbers-crunchers in the starry
cascade of *play-it-as-it-lays*,
a green paper moon achieving
North Pole credibility in the cold
and icy hot.

Dizzy as azure the crybaby sky
concurrent with twice-told flowage
foments the moment directly
after the first frost claims our
grapefruits in a frozen Floridian
misfortune.

MIKE SILVERTON

Icy Conceits

POULTRY

If I say "Poultry" or "The March of the Boyars,"
would that be a poem?
Would shrapnel make a difference?
I feel so alone.

DIGNITY

So, today, and maybe tomorrow,
we come face to face with dignity.
Inaudible frequencies compete for dignity.
(Emphasis: inaudible. We take this on faith.)
Autumn accomplishes autumn with effortless dignity.
During Lent one is especially alert to dignity.
Conversely, one learns to ignore star toots.
Tooting stars violate dignity.

RED CHINA ON YELLOW TABLECLOTH

Chairman Mao at People's Sundown
orders the People's Sunrise. Elsewhere, I don't know
the Chinese term for diktat or how to prepare
sticky Chinese pork belly. I also cannot distinguish
trembling lumps from chilly idiots,
nor do I find papier-maché lifeboats amusing.

KAPOK

Poems begin in the mouth.
I'm thinking of kapok.
k'*pok!* k'*pok!*
Like gunfire with corks.

VIZ.,

We gather for the hemorrhage.
We slap each other.
A horn blows. We cheer.
We pour ourselves some smoke.
We punch dead horses.
One of us dies (viz., the hemorrhage).
It's useless, these syrupy poses.

Exquisite

It is exquisite, driving to see Seattle.
It is also exquisite driving to see Sasquatch,
his soggy feet, his russet buboes, all exquisite,
all forgivable. Exquisite rural alarums and excursions,
we forgive them, likewise an exquisitely crafted tower where
someone is waving, perhaps at you. It is also exquisite
here on the boiled carpet.

My Poems

I like to think of my poems seeking solace
under old wallpaper, insubstantial
as Schrödinger's Chihuahua.
I sometimes think of abandoning my poems
at a lakeside wharf, where, on a cloudy afternoon,
you and I evaporate.

Tercet

Do you often mow the lawn where
homicidal maniacs
doze?

My Little House

Hunkered down in my little house,
I conceal many large-caliber revolvers about my person.
To the casual intruder I look lumpy.
Turning my little house like a page is difficult.
Nor does the doorbell work.
This pleases me.

Per Haps

Between you and the eulogy per
haps something's ed
ible.

Zola

Among the asterisks, mollusks. Zola
(nom de plume), envisions warts on nihilists
out there, somewhere, taken on faith, lost as we are
in a morning's diaspora.

Wednesday

It's Wednesday, dear diary,
an event Mother Nature
notes from her trench.
Water not the turnstiles!
They are not tulips!

Who Knew?

My plaisir, my ragout,
your plaisir, your kazoo,
et voilà Stu! Peut-être Peru!

Saga

A man, Come Here to Me at Once Which Went to Him at Once,
tilted Hairy's chin. Moskuld's mother was Thorgeld,
the daughter of Redder and of Oofa the Whiter, and Ingald Nowhere,
also of Helgi and Thora Du Du and Shake a Snake,
 the son of Hairy Breaks and Aud the Deep Minded, the daughter of
Chastised with a Kettle, the son of Boner, the first Bishop of Ice Land,
also of Yetti and Snake in the Grease, whose father tilted
Hairy Breaks. Hoskuld Hvitaness Priest put on the cloak, fistmele
in one hand, nothing in the other. Njalsson sailed from Orkney.
Sigfusson was also preparing to sail.

Ipecac, a Love Story

Ipecac! Dearest! What our seeds made us,
where our deeds took us, creeping,
weeping, O how they shook us,
O how they baked us! O how they raked us!

Ipecac! Belovèd! Mouths are for shouting,
but nobody's listening,
nobody's smiling for miles and miles,
nobody's glistening, nobody's floating, nobody's creeping,
nobody's scowling, nobody's pleading,
nobody's bleeding.

Ipecac! Divine! Backup? Hiccup?
That you, Bacchus? Bring the wine?
Roast the swine?

Zoom

Zoom! The poet leaks through a slot in the gloom!
The poet prevails! Down with impediments! Religion,
to you the poet makes this gift of sailing earth
he invites you to call an avalanche.
Thank you. The poet's blindest friend rolls cigars.

Vocations

And of the colleagues huddled at the silo sorting silage,
and of the flicker of passerby seborrhea
anticipating snow.

Homeopathy

A homeopath moves to a prairie.
He finds me must deal with bison.
He lies in wait at night, making threatening noises
in the midrange (500Hz to 2kHz) that
bison find intolerable.

Nothing Fits

Nothing fits.
The dog disappears.
The palm fronds creak.
You smile drowsily,
rub the sleep from your eyes
and jump up and down on the hammock.

Under Pajamas

In formality's embrace, a poet asks,
Where's my hat? Who took my coat?
From an icy conceit to a stool in a bar, a poet asks,
Is it possible to write poems that don't mention Nazis?
Of course it is! Poems should be about
small floodlights under pajamas.

Literature + Illness = Literature

Gad's Book
Dylan Bassett
Outpost19, October 2023

I'm inventing a machine
for concealing my desire.
And I'm inventing another
machine for concealing the
machine. It's a two-machine
system, and it sounded like
laughter. And I'm inventing
a machine for concealing
the sound.
—Aaron Kunin, *The Sore Throat*

In the center of Dylan Bassett's novel *Gad's Book*, the narrator, an unnamed novelist who never writes anything, describes a novel he is (not) working on. The novel (not) within the novel centers around another novelist who is having a hard time completing his novel and whose name is Gad, which is not a name I know how to pronounce. I know the acronym GAD, which stands for Generalized Anxiety Disorder, and I know a man named Gadi, who goes by Gad for short, which is pronounced "God." In the Abrahamic tradition, God is not so much a name as it is a pseudonym for the deity, like a pen name. Gad "has not been able to write because, as he puts it, he wants to write something original, to imagine or invent something out of thin air. He wants to tell an old story in a new way, or a new story in an old way. Old—as old as the Greeks and Children of Israel and older, as old as war, as grand as mythology."

This is a familiar conundrum. Gad is stuck between the past and the future: he wants to write something new, or novel, but he wants to invest it with the holy canonicity of tradition, in this case in the form of the novel, which is old. Eclipsed by this tense tearing between the past and the future is of course the present, and Gad rejects his present: "Eventually, Gad decides that he must simply tell his own story and no one else's—the only story he's allowed to tell. Not an

invention, but a confession. But the problem is this. He has no story of his own—nothing to confess. His life, so far, is boring, mostly, or at least uneventful. So far." Throughout the story Gad calls his project a novel, but it more closely resembles nonfiction, or even autofiction. Less a genre and more an element of all fiction, autofiction also represents an impossible (but familiar) conundrum that hinges on a tension between invention and documentation. Autobiography's pact with the reader is that the author invents nothing; fiction's is that it invents everything.

Some of the oldest and best western literature (literally literature you could find at a Best Western) employ autofiction. Chapter 9 of Miguel de Cervantes' *Don Quixote*, arguably the first modern novel, features Cervantes "himself" roaming the streets of Toledo, and then happening upon a pamphlet written in Arabic that contains the entire story of Don Quixote, authored by an Arab historian named Cid Hamete Benengeli. This autofictional move frames the novel as a work of history, and the novelist as a scribe or secondary historian—a move that is itself fictive—while also bringing into ontological question whether History is itself a work of fiction. Add to that the plot of the *Quixote*—a man who wants to resurrect the Christian chivalric tradition two hundred years after its death, and who does so by hallucinating past fictions over present realities—and not only is time suddenly Janus-faced, oscillating between an imagined past and a historical present, but even Western literature's "own story" is posited as belonging to Arabic culture. The founding gesture of the modern novel, then, radiates an autofictional core that infects notions of Invention and Truth with a kind of generalized anxiety disorder, or GAD. Bassett's *Gad's Book* references the *Quixote* frequently, as one of its anxieties of influence.

The narrator—similarly Janus-faced and stuck with writer's block—is being interrogated about his non-novel by his love interest and confessor, "Janice":

Is it one of those lit bro novels?

What's a lit bro novel?

Is it about a sad man who feels sorry for himself? Is it one of the huge books that wants to impose a phallic vision onto the world? Are you one of those dude writers who only describes women's tits?

I hope not.

The narrator describes Gad as "a large man [who] has cultivated what he considers to be a historically masculine look," whose literary crisis begins when his wife writes a successful novel describing a protagonist that has all Gad's characteristics, except for his penis, which in his wife's literary treatment is, well, hilarious: "A short, stalky motherfucker, weirdly compressed, flattened even—a condensed baguette, a smashed-down soda can [. . .] and it was of no use to me." Literally literarily emasculated, Gad withdraws into himself and the marriage dissolves, and then he seeks to write a "revenge novel" that tells the true story of himself as the victim, seeking to correct the impression his wife's vision of his phallus has left on the world. Janice, in other words, is an accurate observer of the narrator's life; the only thing she doesn't know is that his novel is not only non-existent, it's actually a fictionalized confession, an inadvertent autofiction. Here is their exchange after Janice presses the narrator for the synopsis:

> It's long, I said, trying to avoid summarizing another novel I wasn't writing. I glanced down at my wristwatch as if to suggest we didn't have time for me to tell it.
>
> Give me the pitch, she said. Go.
>
> Okay. I decided to take this as an opportunity to impress Janice, maybe, so I made something up. A story. A long one. The longest yet. It took half an hour to tell. It went something like this:
>
> There's this guy, Gad is his name, who, when the novel begins [. . .]

Throughout *Gad's Book*, the narrator is asked about the novel he is working on, and invariably the narrator fabricates a fiction about his fiction. Each protagonist seems to be a surrogate for our narrator: there's Gad, of course, but there's also an unnamed clown who's alternately viewed by the public as an artist or as an incel troller; there's Vernon, a novelist who cannot write past the first sentence of his novel, and who either accidentally or purposefully walks into traffic; there's Jed, a failed writer who is addicted to masochism; and there's Franz who, in a sort of meta-narrative of self-harm, murders the aforementioned Vernon,

but no one will believe his confession, and so he commits suicide. The narrator reveals himself to be a storyteller more than he is a novelist, and under duress, under conditions of extraction, the narrator does precisely what his characters (especially Gad) cannot: he improvises, he creates, he tells an old story in a new way. By creating surrogates through which to confess, the narrator discloses through the protective cloak of fiction, or even autofiction, the fact that he cannot write, that he does not believe in himself or in his life, and that he fears as much as he desires self-destruction. He is safe because it is his characters who cannot write, while his interlocutors—unknowing confessors—have no idea.

Except that they do. Like the ancient tragic heroes who are blind to their inevitable fate, the narrator seems unaware that his novel summaries are autobiographical disclosures. He seems unaware of a lot of things, actually: "I decided to take this as an opportunity to impress Janice, maybe, so I made something up," reveals that the narrator *does not even know* why he is making it up. He is instead acting out. He is hoping to impress others instead of impressing words upon paper. After telling Gad's story to Janice, Janice tells the narrator she understands his story:

> It's an allegory, she said. Gad is an observer in his own life. A tourist or a consumer inside it. And what he consumes is experience. But he wants a bigger narrative.
>
> Maybe.
>
> But the problem is that narratives are dead, she said. That's what Gad's book is about, isn't it? The existential fatigue of stories. Gad tries to turn his life into a story—he lives out a plot of adventure. A quest narrative.
>
> Now Janice paused and looked at me, as if suddenly recognizing a stranger. Her face lit up. Big eyes.
>
> Now, she said, I know why you joined our community. This is why you're here [. . .] to reclaim the narrative. She laughed.
>
> I wanted to tell her that I didn't know anything about her community, but I was afraid of how she might react; and I wanted to tell that I had pulled Gad's Book out of my ass, that it meant—as far as I could say—nothing to me.

When Janice sees that her synopsis of the narrator's fake synopsis is being denied, she says, "It's true what they say. The poet does not know from whence he speaks, dude. You cannot hear what your own story is saying."

There is a strange irony in Janice's diagnosis-judgment, and it is two-pronged along the same hyphenated lines: the diagnosis is correct, and therefore the judgment is partial and erroneous. Janice has diagnosed the narrator as a poet; in other words, she has called him a writer. This is the strangeness inherent in almost any 1st-person literary narrative, which is that the narrator is both character and writer. Of course, the actual writer is Dylan Bassett, but the fictional conceit is that the narrator is narrating these words which he has written. Thus, as character, the narrator is as ignorant as Janice judges him to be—he cannot hear what his own story is saying—but as poet, or writer, the narrator is reading what he has in fact written about his own story. So the question for me becomes, What do we find in *Gad's Book* that we do not find in Gad's book, for example, or in the works of any of the other surrogates of the narrator?

The answer is illness, or sickness, particularly epilepsy, from which the narrator suffers and at which point the book begins. But even to say the book "begins" at the narrator having suffered a seizure is anathema to the experience of epilepsy, which disrupts linear time, physical orientation, and the situation of the self. In the middle of *Gad's Book* the narrator likens the experience of a seizure to Dante's opening stanzas of *The Inferno*—another seminal work of autofiction, whereby Dante is the book's protagonist, both narrator and character—"In the middle of my life / I found myself lost in a forest dark / For the straightforward pathway had been lost." But the narrator of *Gad's Book* goes further:

> This is what it feels like, except worse. Worse because momentarily, after a seizure, you have no concept of yourself—you cannot say, *myself*. You cannot say *lost* because you do not know what it means. Cannot say *in a forest* because you have no concept of being somewhere that is not somewhere else.

What does it mean that an unnamed narrator who invents surrogates to conceal from others—and from himself—the truth of his experience, would liken the experience of epilepsy to a seminal work of literature whereby an author writes himself into a character that is fundamentally and spiritually lost? In his essay "Literature + Illness = Illness," from the collection *The Insufferable Gaucho*, Roberto Bolaño defines illness societally, as a modern communal affliction. Speaking of a line from a poem by Baudelaire, Bolaño elaborates:

> In that line alone there is more than enough. In the middle of a desert of ennui, an oasis of fear, or horror. There is no more lucid diagnosis of the illness of modern humanity. To break out of ennui, to escape from boredom, all we have at our disposal—and it's not even automatically at our disposal, again we have to make an effort—is horror, in other words, evil.

Baudelaire's line—"an oasis of horror in a desert of ennui"—is also the epigraph of Roberto Bolaño's final novel, *2666*, which *Gad's Book* references several times. Bolaño's 1100+ page book also follows the story of a missing author, but the hole in its center is not a synopsis of that author's work; rather, it is "The Part About the Crimes," a brutal 300 pages of forensic descriptions of women who are the victims of sexual homicide in Santa Teresa in the late 1990s, a fictionalized account of real ongoing horrors in Ciudad Juárez. The killers are never discovered, and what is made manifest instead is the complicity of a misogynistic culture and a viciously corrupt police force. In other words, horror. In other words, evil.

Reading "The Part About the Crimes" is incredibly distressing; getting through it is like passing through hell or, worse, passing through history or, even worse, passing through the hell that is the present, staring the horror in the face. For this reason, in another side-story that we could call "Jed's Book," Bassett gives us another surrogate for the narrator named Jed, a failed writer who is traveling in Barcelona, where Bolaño lived out the rest of his life. Jed comes across a woman reading *2666* at a café, and asks her if she's read "The Part About the Crimes":

> I'm dead in the middle of it, she says. She drops the book on the table. Bolaño is a terrible writer, she says. He's all bad sentences. No style. And he's too academic. She flicks the cover of the book with her middle finger. One, two. Insufferable, she says.

"Insufferable" is an endearingly insufferable wink by Bassett regarding Bolaño's short story collection, *The Insufferable Gaucho* and, obliquely, the essay "Literature + Illness = Illness." It is perhaps Bassett's most autobiographical disclosure. "I'm dead in the middle of it" is to be in the middle of the book, where many women are dead: another wink. The woman's response to the Part About the Crimes, in other words, is not horror, but boredom. This then is the moral challenge of Bolaño's novel: will 300 pages of absolute horror bore you? Will the "literature" part of the equation do nothing to change the sum of "illness"? While I do think it's somewhat tone-deaf to write a female character who is pretentiously blasé about this part of Bolaño's book, her critique is noteworthy: the violence isn't aestheticized enough. It doesn't cover up reality sufficiently with art; it is too real, or, as Jed says, it is too much like a book:

> A book, [Jed] thinks, is a vast field of objects under which have been buried an untold number of dead bodies. I must dig them up. I must cleanse the field of them.

While Jed is here referring to the job of text-editing and grammar correction, the passage also reminds directly of the murdered women in The Part About the Crimes, which is "boring," which is not aesthetic enough. A more aestheticized and classical example would be the Persian *1001 Nights*—often also known as *The Arabian Nights*, a frame tale that strongly influenced Miguel de Cervantes' *Don Quixote*. The framing of the *1001 Nights* is that each story is a tale spun by Sheherezade. A despotic king threatens to kill her every night, and the one way she can survive is to tell the king fantastic tales that last until dawn, and while these tales are what make up the vast majority and the popular memory of the *1001 Nights*—the movie *Aladdin*, for example, is not presented as one of many stories told by Sheherezade, because that would not sell—they are nonetheless framed and undergirded by the threat of death. *1001 Nights* is about a woman scared to death every night *for nearly three years*. The aesthetics of it save her: they are oases of entertainment in a desert of horror.

Our narrator, on the other hand, tells tales to those who pressure him in his social life, such as new acquaintances that want him to prove his mettle as a novelist, to Janice who asks for "a pitch" and from whom the narrator wants to ask for love, to his therapist to whom the narrator constantly lies, wanting to prove his normalcy. In other words, our narrator is an anxious person; unlike Sheherazade, his confession is not coerced. But this anxiety is also diagnosed as a social problem, whereby his selfhood, his "i," is disrupted by and replaced by his iPhone, an important character of *Gad's Book*. In a super-condensed, clickable form, it tells Sheherazadean stories throughout the novel, interrupting the principal narrative, and effecting a decentralized dissemination of crimes as communicated by the iPhone's incessant buzzing text reminders of all the horrors of the world, rendered throughout the book in italics:

> Multiple dead in a bombing of a shopping center in Florida. A state of emergency has been declared in Southern California as the region continues to experience aftereffects of multiple earthquakes. Cockroaches are developing cross-resistance to insecticides that can be passed on to their offspring.

If Bolaño offers one oasis of horror in a desert of boredom, Bassett offers several oases of horror, but so many that the boredom and the horror become indistinguishable. This mutual irruption, or fusing of landscapes, is enacted in *Gad's Book* through orthography, in a fusing of textscapes:

> All morning I watched YouTube videos. *Ten misconceptions about polyamory. The underbelly of refugee camps. How eleven people control the world.* The videos kept playing, one after the other. I didn't have to click anything. I watched a video about the Denver International Airport, New Coke, Deepwater Horizon, Alternative Therapy suppression, collapsing media conglomerates, the porn industry, and the rise of Satanism in western governments.

The main fictional narrative fuses into the nonfictional "real" iPhone headlines, in the same way news media fuses into entertainment on the iPhone. Rather than desensitization, it seems to cause a great anxiety in the narrator, robbing him of his autonomy, sense of reality, and well-being:

> My imagination had become real. I felt it. I felt awkward even then, in total isolation, cut off from the social sphere. I was all foggy in the head, and I had to sit down to gather my thoughts. What thoughts? Who put those thoughts there?
>
> You're sick.

Here we see the boundaries of the private and the public crumble, while simultaneously the fictive and the real wear away at one another. The narrator's brain becomes a sort of operating system whereby his thoughts seem to have been downloaded from somewhere/one else. In keeping, "You're sick" is written in the second person, making a stranger of the heretofore 1st person narrator, a perspectival manner of self-alienation whereby "I" talk to "myself" by calling myself "you" or, in a metafictional twist, there really is the voice of that someone "[w]ho put those thoughts there," i.e. the author calling the narrator or the reader sick. The narrator is reporting a profoundly disorienting experience while simultaneously performing a decentering push against his own subjectivity. That, or, in a very canny schism-fusion, Bassett suddenly eclipses the narrator, but uses the narrator's "own" voice, tells the narrator that nothing is his own.

There is an obvious social media commentary here regarding the zombification of the modern citizen, or social media user, whose agency has become replaced by the algorithm, whose thoughts begin to resemble advertisements, etc. Throughout the book there are trenchant arguments in the same vein, regarding the privatization of privacy, and a wariness of therapy that resembles the narrator's wariness towards our spectatorial culture of the confessional mode. This excerpt of a monologue by Zeke, whom the narrator hilariously idolizes as a leader of Antifa (which he clearly is not), very well encapsulates this critique:

> And I realize, he said, that the source of my shame. Frustration wasn't inside of me. It's out there, in the culture of machines and men—in cheap architecture and environmental collapse and addictive politics. It's a goofy thing about depression. Everyone says depression is a chemical imbalance in our brains, in our whole bodies. Something is wrong with us, they say. They use words like disorder, disease, sickness. They give us pills that make us complacent or passive. Neh. But they've got it wrong. We're not sick. Neh. The world is sick.

This reads like a fictionalized version of a main argument in Mark Fisher's *Capitalist Realism: Is There No Alternative?*—a very successful title insofar as it contains its own definition. Capitalist realists are people who believe there is no al-

ternative to capitalism; people who believe otherwise are naïve. Fisher argues that in the realm of Capitalist Realism—a global realm—mental health issues are treated as a natural occurrence that needs to be treated medicinally and pharmaceutically and via individualized therapies, instead of as societal and systemic problems that need to be treated communally, via an *alternative* ideological, financial and political system. Fisher argues that we must stop naturalizing pathology and start politicizing it: that instead of saying "You're sick," we say, "The world is sick."

This critique is operative in the novel, but primarily on the level of content. Stylistically, something deeper is going on here: the language itself seems sick. Again, the instability of the speaker's position in "You're sick" is disorienting for the reader, too. Similarly, Zeke's speech is guttural, heavy, unaesthetic, fragmented, broken in half: *And I realize, he said, that the source of my shame. Frustration wasn't inside of me.* There is an almost hyperrealism at work here, where the punctuation is meant to indicate the pacing of the enunciation in "real time." *They give us pills that make us complacent or passive. Neh. But they've got it wrong. We're not sick. Neh. The world is sick.* is not that convincing, because the "Neh" makes him seem sick. It's not even a word, it's nonverbal.

On the other hand, most literary dialogue buries the body, the real. In capital L Literature, speech is stylized to fit the genre, it is aestheticized into a set of codes that abjects the body, a body being an unruly thing that makes sounds sometimes like "Neh." Literature often abjects sickness, which means literature is repressing something. Or, in other words, literature is sick. "You're sick," I think, is ultimately an argument about sickness, or illness, or madness in literature. Don Quixote's delusions are fictive, and thereby purposeful: they are the creative element of the first modern novel. The narrator muses on this when considering a scene in the *Quixote*, whereby Don Quixote's fantasies are threatened with a reality check, but his faithful sidekick, Sancho Panza, makes a decisive and successful effort to preserve the fantasy, and thereby preserve Don Quixote's madness:

> What struck me was that Sancho's intervention is not pathetic or condescending. His interven-

tion is heroic. He intuitively understands that Don Quixote is not insane, but he entertains a useful delusion. A delusion that gives his life a purpose. And although, at the end of the novel, Quixote does eventually lose his fantasy—and although the loss of that fantasy initiates his metaphoric and literal death—Sancho is, in this moment, I thought, the novel's unironic hero.

Preserving the delusion is tantamount to preserving the fiction: the novel would end prematurely without it. The hero quest's object is to make the delusion *real*; when the real demolishes the delusion, only then does he fall sick and die. He transforms the world into something romantic, into a remote past predating the Spanish Inquisition, while living in a contemporaneous world that has politically and lethally repressed the Jews and the Muslims that had built the cultural foundation of "Christian" Spain. *Don Quixote* is what writer and theorist Rosa Menocal called "A Memory Palace," an ode to an epoch of cultural and linguistic diversity that flourished under Muslim Iberia. Hence the frame tale conceit of *Don Quixote*: a Spanish translation of a historical Arabic text.

I don't know how concerned with this *Gad's Book* is, but it still stands that the first modern novel was written by an author who found the world to be sick, and who found that any expression to the contrary would have him considered sick. And so the hero quest of literature begins at sickness and, in tragic form, ends at the hero's cure.

I do think a lot of this essay begs a certain question: if the protagonists of the stories are all surrogates or mouthpieces for the unknowing narrator—if they're marionettes he doesn't know he's puppeteering, if they're his subconscious becoming conscious to everyone but himself—who is the narrator in relation to the author, Dylan Bassett?

Here is Bassett's bio on the book's back flap:
Originally from Las Vegas, Dylan Bassett has lived many lives: a pastor in Russia, a semi-professional soccer player in Brazil, a translator in Kazakhstan, a local Democratic campaign manager in Utah, and now a professor of literature near Philadelphia. Bassett has an MFA from the Iowa Writers' Workshop and a PhD from the University of California-Santa Cruz.

A few months ago I did a reading with Emma Wood and Dylan Bassett, who are married. Emma read poems about being a mother, which were astonishingly funny and brutal and tender and, well, honest? But how do I know when something is honest? What is the literary device of honesty? Conner—I know Dylan Bassett as Conner—read an-in-progress autobiographical cycle about conversations he has had with strangers at airports, about radical disclosures and intimate stories he has told to and has had told to him by strangers. Many of these stories described what it is like to live with epilepsy. And I thought, Who are these people? Who are these people that I am supposed to know already? I've attended two different graduate schools with Bassett and, like the anonymous narrator, and like me, he writes under a pseudonym. After the reading I was talking to Conner and Emma, and we talked about *Gad's Book*. I said to Conner about the book, "I felt like I wrote it, or recognized it. I've loved a lot of books before, but this feeling was different. I felt this thing I've never felt from a book before, like I was genetically related to it, like it's my brother, or something."

And Emma said, "You mean you related to the narrator?" And Conner said, "No, he means to the writing, to the writing itself. I get that. I felt the same about your book."

plinth.

Palazzo Rodriguez

REYoung's Best Po-Po-Pop!©

DAAA...SnowBiz!
REYoung
TageTage Press, January 2024

It's tough to stick the landing. Ask acrobatic author REYoung as he soars above his endless cinematic circus, so much airtime spiraling alone through all those lights and sounds beneath the big top, pulling double-duty as announcer and bellowing to the crowd in long strings of inventive verbiage that keep it spellbound and salivating. Yet, there is no need to worry anymore. Only recent converts and curious audience-goers drawn in by the barkers outside are still wondering what *might* happen. The fall. The crash. The scream cut short due to a hand unable to reach that next splintery wooden bar in time, a plummet towards the dirt below. No. No need to worry. We few who have been here before (mostly affording the nosebleeds) know there is no need. He always sticks the landing. And besides, this is Snowbiz baby, and *Daaa...Snowbiz!* is no different.

Those in the know have been following along for a while. REYoung's writing career began with an initial emergence from his "cave" (check the About the Author blurb on all his books) in 1997 with the O'Brien Era Dalkey Archive Press publication of *Unbabbling*, a cult hit reviewed *somewhat* positively by Harvey Pekar (yes, that one) and elsewhere described as "if Beckett were an American monster". It created some buzz upon release but REYoung, ever-elusive mononym, rather than capitalizing on this, decided to instead disappear back into his cave for twenty years.

At least some of that silent time, if not most of it, appears to have been spent on writing the first book in what would become, upon completion of *Daa...SnowBiz!*, The Snowman Trilogy.

Margarito and The Snowman was released in late 2016 to some excited discussion in internet literary circles and, as usual, crickets from the wider press. Despite the muted response, *MATS* is without question one of the more linguistically inventive and heartfelt pieces of American writing thus far this century, and a solid contribution to the broader canon of American working-class fiction running from Twain and Melville through Dahlberg and Selby Jr., though with some theatrical and psychedelic twists entirely REYoung's own. It set the stage for what would come after from this singular artist, and particularly this series. With its surrealist blending of overlapping narrative layers (are we reading a book by REYoung about Margarito and said Snowman or watching a Boone Weller movie—don't miss that Buñuel reference—about some guy named Snowman played by someone else named Billy Bob Bengay?), a bricolage quality in its referential streams of detail, elements of minstrelsy and vaudeville, blue collar frustrations, and truly heartfelt moments of companionship and lost love, *MATS* became a calling card of sorts to many who read it and felt seen by its hilariously confused characters and tones of longing.

Between then and now there have been some detours. In quick succession after *MATS* came *InFLATion* (2019), *The Ironsmith* (2020), and *Zol* (2020), that final title being the second volume of The Snowman Trilogy.

Z. proved that there was still more than enough juice left in the series (our wait for Boone Weller's sequel to *Abominable Snowman of the North* was surely well worth it) and that REYoung was capable not only of extending and explaining the many narrative threads left loose at the end of *MATS*, but also doing a degree of tonal and thematic reimagining of his own material. If *MATS* is for fans of films such as Paul Schrader's *Blue Collar* (1978) and Kevin Smith's *Clerks* (1993), then *Z.*, with largely the same cast and continued story, is for fans of Alejandro Jodorowsky's *El Topo* (1970) and Alex Cox's *Walker* (1987).

Now, four years since *Z.*, a long enough time to make one concerned we might be looking at another twenty-year gap between books, we have *Daaa...SnowBiz!*, and it feels like a triumphant culmination of all that has been produced in the series prior. And that's not just because it's the longest in the series by over a hundred pages. Mark this one for fans of Robert Altman's *The Player* (1992) and The Cohen Brothers' *Burn After Reading* (2008).

SnowBiz opens with a visually older and more grizzled Snowman than we are used to (this is after the disembodied sleazy showman prologue paragraph, of course), who is emotionally much more angry, cynical, and frustrated than his last incarnation (which seems fair considering the events of *Zol* ie. everything from loss of loved ones to psychosis to outright physical torture). The Snowman trundles through the streets of Osberg (read: Austin, TX), snarling through waves of people and negative emotions and selling frosted treats out of an ice cream cart he wheels before him. The treats, Po-Po-Pops©, have a magical effect on their consumers, bringing an oceanic feeling of peace and contentment akin in description to a low dose of MDMA. Folks of all ages, races, and classes consume the frozen confection and swirl away in the puffing rainbow cloud released upon pulling the tab of the wrapper. But this is a REYoung novel, and it is not long before something sinister and suspicious makes itself apparent behind even the most benign or happily magical of happenings. The Snowman, continuing his peregrinations as Boone Weller continues, all these years later, filming him, receives a phone call that *appears* to be about a large-scale business deal (legality left to readers imagination, at first), and then it's off to the races. We digress through a tour of the homeless population, zoom cinematically outward and into the midst of academic politics at the local university, where we are also introduced to multiple important figures including the mercurial-in-all-manners Dr. Levant and the invisibility maestro Oscar, and it just keeps on expanding, compressing, or rolling from there.

By the end of the book the plot encompasses everything from international political conspiracy to asides on etymology and entomology. Disquisitions on silence and disappearance are punctuated by minstrel shows. Hyper-modern thoughts and topicality are layered or woven with seeming centuries worth of filmic reference and art history. Like much of REYoung's fiction, *Snowbiz* sits firmly in the vein of the post- (post-post?, meta-? -) modern milieu in which it was born, with scattered influences ranging from Robbe-Grillet to Bradbury to daytime television to monster movies, consistently presented with a healthy dose of humor to keep things appropriately unsentimental.

Similar to REYoung's very first work, *Unbabbling*, the Snowman series seems to function on a rule of threes. Though in *Unbabbling* the tripartite character is on a cyclical trip downward (and this is a good thing leading to a freedom in burrowing, a comfort in caves) here in the Snowman's frozen world the Snowman finds himself drawn almost conspiratorially upward (and this is a bad thing, leading to a far worse life than any of the Snowman's many lonely bathtub and beer nights that the *MATS* days may have amounted to). *MATS* is a day in the life of a worker this side of the border, bottom rung life of drudgery, but consisting of camaraderie and occasional flashes of fun. *ZOL*, then becomes a complexification of this, and the Snowman finds himself on the other side of the border, dustily sifting through social stratifications wrought by the capitalism he once worked comfortably inside of. Here, as he enters the *Snowbiz*, he arrives at the top rung of everything to witness the destruction wrought by the climb. It is a climb the Snowman remembers only slowly over the course of the novel, and what a ride of remembrance it is. One senses that if the trilogy were published as a single omnibus volume, a tome for all time at its 1200 plus pages, that it would be embraced by the American cognoscenti quickly as another genius exercise in the encyclopedic novel lineage of Pynchon, Gaddis, and Wallace.

Because REYoung IS experimental and seems to write with both the scatter approach of a Sufi mystic as well as the furious forward intensity of Thomas Bernhard. REYoung IS challenging and brethren with dense linguists like Hawkes and Gaddis. But REYoung is also fun and funny like Twain or Thompson, and endlessly inventive to boot and nowhere is that more on display than here in *Daaa . . . Snowbiz!* And hey, if you don't feel like sticking around for the philosophical asides and movie references then stick around for the dancing insects and one-liners. He'll be here all week, and hopefully another twenty years after that.

There are many readers that all the shticks and tricks may not be for. But in the context and lineage that REYoung has always seemed to be pulling from, sometimes ironically and other times sincerely, it all falls into place. Think the carnival barker. Think the one-liner comedian shuffling his way through a series of bits in desperation for a cut of the door or the tummler tugging his collar as he breaks out in nervous sweats. Think the death of vaudeville. And we do mean all of this as a good thing. The worlds lengthiest Aristocrats joke that somehow has a heart of gold. There is a *Ha-Ha-Ho-Ho* nature to much of the presentation in the early scenes, when the veil must remain up to hide OZ, a degree of "please, somebody take my wife" one-linerism, but this has always been in service (and quite effectively) to a quiet anger, simple sadness, and deep longing, that begins to seethe forth from the relentless stream of verbiage always attempting to keep you at arm's length. A general understanding of the fuckedness of our collective situation, all ways out of the precipice we find our world teetering on. A kind of Pagliacci story for all time.

All said and done, the most effective moment of the whole book, the whole series even, comes at the very end in a section titled 'Cutting Room Floor'. There is no need to spoil the scene, but one gets the feeling that this inexplicably moving image cooked up somewhere in the fiery middle of REYoung's imagination, will resonate most with those who cry when HAL is unplugged in Kubrick's *2001 A Space Odyssey*. The moment is a display of what we can only hope we see more and more of from this writer as long as he will keep producing these delicious treats of text with their weighty centers, a strange hyperreal sympathy set against a surrealist stage, a sort of cosmic understanding as delivered by a stoner Buddha forgetting his place in the meditation. This final section is a moment of writing (as we have seen before from this writer but perhaps never quite so strongly) that will leave one wondering if they are crying by the time the final sentence runs (final reel rolls) and you stumble from the theatre, blinking into the sunlight. But relax, maybe those aren't tears. Maybe, like the Snowman, you're finally just melting.

Oscar Mardell

The Atolls of Ecstasy

The Oceans of Cruelty
Douglas J. Penick
New York Review Books, October 2024

Douglas J. Penick's *The Oceans of Cruelty* is a collection of twenty-five stories—twenty-six, if we include the frame-story (in which the nefarious Yogi Valkalāśana tricks the legendary King Vikramāditya into bringing him the Vetāla—the corpse possessed by the spirit of its former inhabitant—which narrates the core twenty-five to the King along his journey). Their origin is in the *Vetala Panchavimshati* whose earliest written recensions date from between the Eleventh and the Fourteenth Centuries CE, but whose own origins lie in oral traditions so timeless and so protean that it would hardly make sense to discuss them in terms of 'origins' at all. How, then, with none of the usual certainties afforded by a definite genesis, should we begin to interpret them?

Perhaps the immediate temptation is to attempt some kind of feverish crosschecking—to analyse *The Oceans of Cruelty* in terms of its borrowings and departures from the other recensions. But such an approach would miss the sheer accessibility of Penick's text, which demands no prior expertise on the part of its readers (and is certainly not, say, a series of in-jokes for aficionados of the *Vetala Panchavimshati*). That, and it would quickly become completely absorbed in the text's own artifice. The Vetāla intends to 'get this King [Vikramāditya] to respond to each story as if it were real', and *The Oceans of Cruelty* requires that its own audiences respond in much the same way. Of course, meeting this requirement is harder than it sounds. *The Oceans of Cruelty* is constantly drawing attention to its own artifice, reminding us at every opportunity that it is not the slightest bit 'real'. Furthermore, it is quietly scathing of those audiences who completely 'immerse' themselves in stories—that is, of audiences for whom fictions *are* real—eventually warning us (albeit, with comically late timing) of an apocalyptic future in which 'Men and women would soon be completely unable to distinguish the human realm from stories about the human realm'. The challenge here is to know full well that the twenty-five (or twenty-six) stories are outright fabrications, painstakingly (co-)constructed over multiple centuries, whilst treating them as if they were not. Fiction is a subjunctive art, and *The Oceans of Cruelty* is no exception.

To complicate the question of origins, *The Oceans of Cruelty* offers its own account of the genesis of the twenty-five:

Brahman [who subsequently becomes the Vetāla, his corpse possessed by his own spirit] slept next to his wife and dreamed . . . He dreamed he saw Śiva and Pārvatī, whispering one story, then another, twenty-five in an unbroken stream. In the morning, when he woke, Brahman could not help himself. He made love to his wife and told her these stories as he heard them.

Of course, it is easy to remember that this story is itself a further fabrication (indeed, if we do succumb to the temptation to crosscheck, then we can even guess at *when* it might have been fabricated, for the device in which Lord Śiva is the ultimate source of the Vetāla's stories appears in Somadeva's *Kathāsaritsāgara* from 1070 CE but not in Kṣemendra's *Bṛhatkathāmanjarī* from 1037 CE). But how does our interpretation change when we treat this fabrication 'as if it were real'? The rub here is that it does not. As Chandra Rajan explains in the introduction to her 1995 translation of Śivadāsa's recension:

> By positing such a hoary antiquity to story-telling and projecting it far back in time to the quasi-eternal and temporal abode of divinity, and by making the divine pair Śiva and Śaki (Parvati) as the primal narrator and audience, tradition is pointing to a very ancient and undateable origin for it. This apocryphal story underlines what is central to the genre of oral storytelling, and defines its special nature. Storytelling is timeless. Like fire it is brought down to earth for man's use and entertainment. A narrative is a *re-telling* and will always be that. However far back in time it is traced to it always remains a *re-telling*. We are still left, not with an 'original', not with 'absolute beginnings' of a narrative, of any narrative, but with successive *re-tellings* . . . To place the initial, the original narration on Mt. Kailāsa, in the divine world of the timeless, is simply to state this ineluctable fact in a mythic form.

Whether we prefer to accept the fact that *The Oceans of Cruelty* has come down to us via tradition's grapevine, or to entertain the idea that it has come down to us from Śiva himself (or—ideally—to do both at once), the result is the same: *The Oceans of Cruelty* derives its affect from its being an imperfect, mutant text, distorted and corrupted—a single moment within a long process of entropy. The important thing here is not to attempt to reconstruct the entire process, but simply to trace the particulars of the iteration at hand.

What are those particulars? To repeat: *The Oceans of Cruelty* is constantly drawing attention to its own artifice. It is not simply a collection of stories but a near-exhaustive demonstration of storytelling's every device—a heaving compendium of mistaken identities, calculated revenges, surprise revelations, and reversals in fortune. But what makes it especially hard to 'respond to each story as if it were real' is the abundance of additional, embedded stories. Some good examples occur in 'Wise Birds' (which, of course, is itself embedded within the story of Vikramāditya's bringing the Vetāla to Valkalāśana): King Rūpasena, who keeps a pet parrot, marries Princess Surasandarī, who keeps a pet mynah. The parrot propositions the mynah with sex. The mynah is not interested, and in her defence tells a story about her previous owner's daughter, Ratnavati, who was seduced, murdered, and robbed by the deceitful philanderer, Dhanaksaya. Partway through this story, Dhanaksaya himself starts regaling a merchant with a (false) story about losing merchandise in a shipwreck. We have, to put it bluntly, a story within a story within a story within a story. The parrot responds by telling a story of his own about his previous owner, Jayshri, whose husband, Śridatta, was killed in bed by thieves without Jayshri's realising. Partway through this story, moreover, Śridatta starts regaling Jayshiri with a story of 'his voyages and how he had longed for her'; Jayshri, however, 'covered her ears and grimaced'. The joke here is that the device has already been taken too far—that the actual audience, Penick's flesh-and-blood reader, has already been subjected to one too many embedded stories and that anything more will result in unmanageable chaos. *The Oceans of Cruelty* is not simply a showcase of the storyteller's art but a delineation of its outermost limits—one that constantly pushes it to the point of breakdown.

Making it still harder 'to respond . . . as if it were real', *The Oceans of Cruelty* often reads like an allegory of the actual mechanics of storytelling. 'True Love', for example, begins with a Princess making signs—that is, telling a story (or narrating excerpts of her biography)—to Prince Vajramukuta:

> The Princess . . . took a lotus flower that she had twined in her hair and held it to her ear. Then

she bit the flower, stopped, put it under her right foot, then retrieved it and placed it between her breasts.

But the Prince's friend, Buddhisena, proves to be the more sensitive audience, and it consequently falls to him interpret these signs—to 'hear' or 'read' the Princess' story:

> 'She was telling you her name, the name of her homeland and certain other things too . . . When she moved the lotus from the side of her head down to her ear, she was indicating that she comes from the south, from Karnakubja, the place where Karnatic singing began. By biting the flower, she told you that she is the daughter of King Dantāghatā which means "Bite". Pressing the lotus under her foot, she showed that her name is Padmāvati, 'She who is like a lotus'. When she pressed the lotus to her heart, she showed you that you have entered her heart.'

Sure enough, the Prince and Buddhisena find the Princess at Dantāghatā's palace in Karnakubja, but her response to their arrival appears to contradict the latter part of Buddhisena's interpretation: 'She spat on the fingers of both hands and spread the spit on the sole of one of her sandals. Suddenly she slapped her old nurse on the face with the sandal.' Hence, Buddhisena must provide further interpretation of these new signs:

> Using all ten fingers to wet her sandal, the Princess meant that when the ten nights of moonlight have come to an end, she will meet you in the dark. Slapping [her nurse] meant she had to reject [her] until then.

The Prince and Buddhisena return in ten days' time, but still the signs are unfavourable: 'the Princess had put saffron paste on three of her fingers . . . lashed out and again struck her old nurse'. Accordingly, Buddhisena provides still further interpretation, this time claiming: 'The Princess is in the state that afflicts all women every month.' The remainder of Buddhisena's initial reading is finally validated three days later when the King returns and is told by the Princess, 'I wish only to serve you, great lord'. Before long, however, she starts to spin false signs, to tell fictional stories: when the Prince requests to visit Buddhisena, she indicates that she is happy for him to do so, but then attempts to poison both men. The Prince and Buddhisena take revenge by concocting a fictional story of

their own—that the Princess is a rabid nymphomaniac who gave the family treasures away to a Yogi in exchange for further sexual prowess—and by manipulating the signs (even *marking* the Princess' leg with a trident) so that their fiction appears to be real. Convinced of her guilt, the Princess' father punishes her by editing her out of the world of stories altogether:

> He didn't want her in his mind for another second. He would no longer speak her name. He commanded that this terrible child be placed in a palanquin and taken immediately to the wilderness outside his kingdom's border. The guards were neither to explain nor speak to her.

The Vetāla eventually has King Vikramāditya interpret the whole story, the entire system of signs, asking him: 'Who, of the five people in this tale . . . deserves the lowest rebirth?' The King's answer is a revealing one: 'the King, Padmāvati's father, should never have judged her without questioning her directly.' Here, the harshest judgement falls on the story's worst audience, its most incompetent reader, the person who fails to properly interrogate the signs. When, at the end of 'A Question With No Answer', King Vikramāditya finds himself unable to interpret any more—when, as 'A Wave Beginning' phrases it, 'words fail him'—there is, once again, a sense of having reached an outermost limit, a breakdown in meaning:

> It was a chaos of simultaneous possibilities . . . It was the kind of irresolvable confusion that, as he knew, often follows war. There was no untangling it.

The Vetāla's stories eventually bring us, in other words, to the very place where stories fail: to the real itself—unspeakable and unreadable, disorganised and infinite.

In addition, much of *The Oceans of Cruelty* appears to present something like a coded apology or manifesto for storytelling. Its most common line of defence is that storytelling offers a diversion from the trauma or 'cruelty' of the real. Just before he starts narrating 'True Love', for example, the Vetāla whispers to King Vikramāditya, 'this world we now traverse together is, as you know, a sea of insatiable desires and cruel deceits. Let me distract you with stories from other places and times'. The distraction motif recurs throughout *The Oceans of Cruelty*, but what is brilliant about it (and what ultimately enables us to respond to *The Oceans of Cruelty* 'as if it were real') is that it too breaks down. On the one hand, the Vetāla's stories are every bit as teeming with 'insatiable desires and cruel deceits' as the world which King Vikramāditya inhabits (and perhaps even as the world which we, Penick's flesh-and-blood readers, inhabit). On the other hand, the distinction between the real world and the Vetāla's fictions turns out to be eerily unstable. In 'Uncaused', for example, we are told that 'The Corpse-Demon's stories which he offered as distractions had become the most real part of the King's journey'. In 'Unchanging', we learn that:

When the Vetāla spoke, the outer world faded and the stories grew real. At each tale's conclusion, King Vikramāditya knew he would be required to make judgements as if he ruled in these storylands. Then, briefly, storytelling would end, and the outer world return ever less substantial.

Likewise, in 'Love and Ruling (2)', we find that 'The painful tedium of the King's labors dissolved within the reality of another tale.' The implication is that storytelling does not just offer an escape from the world, but a more immediate point of access—a purer and more concentrated distillation of reality than life itself ordinarily provides.

Concurrently, *The Oceans of Cruelty* makes the case that stories do not just distil life, but actually enable us to live—especially, beyond the physical and temporal limitations of biological life. In 'Love and Chaos', the Vetāla reminds King Vikramāditya, that 'we the dead, live only as tales are told.' Similarly, having finished telling his twenty-five tales, he announces:

O Great King Vikramāditya, the twenty-five tales I told have long been the essence of my being. Now they live in you; they are part of your life, and you will carry me into millions of places and times. My existence is inseparable from the story of your life and will continue in whoever hears your history. I will be woven into them. As one tells another, in hundreds of millions of minds, I will become part of hundreds of millions of beings. In eon after eon, I will come to life in times and circumstances beyond imagining and without limit. But, O Merciful One, my continuing depends on your survival. Your story must not end.

Of course, King Vikramāditya's story does not end. The final words of *The Oceans of Cruelty* are these:

Legends about King Vikramāditya began at once, and were written down in the Brihatkatha, the Hatha-sarit-Sagara, the Gatha-Saptasati, Vasavadatta, and in innumerable later texts, dramas songs, and spoken stories which are current now.'

The thesis developed here, as Penick phrases it in his Foreword, is that 'Our existence beyond the bounds of a single life, as well as our posterity, depends entirely on [stories], on becoming one of them.' But what is brilliant here is that this thesis has a catch: to live beyond the physical and temporal limitations of biological life is essentially to be a corpse-spirit. Earlier, Penick's Foreword explains that 'a story is something that takes possession of whoever reads and hears it', adding that 'it is the Vetāla itself that embodies this demonic aspect of narrative'. To exist in other people's accounts of oneself, then, is to possess those people, to be a demon, to lack a properly embodied existence of one's own. It is to be, as 'A Wave Beginning' says of the Vetāla, 'filled with seething mist, neither live nor dead'. Vikramāditya eventually sacrifices the Vetāla, triumphs over the Yogi Valkalāśana, and thus becomes an immortal legend; in doing so, however, he also becomes a kind of Vetāla. (As it happens, the historical record concurs: it remains inconclusive as to whether Vikramāditya was a real personage, a composite of several real personages, a mythologised version of one or several real personages, or an outright fabrication. He has always been, in a sense, 'neither live nor dead'.)

But *The Oceans of Cruelty* also contains a further defence of storytelling: that it offers a sort of existential geometry—a set of shapes and delineations with which to order our experience of the world; that we can navigate or make sense of the chaos of existence by organising it into a compendium of mistaken identities, calculated revenges, surprise revelations, and reversals in fortune. On learning that his stories for Pārvatī have been overheard and retold,

The great god [Lord Śiva] was enraged that the intimacy of his love, the merging, caressing passions, the scents and colors and textures emerging and dissolving as he moved within the great goddess, whispering and licking, that this play of love should somehow be overheard, that its expressions be somehow stolen and used to debase a world and corrupt it by names and forms.

Without narrative, then, the world is—as in Genesis (and Jeremiah)—'without form'. Here, however, the emergence of storytelling is a catastrophe, a fall from grace. *The Oceans of Cruelty* does not have a beginning as such (that is, it does not begin, like Genesis, 'In the beginning', but 'Before Beginning'—or, more accurately, with two 'Before Beginning[s]'), but its opening words are these:

As has been told:

Primordial space, the undivided, the signless, where sentience and non-sentience, awareness and unawareness have not divided, where there is neither life nor death, nor time, nor stasis, continuity or discontinuity, void or phenomena. Primordial sea undivided. Primordial Sky undivided. Primordial Darkness undivided. Primordial Light undivided. Chaos moving and alive without reference to order or disorder. Neither noun nor verb. Continuity continuing in its own reference. A vast and empty luminous expanse.

What is crucial (or divine) about the ur-stories, the proto-narratives with which Śiva pleasures Pārvatī, is that they do not disrupt this 'primordial space'—that they do not divide 'the undivided' nor carve up 'the signless' into neat little signifiers and signifieds. They are, as the text puts it, 'stories unconstrained by meanings, shaped from chaos' (and not, say, in opposition to chaos). By contrast, the stories told by us mortals de-eroticise the world. They are a turn-off. What is more, the obverse proves to be true as well: in 'Three Fathers', a Brahmin's daughter, Mohini, attempts to describe her first sexual encounter, explaining, 'I lost all consciousness of being myself'. Sex, in other words, is messy. Like Primordial space, it muddles divisions—in particular, those between self and other.

The final paradox—and, in fact, the reason why storytelling continues to be worthwhile (that is, in spite of the terrifying/tedious ubiquity which stories have assumed in our own era)—is that the only way out is through: we can only arrive at the unnarratable by means of narrative. It is not just that 'Primordial space' is only known to us because of the existence of tales—including Penick's—about 'Primordial space' (although, in one sense or another, this is almost certainly the case). It is that the world which exists prior to or beyond storytelling—the world in which all divisions (not just those that are muddled by sex—that is, between self and other) are effaced beyond recognition—is most directly and fully accessed via the breakdowns in storytelling itself: in stories which push their own devices to their limits, which allegorise their own unreadability, which are insufficiently distinct from reality, which fail to immortalise their subjects, which are incapable of providing life with form, which do not manage to begin and end, which lack definite geneses. *The Oceans of Cruelty* is a collection of twenty-five such stories—twenty-six, if we include the frame-story. It is, in a manner of speaking, 'better than sex' (at least, the sex practised by us mortals).

Greg Bem

Two Recent Books by Cecilia Vicuña

Internationally renowned, Chilean-born Cecilia Vicuña has recently seen a surge in translations of recent and past works, further introducing and solidifying her voice in the English language. Two recent titles are of monumental significance in extending conversations that first emerged decades ago. In this double review, I examine two relatively new releases: *Deer Book* and *Word Weapons*, each entirely unique, awe-inducing collections that equally shed light onto this artist and her written and visual worlds' worth of work. These books have arrived at the English-language world offering a glimpse at the vastness of Vicuña's decades-long career through two unique projects, each of their own timelines, each of their own expressions and connectivity. They are unique yet inseparable. We see Vicuña's worldview, her poetries of word and picture and installation and performance. These new portals are a fantastic milestone of translation and artistic wonder as we are invited in and invited in again.

Deer Book (*Libro Venado*)
Translated by Daniel Borzutzky
Radius Books, 2024

The massive *Deer Book* (or *Libro Venado*) is unlike any other book I've encountered. Layers upon layers of sequences are contained on unnumbered pages with beautiful and striking patterns and papers. This is a book that feels like an experience before the cover is even opened. The art of the tome is captivating, the deer emblems and icons glancing mysteriously on the cover. Upon opening, we are greeted with the announcement: this is *Deer Book*, by Cecilia Vicuña, translated by Daniel Borzutzky.

The table of contents unfolds. It is several pages long, all connected with handwritten text in black on yellow paper. It is the "Deer Book Map." It moves us along to a page that is a pattern, a textile, and then a transparency, a totemic or emblematic image of a being with arms stretched out, a beam or antler or horn or crown emerging from its head. We are greeted with "The Animal Poem," the first major section of the book.

Each of the book's sections are presented with an inventive variation of translation, permutations of arrangement and style, as we explore language in the creative, amorphous way that signifies and spurs much of Cecilia Vicuña's art. The type is clean, has a punch to it, moves the gaze across the page methodically, hypnotically, often moving between Spanish and English across geometric arrangements and color choices in the font.

Deer Book is filled with original and borrowed language: a collage across time and space. A translation of Eliot Weinberger opens "The Animal Poem":

> The poem
> > Is the animal
> > Sinking its mouth
> > In the stream.

The page later closes "Thirst is the thread." We are transported. Or transposed, if only temporarily. Vicuña layers on language, the poetry and prose weaving along from page to page, pages absent of numbers, a flow of moments, a process that absorbs the reading experience and turns it into something else, something other, but still familiar: awash with ideas, language. A fuller literary emergence, undistracted.

> "A poem lives in the in-between, the interval between languages."
> (from "The Animal Book")

The text guides us through a fluid, mystical history. It is a book about Deer. Who is deer? Where is deer? Vicuña invites us to learn: "In Mesoamerica, deer worlds exist in a web of 'mutually constitutive' relations associated, since time immemorial, with sacrifice, fertility, speech, flowers, and the fluidity of water . . . in other cultures, deer is a translator, a sacred teacher called 'the root of empathy,' or the 'Guardian of the Dharma,' a master of trans-formation."

As we move forward into the text, the resemblance of Deer behind the pages pulls everything together. But, as marionettes or bundles of energy, we are the ones with the motion. Deer sits behind (or within) each page, appearing to peer just as we appear to peer, a being or no-being of presence and documentation. A witness. A keystone of translation and translated experience.

Deer Book contains typed text and handwritten text, photography and hand-scrawled language. It is filled with cryptic wisdom and engaging wordplay. It is filled with indigenous knowledge and reflections on indigeneity in the corrupted and corroded present. It is also informed by transience and loss, the brutality of circumstance with ecological change.

Cecilia Vicuña started this book in multiple potential spaces, as she explains in the book's afterword: in 2004 during a visit to the Lower Pecos River, located in what is commonly known as New Mexico, USA; in 1985 when she "encountered deer in the *15 Flower World Variations, the Deer Dance of the Yaquis* by Jerome Rothenberg." "I translated it into Spanish, but in truth, the poem translated me" writes Vicuña, a book of transformations born of transformation.

But transformation of what and to what? Within the artist's mind, simple explanation is always matched with the infinite: that we may understand through total, complex engagement. *Deer Book* is one of these moments of infinitude, where we can encounter "Death of the pollinators," where we can spread out across "The I of Sound," where the section "Breath Flower" can find us and bind us through breath to the entirety of the book.

And as we are bound, as we breathe, so too do we hear. And "To hear is to heal" the artist lets us know (in "Sound Flower"), as we move in all directions toward center, no center, toward past, and toward future.

Word Weapons
RITE EDITIONS, 2023

T he colorful cover of *Word Weapons* draws us in. A bright red, hardbound cloth cover with beautiful blue scrawl and "Cecilia Vicuňa" in a bold yellow. The new book, a mere 750 copies from RITE EDITIONS and the CCA Wattis Institute of Contemporary Arts is an experience of welcoming, of conversation, of exploration. It is also profound in its scope and scale, and a beautiful book to peak or dive into.

Upon opening the book, we immediately find the *Palabrarmas*, the word weapons, small, agile, vispo icons that move between word and firearm. The yellow on sky blue is electric and striking. Is strikes, and it sticks. We are greeted with these initial moments of presence, the imagery slowly sinking into the page. Its origins, the causation: this is the foreshadowing, this is the curtain lifting upwards toward the clouds.

Word Weapons is the result of a communal project, a Faculty Group composed of fourteen individuals committed to exploring Cecilia Vicuňa's work: "This book is published in conjunction with *Season 7: Cecilia Vicuňa is on our mind*, a year-long season of private meetings and public events about and around the work of Cecilia Vicuňa." The "research season" went from September 2020 to August 2021, a cycle that led to this profound compilation.

The majority of *Word Weapons* is contained with "Visions," a nearly-90-page section that presents Cecilia Vicuňa's *Palabrarmas* work from as far back as the 70s. A collection of handwriting and illustration printed on pages, scanned imagery, and photography from the artist's performance art is all presented here page after page, with brief captions only providing minimal context. The reader is welcomed in, welcomed to browse, to scan, to select, to layer into meaning.

The collectors, the designers, the anthologizers, they have created a collection that creates a story, a single approach to a lifetime journey of art created by Cecilia Vicuňa and the communities she worked within. It is an assortment that is humbling: to show snapshots and single frames from the word weapons, which are projectiles, which are enticing in their motion, and given space to sit and slowly open, emerge, arrive in this space.

In a form that mimics Cecilia Vicuňa herself, the book is introduced only after the ritual of presenting the artist has been complete: we are then greeted with an introduction by Jeanne Gerrity that is both brief and thorough across its four pages. Context is reinforced with a second voice.

We learn that "words are acts" from Octavio Paz. We learn of Vicuňa's decades-long exploration of the intersection of language and images (page 99). The book is a collection, a series, the "urgent need for political engagement, coupled with a resolute love for humanity" (page 02). Gerrity's pull is a triangulation, the mode towards conversation and community, to set the book upon itself with multiple visions, gazes, lenses.

Cecilia Vicuňa herself is the third voice, appearing in a subsequent piece with beautiful description's of the palabrarmas, the puns, references, and quirks of the vispo (and beyond): "To Work Words More." What starts as a poem moves into a personal recounting of the word weapons, the first person experience, in all of its awe and psychedelic wandering.

This would be enough. This would be a powerful text, an enduring retrospective on the longitudinal beauty and the aspects of time that are necessary for Cecilia Vicuňa's work to exist. But there's more. Gifts of ellipses in the form of additional essays, additional perspectives: "Mobilizing Words" by Mónica De La Torre and "Labor the word, spill the sound, unleash the tongue," by Carla Macchiavello Cornejo. Two critical works that supplement history and inference with more details, more context, more triangulation.

The book closes with a final section: "Languages," which serves as an appendix: bringing forward older, inspiring works that influenced and guided the artist: "From Rasa, or Knowledge of the Self: Essays on Indian Aesthetics and Selected Sanskrit Studies" by René Daumal, translated by Louise Landes Levi; "Sacred Language: Wordplay in Andean Cosmology" by Robert Randall, translated by Juana Berrío; and "Luces y virtudes sociales / Social Virtues and Illuminations" by Simón Rodríguez.

The book opens with mystery and closes with community. Thus, we have a toolkit, a process, a method of conjoining the multitudes of inquiry and commitment. This is a book of refraction and reflection, where we are gifted multiple approaches, multiple angles towards a center across space, time, and context, all of which aids us in movement through art, to reach wisdom, to explore language and its teachings in bold, living ways.

REVIEW | Jesi Bender

Easy Victims to the Charitable Deceptions of Nostalgia
Emily Schulten
White Pine Press, 2024

Easy Victims to the Charitable Deceptions of Nostalgia is a poetry collection is immersed in its surroundings: in the beach, the ocean, aquatic flora and fauna, and the peculiarities of Florida. This book reads more like a prose writer telling different stories; scenes from the author's life are refracted back in short passages filled with abundant coastal mise-en-scène. The language is straight-forward and less abstract (as is often encountered with poetry) so it becomes reminiscent of confessional poets, though more Paul Hetherington than Sylvia Plath.

A good portion of the poems explore the poet's attempts at conception or puts the author's voice in relation to to men in her life, be it fathers or partners or friends, etc. The feminine voice exploring these scenes would be relatable to a wide audience, especially for women. Fans of atmospheric, confessional poets or movies like *The Florida Project* would enjoy this book. Particular

gems in this collection include "To Make a Paradis Out of Paradise," "Love Poem, Interment," and "Lovebirds". At its heart, *Easy Victims to the Charitable Deceptions of Nostalgia* is a woman's exploration of different forms of love and loss where her surroundings become a tool through which she is able to understand her internal world.

I say to burn and you say to bury, and the rest
we agree on—we will become nothing together,
we will expose the entirety of our bones,
to dry and be bleached white in the sun.

REVIEW | Charles Holdefer

A Walk with Frank O'Hara
Susan Aizenberg
University of New Mexico Press, 2024

To refer to a book as "capacious" might at first blush seem a likely description of a fat, maximalist novel, but the term can also apply, in the case of Susan Aizenberg's *A Walk with Frank O'Hara*, to a svelte volume of poetry.

Divided into three sections, these 45 poems range from the speaker's personal history to contemporary politics to events in previous centuries, sometimes in the same poem. A number of poems begin with lines from other poets, or, as in the title poem, with the reimagining of another poet. The result is a heightened sense of connectedness.

The speaker's parents often provide a springboard into the past. The poem "Hunger" is a sober portrait of an unhappy father that uses food to conjure up an entire era. His is a world of potatoes every night ("Idahoes the size of baby / shoes in their blackened skins—") with Walter Cronkite on the black-and-white TV. The man's anger serves as "the kindling that kept him thin." The Vietnam War looms large in several of Aizenberg's poems, while the speaker's mother appears at various stages in life, from hopeful youth to final decline and death. The poems "Three Rispetti" and "First Light" are among the most moving in this collection.

Formally speaking, Aizenberg often favors unrhymed couplets to create discrete units of thought that can stand on their own while also being flexible enough to serve as pieces of longer, more discursive meditations, as in "The Beautiful American Word *Baby*." The poem is too long to quote in its entirety here, but the speaker amusingly explores sociological nuances of *baby, babe, sugar baby, honey baby, baby doll, dear baby*, etc.

> . . . *Honey*
>
> Was for drag queens and sitcom husbands—
> campy as a big wig and falsies, homely as Schlitz
>
> and socks on the bedroom floor. *Doll* reeked
> of menace, cold eyes, hard slap, sharp
>
> flick of a switchblade. *Dear* was unthinkable—
> Ozzie and Harriet, virginal librarians

There are also a number of ekphrastic poems, across a variety of media. "*La Liseuse*" addresses Mary Cassatt's portrait of her sister, and meditates on the life of the model, and her importance as a help-meet to the artist. "At the Chicago Art Institute" considers a Brancusi sculpture, while other poems, like "Tea Boys" (about *Salaam, Bombay!*), "Forced March" (about the real-life Hungarian poet Miklós Radnóti) and

"Michael Corleone Prepares for Bed" (about *The Godfather II*) explore the power of film, moving deftly from aesthetic appreciation to the highly personal. Regarding Corleone, the speaker observes:

> . . . the scene's
> not meant to be erotic,
> but because you are gone
> I'm seized with a longing so strong
> I could raise a car with it.

Contemporary culture—coronavirus, CNN, the Taliban—is sometimes mentioned in these poems but Aizenberg generally avoids the fodder of the news cycle and quick, easy judgments. "Errata" is an fascinating, sadly wise poem about human limitations, cruelty and our capacity for self-deceit. But though the poet does not preach, she is also unsparing. For instance, "Not One Woman I Know Hasn't These Stories" is the best poem I've read about sexual harassment.

A Walk with Frank O'Hara is probing and wide-ranging, highly personal without being solipsistic, and, for its variety, refreshingly unpredictable from one poem to the next. This is first-rate work.

CHRISTOPHER BOUCHER

THE CLAMS

I still regret not seeing more of their shows—the Clams were one of my favorite bands! But I thought sure they'd tour again. Apparently there was an altercation in a hotel room in Sydney, though, and the band's lead guitarist, Exacting DeRose, threw a glass table at singer Clam Watson. A drunk Clam stumbled out of the room and flew home to the States on his own dime, and that was pretty much it; the rest of the tour was canceled and the Clams disbanded. Madge Sycamore joined the Baltimore Philharmonic soon thereafter, and zitherist Dollar Bill quit music altogether and moved to Japan. I don't think Clam and Exacting spoke to each other ever again.

I did have the chance to interview the band once, back when I was writing for the magazine *Cursory* and the Clams were touring to promote their album *Barrel of Which Blossomed Into a Flowering*. I spoke with them backstage before their show at the Parlor Horse. Clam declined to be interviewed, but Exacting would've talked for hours if we'd had the time. He told me all about the band's founding – about how Clam was touring with the band Ear Regression when their bus broke down in Cleveland, and Exacting was driving the tow truck that came to assist. "Clam was smoking a cigarette outside the bus, and I happened to be humming this tune while I changed a tire," said Exacting. "He asked me what the tune was, and I told him I made it up. He said, 'You made that up?' I sang the song a bit louder and Clammy started harmonizing to it. Then he asked me, 'Got any other tunes?' 'I got dozens,' I said. He quit Ear Regression that same day."

I also asked about their new album, which Dollar was especially excited about. "We're becoming artists in real time," Bill said, strapping on his zither. "Yeats of the baleful influence, all that." I had no idea what that meant, and I'm sure I looked confused. "The unicorn has gored the hound," Dollar said, as if that clarified anything. Then the band's manager leaned through the doorway and told them it was time to take the stage, and the band quickly donned their instruments and filed out. I wrote down Dollar's cryptic quotes in my notebook and ran out into the audience to catch the beginning of the show. I got to my seat right as the house lights went down. "Ladies and gentleman," boomed the announcer, "please welcome . . . the Clams!" Then the stage lights shouted on and Clam howled the first words of "Admit a Reappearance." "Top of the stairs!" curdled Clam as the band thundered behind him. "Jasmine iridescence cloys the comfort zone!"

"The comfort zone!" echoed a falsetto Exacting.

That was one of the oddest concerts I'd ever seen. The stage was full of actual clams, first—clams that Madge and Exacting hoisted into the crowd during "Academy of American Poets" and "Turn On All the Lights." They wore hats shaped like red roses for "Arose a Rose's," and dressed like dollar bills during "We'll Pay You More."

But as I watched and listened, I realized that what Bill had said—if I understood him correctly, at least—was true: this was a band finding their footing, pushing themselves, reaching new heights. And the crowd was responding. During their encore, "To Vienna and the House Became Engulfed," everyone leapt their feet and sang the chorus together:

Thalassa! Ah!
Thalassa! Ah!
It's Not a Spoonful of Sugar
Or a Generous Array

Thalassa! Ah!
Thalassa! Ah!
find yourself
being pulled away

I did detect some tension at that show, though. For most of the performance, Dollar Bill wore one of those beer hats—the hard hats with the straws—that he'd retrofitted to hold two bottles of wine. And I don't think Clam looked over at Exacting the entire show—even during "Aluminum Folly." When they walked off after the encore, Exacting went to one side of the stage and Clam to the other.

The glass table incident was just a few nights after that, but it wasn't until much later—just a few years ago, in fact—that Madge told *Oyster/Pearl* what the fight was about. Apparently Exacting had brought the band a bunch of new demos—early versions of the proggy songs that would later appear on his first solo album, *Uttressbay*—that Clam had flat-out rejected. "Clam said they were 'houses of cards,'" Madge said in the interview. "I think the words he used were 'flimsy' and 'soulless.'"

Shortly after their demise, a deeply in debt Clam tried to reform the Clams without Exacting, but Exacting sued him for using the band name and won. Exacting, meanwhile, released two more solo albums—*Pointed at the Gorillas* and *Numbered Not Named*—before filing for bankruptcy. I guess he later sent a few postcards to Clam, hoping to restore at least some level of contact, but he never heard back.

Clam died in a freak "flowers bursting in resplendent glory" accident two years ago. A posthumous album of new songs, *Adieu, Stale Eggs*, was released the following summer. Shortly after that, Exacting took a revival band called Clamshell on the road. If I'm being honest, though, it was a blue impasto: a paunchy, teary-eyed Exacting singing the low part with no one to harmonize with and backed by a band of studio musicians. Towards the end of the show, before singing a slowed-down version of "Aluminum," Exacting said into the microphone, "This one goes out to my friend Clam Watson." Then he winced and said, "Clammy, you're a ripple in the heated velvet breeze."

Contributors

Kirstin Allio's new story collection is *Double-Check for Sleeping Children* (FC2, 2024). Previous books are the novels *Garner* (Coffee House Press), *Buddhism for Western Children* (University of Iowa), and the story collection *Clothed, Female Figure* (Dzanc). She lives in Providence, RI.

Greg Bem is a librarian based in Spokane, Washington.

Jesi Bender is an artist from Upstate New York. She helms KERNPUNKT Press, a home for experimental writing. She is the author of *KINDERKRANKENHAUS* (Sagging Meniscus, 2021) and *The Book of the Last Word* (Whiskey Tit 2019).

Israel A. Bonilla lives in Guadalajara, Jalisco. He is author of the micro-chapbook *Landscapes* (Ghost City Press, 2021) and the story collection *Sleep Decades* (Malarkey Books, 2024).

Christopher Boucher is the author of the novels *How to Keep Your Volkswagen Alive* (Melville House, 201), *Golden Delicious* (MH, 2016), and *Big Giant Floating Head* (MH, 2019). He teaches writing and literature at Boston College and is Managing Editor of *Post Road Magazine*.

Marvin Cohen is the author of many novels, plays, and collections of essays, stories, and poems. He lives on the Lower East Side of Manhattan.

Mitch Corber is a poet, weekly NYC *Poetry Thin Air* cable producer, and 30+ year founder/poetry videographer of Thin Air Poetry Video Archives. He is the author of the collections *Quinine* (2009, Thin Air Media) and *Weather's Feather* (2014, Fly By Night Press) and performs regularly at NYC's East Village open mics and feature poetry readings, sometimes with guitar.

Jim Daniels' books include *Comment Card* (Carnegie Mellon University Press, 2024), *The Luck of the Fall* (Michigan State University Press, 2023), *The Human Engine at Dawn*, (Wolfson Press, 2022), *Gun/Shy* (Wayne State University Press, 2021), and *Rowing Inland* (WSUP, 2017). A native of Detroit, he lives in Pittsburgh and teaches in the Alma College low-residency MFA program.

Lyudmyla Diadchenko earned her Ph.D. in Literary Theory from Taras Shevchenko University in Kyiv, and has served as Vice President of the Ukrainian Writers Association. She has published three books in her native Ukrainian, including the award-winning *A Hen for the Turkish Man*. Her first book translated into English, *Magnetic Storms*, appeared in late 2023 as a bilingual collector's edition by Portland, OR's No Reply Press.

Guadalupe Dueñas (1910–2002) was a Mexican author. Four collections of her stories were published during her lifetime: *Tenemos la noche un árbol* (1958), *No moriré del todo* (1976), *Imaginaciones* (1977) and *Antes del silencio* (1991).

Eli S. Evans is the author of *Obscure & Irregular* (Moon Rabbit, 2021) and *Various Stories About Specific Individuals in Particular Situations* (Moon Rabbit, 2023).

Colin Gee is founder and editor of *The Gorko Gazette*, teacher and writer. Stories and novellas in *The Penult* from LEFTOVER Books. Novella *Lips* forthcoming from Anxiety Press.

Jake Goldsmith is a writer with cystic fibrosis and the founder of The Barbellion Prize, a book prize for ill and disabled authors. He is the author of *Neither Weak Nor Obtuse* (SM, 2022) and *In Hospital Environments: Essays on Illness and Philosophy* (SM, 2024).

Tyler C. Gore is the author of *My Life of Crime* (SM, 2022).

Michael Gray is the author of more than forty published stories and six published novels. He earned a MFA from Western Michigan University and lives in Kalamazoo, Michigan, with two cats and a dozen electric guitars.

Tina Gross lives in Moorhead, Minnesota. She sometimes creates found poems based on her work as a cataloging and metadata librarian. Her poems have appeared in publications including *McSweeney's Internet Tendency*, *Maudlin House*, *The Laurel Review*, *Rogue Agent*, and *Poetry City, USA*.

Charles Holdefer is an American writer currently based in Brussels. His latest book is *Ivan the Terrible Goes on a Family Picnic* (SM, 2024).

Diane Josefowicz is the author of *Ready, Set, Oh: A Novel* (Flexible Press, 2022); *L'Air du Temps (1985)* (Regal House, 2024); and *Guardians & Saints: Stories*, forthcoming from Cornerstone Press. With Jed Z. Buchwald, she is also the author of two histories of French Egyptology: *The Zodiac of Paris* (2010) and *The Riddle of the Rosetta* (2020), both published by Princeton University Press. Her translations of Anna de Noailles have appeared in *L'Esprit Literary Review* and were nominated in 2024 for a Pushcart Prize.

Jared Joseph attended the Iowa Writers Workshop, and now lives in Los Angeles and teaches at Los Angeles City College. Recent work has been published in *Action Books, The Iowa Review, The Los Angeles Review of Books*, and *Gulf Coast*, He is the author of are *A Book About Myself Called Hell* (KERNPUNKT Press, 2022), and the novel *Danny The Ambulance* (Outpost 19, 2023).

Vicki Kaye is a writer and artist. Her work has been published in journals including *The Café Irreal* amongst others. Her pamphlet *Fractured Light* (Sampson Low Press) was published in 2022 and she has work in several anthologies. She lives and works in Bristol, UK.

Habib William Kherbek's fiction includes *Ecology of Secrets* (Arcadia Missa, 2013), *ULTRALIFE* (AM, 2016), *Twenty Terrifying Tales from our Technofeudal Tomorrow* (AM, 2021), *New Adventures* (left gallery, 2020), *Best Practices* (Moist Books, 2021) and *Fail Worse* (AM, 2024). His poetry has been published by If A Leaf Falls Press, Arcadia Missa, and left gallery. His collected art writings were published in *Entropia Vol. 1 &2* (Abstract Supply, 2022).

Kurt Luchs is the author of *Tributaries* (SM, 2025), *Death Row Row Row Your Boat* (SM, 2024), *Falling in the Direction of Up* (SM, 2021), *One of These Things Is Not Like the Other* (Finishing Line Press, 2019), and the humor collection *It's Funny Until Someone Loses an Eye (Then It's Really Funny)* (SM, 2017). He lives in Michigan.

Oscar Mardell is a teacher and writer from Aotearoa/New Zealand. He is the author of *Delirious New Lynn*, forthcoming from 5ever Books.

Kit Maude is a translator based in Buenos Aires. He has translated dozens of Latin American writers for a wide array of publications and writes reviews for *Ñ, Otra Parte*, and the *Times Literary Supplement*.

Melissa McCarthy transmits from a tracking station in Edinburgh, Scotland. She's written *Photo, Phyto, Proto, Nitro* (SM, 2023) and *Sharks, Death, Surfers: An Illustrated Companion* (Sternberg, 2019). She's fond of Melville. See sharksillustrated.org for more.

Jim Meirose's novels include *Sunday Dinner with Father Dwyer* (Optional Books), *Understanding Franklin Thompson* (JEF), *Le Overgivers au Club de la Résurrection* (Mannequin Haus), *No and Maybe—Maybe and No* (Pski's Porch), *Audio Bookies* (LJMcD Communications), *Et Tu* (C22 press), *The Private Adventures of Fresh Detective Gerdulon* and *The Box* (Alien Buddha Press), and *Hands Up Shoot Me* (Equus Press).

Anna de Noailles (1876–1933), a writer and poet with close ties to Marcel Proust, was a leading figure of the French fin-de-siècle. She wrote four novels and many volumes of poems, co-founded the Prix Femina, and was an associate of *La Nouvelle Revue Française* which, in association with Gallimard, became one of the leading publishers of her time (and ours). Inspired by de Noailles' extensive travels in Italy, "A Roman Morning" first appeared in her late volume of essays, *Exactitudes*, published in Paris by Bernard Grasset in 1930.

Jonathan Plombon is a writer from Minnesota whose work has been published in *Bourbon Penn*, *Bombay Gin*, *Berkeley Fiction Review* and others. When not writing, Jonathan enjoys watching *Swans Crossing* and pro wrestling. His first book, *Tortured Ambition: The Story of Herb Abrams and the UWF*, was published in 2022.

Eric T. Racher lives and works in Riga, Latvia. He is the author of a chapbook of poetry, *Five Functions Defined on Experience: For Jay Wright* (2021).

William Repass, originally from Los Alamos, currently lives in Pittsburgh, where he works at a used book shop and an art house cinema. His fiction and poetry have appeared in *Bennington Review, Word For / Word, Denver Quarterly, Fiction International*, and elsewhere. His critical writing may be found at *Full Stop* and *Slant Magazine*. www.williamrepass.info.

Palazzo Rodriguez is a shifting assemblage currently writing and line cooking somewhere in the American Midwest.

Robyn Schelenz is from Birdsboro, Pennsylvania. Her chapbook *Natural Healing*, a collection of short poems, prose poems and fables, is out from Bottlecap Press.

Mike Silverton is the author of *Anvil on a Shoestring* (SM, 2022), *Trios* (SM, 2023), and *Yoga for Pickpockets* (SM, 2024).

Julian Stannard's most recent collection is *Please Don't Bomb the Ghost of my Brother* (Salt, 2023). His new novel is *The University of Bliss* (SM, 2024).

Guillermo Stitch is the author of *Lake of Urine* (SM, 2020).

Padma Thornlyre was born in Colorado and now lives in northern New Mexico. He is a founding member of the poetry co-op Turkey Buzzard Press and edits *Mad Blood*. His poetry and translations have appeared in *POETRY, Gargoyle, Yellow Silk, Channel* (Ireland), and *Turtle Island Quarterly*, among others.

Dan Tremaglio is the author of *Half an Arc & Artifacts & Then the Other Half* (Mint Hill Books) and *The Only Wolf is Time* (SM, 2025). He lives in Seattle where he teaches creative writing and literature at Bellevue College and is a senior editor for the journal *Belletrist*.

Thomas Walton is the author of *Unsavory Thoughts* (SM, 2025), *Good Morning Bone Crusher!* (Spuyten Duyvil 2021), *All the Useless Things Are Mine* (SM, 2020), *The World Is All That Does Befall Us* (Ravenna Press, 2019), and, with Elizabeth Cooperman, *The Last Mosaic* (SM, 2018). He currently works as an AI yoga instructor at Ashram Deapphake in Seattle, WA.

Lawrence Winkler is a retired physician, traveler, and natural philosopher. He lives on Vancouver Island and in New Zealand. His writings have previously been published in *The Montreal Review*

Kelly L. Wurth is the author of *That Dish at Gracie's Café* (True to Story, 2020).

www.ingramcontent.com/pod-product-compliance
Lightning Source LLC
Chambersburg PA
CBHW081326020726
47506CB00006B/1192

* 9 7 8 1 9 6 3 8 4 6 3 2 4 *